THE MERCHANT OF VENICE

THEORY IN PRACTICE SERIES

General Editor: Nigel Wood, School of English, University of Birmingham

Associate Editors: Tony Davies and Barbara Rasmussen, University of Birmingham

Titles:

THE MERCHANT OF VENICE

EDITED BY
NIGEL WOOD

OPEN UNIVERSITY PRESS
BUCKINGHAM · PHILADELPHIA

Open University Press
Celtic Court
22 Ballmoor
Buckingham
MK18 1XW

and
1900 Frost Road, Suite 101
Bristol, PA 19007, USA

First Published 1996

A catalogue record of this book is available from the British Library

ISBN 0 335 19237 8 (pb)

Library of Congress Cataloging-in-Publication Data

The Merchant of Venice / edited by Nigel Wood; [contributions by]
    John Drakakis . . . [et al.].
        p. cm. — (Theory in practice series)
    ISBN 0–335–19237–8 (pb)
    1. Shakespeare, William, 1564–1616. Merchant of Venice. 2. Jews
    in literature. 3. Comedy. I. Wood, Nigel, 1953– .
II. Drakakis, John. III. Series.
PR2825.M47   1995
822.3′3—dc20   95–32145
                                                           CIP

Typeset by Colset Pte. Ltd, Singapore
Printed in Great Britain by St Edmundsbury Press,
Bury St Edmunds, Suffolk

Contents

The Editor and Contributors

JOHN DRAKAKIS is reader in English Studies at the University of Stirling. He has written widely on Renaissance writing, including the editing of *Alternative Shakespeares* (1985), the Longman Critical Reader on *Shakespearean Tragedy* (1992) and the New Macmillan Casebook on *Antony and Cleopatra* (1994).

GRAHAM HOLDERNESS is professor in English at the University of Hertfordshire. His most recent work in Shakespearian studies has been as the general editor of the *Shakespearean Originals* series, in which he has been the editor of the *King Lear* volume (1995). Other recent work has included the New Macmillan Casebook on *The History Plays* (1993), and *Shakespeare Recycled: The Making of Historical Drama* (1992).

KAREN NEWMAN is professor of Comparative Literature and English at Brown University. Her books include *Shakespeare's Rhetoric of Comic Character* (1985) and *Fashioning Femininity and English Renaissance Drama* (1990) as well as articles on a range of topics in Renaissance studies and feminist theory. She is presently finishing a book on the representation of obstetric knowledge in the early modern period and beginning a project on urbanization and cultrural production in seventeenth-century London and Paris.

SCOTT WILSON is lecturer in English at the University of Lancaster.

He has published several articles on the significance of Bataille's work for literary criticism, and is preparing a study of heterological approaches to Renaissance playtexts.

NIGEL WOOD is senior lecturer in English at the University of Birmingham. He is the author of a study of Jonathan Swift (1986), and of several essays on literary theory, has co-edited essays on John Gay (1989), edited a selection from Frances Burney's diaries and journals (1990), and is general editor of the *Theory in Practice* series. To date he has edited the volumes on *Don Juan*, *The Prelude*, *Mansfield Park* (all 1993), *The Tempest* and *Henry IV*, *Parts I and II* (both 1995), and co-edited (with Tony Davies) the volumes on *A Passage to India* and *The Waste Land* (both 1994).

Editors' Preface

The object of this series is to help bridge the divide between the understanding of theory and the interpretation of individual texts. Students are therefore introduced to theory in practice. Although contemporary critical theory is now taught in many colleges and universities, it is often separated from the day-to-day consideration of literary texts that is the staple ingredient of most tuition in English. A thorough dialogue between theoretical and literary texts is thus avoided.

Each of these specially commissioned volumes of essays seeks by contrast to involve students of literature in the questions and debates that emerge when a variety of theoretical perspectives are brought to bear on a selection of 'canonical' literary texts. Contributors were not asked to provide a comprehensive survey of the arguments involved in a particular theoretical position, but rather to discuss in detail the implications for interpretation found in particular essays or studies, and then, taking these into account, to offer a reading of the literary text.

This rubric was designed to avoid two major difficulties which commonly arise in the interaction between literary and theoretical texts: the temptation to treat a theory as a bloc of formulaic rules that could be brought to bear on any text with roughly predictable results; and the circular argument that texts are constructed as such merely by the theoretical perspective from which we choose to regard them. The former usually leads to studies that are really just footnotes to the adopted theorists, whereas the latter is effortlessly self-fulfilling.

It would be disingenuous to claim that our interests in the teaching of theory were somehow neutral and not open to debate. The idea for this series arose from the teaching of theory in relation to specific texts. It is inevitable, however, that the practice of theory poses significant questions as to just what 'texts' might be and where the dividing lines between text and context may be drawn. Our hope is that this series will provide a forum for debate on just such issues as these which are continually posed when students of literature try to engage with theory in practice.

Tony Davies
Barbara Rasmussen
Nigel Wood

Preface

Thanks are due to the students of the Theory seminar at the Shakespeare Institute (University of Birmingham) at Stratford-upon-Avon, who may find some of the volume eerily familiar. I am also indebted to all of the contributors, who have helped make this a genuinely collaborative enterprise.

Nigel Wood

How to Use
this Book

Each of these essays is composed of a theoretical and a practical element. Contributors were asked to identify the main features of their perspective on the text (exemplified by a single theoretical essay or book) and then to illustrate their own attempts to put this into practice.

We realize that many readers new to recent theory will find its specific vocabulary and leading concepts strange and difficult to relate to current critical traditions in most English courses.

The format of this book has been designed to help if this is your situation, and we would advise the following:

(i)   Before reading the essays, glance at the editor's introduction where the literary text's critical history is discussed, and

(ii) also at the prefatory information immediately before the essays, where the editor attempts to supply a context for the adopted theoretical position.

(iii) If you would like to develop your reading in any of these areas, turn to the annotated further reading section at the end of the volume, where you will find brief descriptions of those texts that each contributor has considered of more advanced interest. There are also full citations of the texts to which the contributors have referred in the references. It is also possible that more local information will be contained in notes to the essays.

(iv) The contributors have often regarded the chosen theoretical texts as points of departure and it is also in the nature of theoretical discussion to apply and test ideas on a variety of texts. Turn, therefore, to question and answer sections that follow each essay which are designed to allow contributors to comment and expand on their views in more general terms.

A Note on
the Texts Used

Quotations from *The Merchant of Venice* are from the Oxford University Press edition, ed. Jay L. Halio (1993). In addition, the following Shakespeare editions have been consulted:

Anthony and Cleopatra	ed. Michael Neill (Oxford, 1994)
As You Like It	ed. Alan Brissenden (Oxford, 1993)
Julius Caesar	ed. Marvin Spevack (Cambridge, 1988)
Love's Labour's Lost	ed. G.R. Hibbard (Oxford, 1990)
Much Ado About Nothing	ed. Sheldon P. Zitner (Oxford, 1994)
Othello	ed. Norman Sanders (Cambridge, 1984)
The Poems	ed. John Roe (Cambridge, 1992)
King Richard II	ed. Andrew Gurr (Cambridge, 1984)
The Sonnets and Love's Complaint	ed. John Kerrigan (Harmondsworth, 1986)
The Tempest	ed. Stephen Orgel (Oxford, 1987)
Timon of Athens	ed. G.R. Hibbard (Harmondsworth, 1970)

The edition used of Ben Jonson's *Volpone* is that by Philip Brockbank (London, 1968) and that of Christopher Marlowe's *The Jew of Malta* by N.W. Bawcutt (Manchester, 1978).

Introduction

NIGEL WOOD

BASSANIO: Do all men kill the things they do not love?
SHYLOCK: Hates any man the thing he would not kill?
(IV.i. 65–6)

To pitch it in another key, how strained can the quality of mercy become before it loses its familar shape, and restraint is set by? What can intercede between desire and action to preserve civilized manners and keep the state intact? As Shylock discovers, special cases can always be made if the spirit is willing, and the most forensic and tightly bound formulation can be set against itself. For Portia, the Belmont perspective takes account of the 'throned monarch' (IV: 186) and his power – but sets a metaphysical quality above and beyond them both:

His sceptre shows the force of temporal power,
The attribute to awe and majesty,
Wherein doth sit the dread and fear of kings;
But mercy is above this sceptred sway.
It is enthronèd in the hearts of kings;
It is an attribute to God himself, . . .

(IV.i.187–92)

Whatever *The Merchant of Venice* could be said to dramatize, most critics and audiences have traced a split between the Venetian province of exchange and hazard controlled by a soulless observance of the law of contract, and its antidote: the moral imagination of Belmont, which is found in hearts, not bonds.[1] As a comedy, the play is predisposed, one might think, to deliver a world secure from the literal and standardized. The concluding episode, therefore, celebrates the union of

Venetian adventurers (and their temporary financial saviour) with the landed probity of Belmont.

But in what can law inhere, if secular justice is to be administered with equity and liberty assured all those who sue for redress? This is not a perverse question to ask of the play. Can Law bypass the verbal or textual to embrace its supposed spiritual basis? Can Justice emerge without the notary? As Isabella advises Angelo in *Measure for Measure*, Mercy can (with profit) be placed against 'proud man,/Dressed in a little brief authority' (II.ii.121–2), and yet, last judgements aside, authority is effective, and 'Hath . . . a medicine in itself/That skins the vice o'th'top' (II.ii.139–40).[2] Only the heart's knowledge can off-set the pragmatism of thrones and expensive robes, and so ignore authority's cosmetic surgery. In *The Merchant of Venice*, however, the Belmont perspective is not the only one, even if it is given the last word. This is a play that examines obligations of many and varied kinds, from Portia's own observance of her father's will, to the under-takings of her three suitors, to the polite 'bonds' of gratitude that assail Bassanio where Antonio is concerned, to marriage vows embodied in the exchange of rings, to Gobbo's defection from 'the Jew', to tribal loyalty that apparently weighs so heavily with Shylock and to the filial relationship that apparently does not with Jessica. No matter how disparate the sources put to work in the play, the final product circles and returns to this dialectic of theory and practice in a variety of discourses and contexts – and not all of them achieve comic resolution in Act V.

The Laws of Belmont

Portia/Balthasar must surely be speaking in alien accents when Vene-tian decrees appear so 'establishèd' (IV.i.216) that future precedents are predestined or else 'many an error by the same example' would 'rush into the state' (IV.i.218–19), as this is materially the same point that Shylock makes earlier in the scene, when he applies to law and decree to make good his claim on Antonio's flesh, or else the Venetian claim on 'purchased' slaves would have to lapse, and the distribution of slavish subjection and the rights of possession be radically affected (IV.i.88–102). The Duke's immediate response, to 'dismiss' the court 'Upon [his] power' (IV.i.103), is no answer to Shylock, merely the arrogation of power to refute what it cannot resolve. Indeed, Shakespeare's structural decision to separate this local skirmish from

Portia's eleventh-hour disquisition on Mercy by some 70 lines can be interpreted as dramatic timing of the highest order, as a calculated display, not of evasion, but of transcendence: part of that call for a heart's knowledge that is incommensurate with law, but if law is uncoupled from justice here, the irony of having the former unexpectedly serve the other when the pound of flesh is taken to mean literally and unnaturally just that at the play's most memorable denouement comes dangerously near to soldering both together. The words of legal formulation are interpreted ingeniously, with 'spirit' – but only so as to return us to their strict denotation. We might also register that the ring badinage of Act V is comic precisely to the degree that the vows of Bassanio and Graziano might *not* be mitigated by changed circumstances. Their discomfiture is comprehensible in comic terms only as long as we are aware of the wider ironic strategy that lingers after the climactic trial scene: we allow an excuse of their venial sin of infidelity only if we accept that vows and promises are never irrevocable, and can only literally bind us as long as the context in which they are first entered into persists. As both Karen Newman and John Drakakis point out (this volume, pp. 117–19, 51–3), the bawdy pun that awaits any close inspection of Graziano's last sentiment of fearing 'no other thing/So sore as keeping safe Nerissa's ring' (V.i.306–7), is a deflection of the potentially paradoxical and resonant on to the apparently straightforward and local – from *gest* to jest.

If the play dramatizes the difficulties inherent in passing between equity and morality, then it could just as viably be regarded as an attempt to find for words some 'presence', or true referentiality. Rings should betoken a vow of faith, a choice of the correct casket should be no mere bagatelle and bonds can never ultimately be merry. Our understanding that the play may be a comedy only suggests, not that these matters are out of court, but that comedic relief has powerful and intractable ghosts to exorcize. Bassanio realizes an important truth involved in his choice of the lead casket (indeed, romantic readings stress this as part of his sentimental education):

So may the outward shows be least themselves.
The world is still deceived with ornament.
In law, what plea so tainted and corrupt
But, being seasoned with a gracious voice,
Obscures the show of evil? In religion,
What damnèd error but some sober brow

Will bless it and approve it with a text,
Hiding the grossness with fair ornament?

(III.ii.73–80)

That there is evil and error Bassanio is convinced; that we might not be able to identify them, without relying on the 'gracious voice' or sober-sounding 'text' is the problem. As Jonathan Culler (1983: 81) terms it, reading forms an 'attempt to understand writing by determining the referential and rhetorical modes of a text, translating the figurative into the literal, for example, and removing obstacles in the quest for a coherent result'. Interpretation must be an identification of what is described aside from the means of description, but it is also inevitable that rhetoric, as Paul de Man (1979: 131) noted, 'puts an insurmountable obstacle in the way of any reading or understanding'. Far from a cause for regret, this is a provocative deconstructive perception, and leads Jacques Derrida to acknowledge that 'traditional' philosophy depends on distinctions that do not merely provide 'a peaceful coexistence of facing terms' but rather 'a violent hierarchy', where there is domination of one item (the Jew, the feminine, or the Orient, for example) by the other (gentile, the patriarchal or the West). Deconstruction is a reversal of this hierarchy 'at a particular moment' (Derrida 1981b: 41), by recognizing that its claims to truth are a trope, a rhetorical effect, rather than self-evidently demonstrated. Consequently, the perverse attention to detail that a deconstructive reading demands actually sets the overt logic of the writing against itself, not only to reverse the classical distinctions that privilege one term above others, but, further, to displace the whole system of such discrimination: 'It is on that condition alone that deconstruction will provide the means of *intervening* in the field of oppositions it criticizes and which is also a field of non-discursive forces' (Derrida 1977a: 195). Shylock believes that such intervention can be mounted on a platform of judgement, law and contract, and finds to his great cost that there are powerful 'non-discursive forces' that control language, and that it is these that yoke signifier and signified, not some freely available and transparent rationality.[3]

That *The Merchant of Venice* ends happily for most of its *personae* could simply be a recognition that this array of 'non-discursive forces' needs to be kept in place. That the action culminates in Belmont, and can take in Bassanio, Jessica, Lorenzo and Graziano as well as Antonio (temporarily), is, one could point out, as much providence as a proposition about the world as a whole. If the action were to conclude in

Venice, then the particularly fraught consequences of administering secular law could not be as successfully transcended. In Belmont, signs betoken a greater reality without spillage or an effort at interpretation:

> PORTIA: That light we see is burning in my hall.
>   How far that little candle throws his beams –
>   So shines a good deed in a naughty world.
> NERISSA: When the moon shone, we did not see the candle.
> PORTIA: So doth the greater glory dim the less.
>   A substitute shines brightly as a king
>   Until a king be by, and then his state
>   Empties itself as doth an inland brook
>   Into the main of waters. Music, hark!
> NERISSA: It is your music, madam, of the house.
> PORTIA: Nothing is good, I see, without respect.
>
> (V.i.89–99)

The 'naughty world' lies outside Portia's domain, and, within it, even the music is owned. 'Respect' bestows value, but not directly in a Derridean sense: kings have an innate superiority that dims the apparent glories of lesser beings as soon as comparison is possible. Just as 'inland' streams flow in tribute to the ocean, so should the 'state' of homage be paid to self-evident status. As a last gesture, to ensure the providential conclusion to the action, the letter carried by Portia that announces the unexpected existence of three of Antonio's argosies, and the 'deed of gift' Nerissa hands over to Lorenzo and Jessica (V.i.274–9, 290–3) are as mysterious in origin as they are set off from the logic of the foregoing events. Portia is blatantly coy about how the news has emerged: 'You shall not know by what strange accident/I chancèd on this letter' (V.i.278–9), and concedes that the rest of the Belmont house party may not be satisfied 'Of these events at full' (V.i.297). All the more reason, therefore, to hustle in these fortuitous tidings so near the end of the play, and also claim assurances that will stand up 'upon inter'gatories' (V.i.298) – off-stage.

Comedy's stock-in-trade, one could claim, is exactly this mesh of coincidence and deliverance, and it would be insensitive (to say the least) to wish a bleaker ending simply because we wished Shakespeare possessed a more materialist (and contemporary) philosophy, but, at the same time, it might be informative to assess just what riders are appended to our closing sense of poetic justice. Here is wealth that is not just inherited but also safeguarded by the same legal strictures that, at the trial of Act IV, scene i, kept slaves 'purchased' and aliens at a potential legal disadvantage. One could also mention Portia's relief that Morocco chose incorrectly: 'Let all of his complexion choose me so' (II.vii.79), and Gobbo's 'witty' play with Jessica's conversion in Act III, scene v, where the 'sins' of a Jewish father lead to damnation. Not every errant father is held to account for sins, not of race, but of commission. Lorenzo's upbraiding of Gobbo's sexual profligacy – 'The Moor is with child by you, Lancelot!' (III.v.36) – only supplies the material for verbal punning (Moor/more), and the 'comedy' furthered by verbal foolery. Portia's virtuous father can leave an inheritance endorsed by Bassanio's (fortuitous?) choice; it is only a comic destiny in its assignation to paternal virtue and calculation – see Nerissa's faith that 'holy men at their death have good inspirations' (I.ii.27–8) – that prevents a marriage to Arragon or Morocco.

Portia's admission of human weakness in the first scene in which we meet her predicts much of what is about to happen in Venice: 'The brain may devise laws for the blood, but a hot temper leaps o'er a cold decree' (I.ii.17–19). Blood is set at odds with the brain. Antonio's 'mind is tossing on the ocean', according to Salerio, in the very first scene (I.i.8), and he admits himself that he 'has much ado to know' himself due to his 'want-wit' sadness (I.i.6–7). One scene later and Portia suffers from a similar *Weltschmerz*: 'By my troth, Nerissa, my little body is aweary of this great world' (I.ii.1–2). This is the problem that the comic action seeks to address: the immersion in *ennui*, and with it, stasis, the prospect of infinite sameness. For Antonio, the prospect of Bassanio's departure and his need of help actuate an offer not only of his 'purse' to be 'unlocked to [his] occasions', but also his 'person' (I.i.138–9). This almost comes literally true, and the intensity of this identification is clearest when Antonio's sacrifice moves from the category of token promise to pressing probability, when the letter from Venice makes it to Belmont at the moment of highest fortune:

> Here is a letter, lady,
> The paper as the body of my friend,
> And every word in it a gaping wound
> Issuing life-blood.
>
> (III.ii.261–4)

This dramatic and textual trope is not isolated to those narrative passages that derive directly from the 'merry bond' plot. At moments of stirring narrative condensation – of images, of dramatic confluence – there is an effort to efface the rhetorical. Poor in thanks, Bassanio accepts Portia's ring, and confesses that he has been 'bereft . . .

of all words', leaving only his 'blood' to speak to her 'in (his] veins'
(III.ii.175-6). This same life-source, indeed, constitutes the only
wealth he offers Portia (III.ii.250-3). Portia herself recognizes the
identity that can exist between 'companions/. . ./Whose souls do bear
an equal yoke of love', and construes that there must be 'a like propor-
tion/Of lineaments, of manners, and of spirit' (III.iv.11-15).

Compared to this innate value and identity the incursion of bonds
and ring tokens introduces a bar between signifier and signified.
'Mercy' is the wedge that forces contract apart from spirit, and the
mix of Bassanio's 'deservings' and Antonio's 'love' compete with Portia's 'commandement' (IV.i.446-7). The ring is nearer in status to a
bond than the ending of the romantic action makes at all explicit.
Unlike the 'blood' language that confirms friendship and the first flush
of respectful gratitude, the value of the ring is a matter of debate.[4]
Disguise accentuates the comic complications, but also spills over
into the perception that the recovery of unmediated understanding
between the heterosexual unions has to happen off-stage.[5] When
Portia exclaims

What man is there so much unreasonable,
If you had pleased to have defended it
With any terms of zeal, wanted the modesty
To urge the thing held as a ceremony?

(V.i.203-6)

most commentators feel that they have to gloss as purely honorific
Portia's description of the ring as a 'ceremony'. With Henry V's set-
piece on 'idol ceremony' in mind (*Henry V*, IV.i.228), one could claim
that Portia is actually choosing a particularly suitable term to describe
the token.

What is here evident is the route such romantic comedy takes to
achieve consonance and lucidity. The aesthetic fitness of the closure to
the play is in exact proportion to its simplification. The letter that
brings Antonio 'life and living' (V.i.286) also bars him from Belmont
and human companionship, especially the friendship of Bassanio. The
deed of gift is a reminder of Shylock at the same time as a mark of his
exclusion not only from Belmont but also from the 'life' he had hitherto
enjoyed. The irony of this gesture is not lost on Lorenzo: this time it
is not the Jew who receives 'manna' (see V.i.294-5). For Derrida, and
in terms accepted and deployed throughout deconstructive readings,
this irony is where analysis might start.[6] Lorenzo, when faced with
Gobbo's equivocation, voices a profound exasperation:

> How every fool can play upon the word! I think the best grace
> of wit will shortly turn into silence, and discourse grow com-
> mendable in none only but parrots. . . . I pray thee understand
> a plain man in his plain meaning: . . .
>
> (III.v.40–3, 52–3)

This quest for 'unwitty' plainness does indeed come near to the rejection of all speech whatsoever.

If what Derrida called for was merely a playing with sense, then
his quibbles would be out of Gobbo's book with a vengeance. In rid-
ding semantics of a complacent trust in a 'metaphysics of presence',
where the thought or object is transparently rendered by language,
Derrida 'plays' in order to displace a whole system of metaphysics – and
so identify the accents of desire or political opportunism that are
supported by it. In the beginning is the word, not the matter signified,
and this to a greater or lesser degree poses as an innocent doubling
of reality, not a proposition about such a notion. The impulse to
ground one's understanding on the 'natural' or 'commonsensical', for
example, is actually to *wish away* the dramatic, rhetorical or verbal:
to return 'to an origin or to a "priority" seen as simple, intact, normal,
pure, standard, self-identical, in order *then* to conceive of derivation,
complication, deterioration, accident, etc.' (Derrida 1977a: 236). To
find this a reflex of understanding is not at the same time to find it
'real' or non-verbal.

If it is admitted that the tropes of the play's dramatic action do not
derive in some uncomplicated way from prior intention, then meaning
is plural and always in process, and only unified and finished by dint
of critical intervention, the power of a 'strong' reading dependent on
audience and timing as well as author. When Derrida carefully identifies a determining factor of interpretation as bound to a 'particular
moment' (see above, p. 4), the qualification is crucial. The revelation
that the deciphering of writing (including here theatrical effects) need
not obey 'logocentric' pressures actually comes to predict very little
about it – or about our own allegories of reading. Not all texts are
equally or identically 'logocentric', just as the workings of *historical*
difference, though always seen through the lens of the present moment
of critical comprehension, provide a locus or grid of analysis where
the local detail may be more resonant than the guiding deconstructive
perception.

To put it bluntly: *The Merchant of Venice*'s immediate strands of
significance – common to *c*.1596, London, gentile, public playhouse –

picture a precise set of cultural contradictions – or, at least, debates – which are foreign to our own. They may not correspond in some unmediated way to a discoverable origin in Derrida's account, but that is because priority and the constant deferring of the signified are mutually exclusive. What we are left with is a patterning of association that the critical view can sum up or alight on provisionally and which emerges as distinct from what we now discover our own to be, knowing it perhaps for the first time. These are explored in both cultural and gender terms by the contributors to this volume. The collocation of hazard and wealth, the body with sacrifice, the sea with both wreckage and the loosening of frontiers and so the powers of definition – all these emerge from the figurative life of the play. There still remains the encounter with Shakespeare's Venice, and, through that, the comprehension of cultural difference.

Radical Comedy

Could Shylock really have existed in London – always accepting that he did, on the Globe stage, as a fiction? In John Gross's perceptive study of Shylock and his stage renditions it becomes quite clear that, while Venetian stage mores encouraged a typification of Shylock's behaviour and character, this has commonly been accompanied by audience reaction that moves in a contrary direction. Shylock is distinctive – both as a name and as a dramatic voice ('Hath not a Jew eyes?' (III.i.55)):

> There can be no doubt . . . that Shakespeare knew what he was doing when he declined to settle for either a common biblical name (as he so easily might have done), or a baldly allegorical one. A Shylock who was called Moses or Isaac would not have been at all the same thing; neither would a Shylock called Lucre or Mammon . . .

On the other hand, we see the gentiles actually take Shylock's name from him:

> A name is a precious possession. Like other possessions, it can be taken away. Shylock is 'Shylock' to his face, but behind his back he is always referred to as 'the Jew'.
>
> (Gross 1992: 51)

Moreover, this is merely what has happened throughout the textual transmission of the play. With James Roberts as printer, its earliest mention in the Stationers' Register for 22 July 1598 is as 'a booke of the Marchaunt of Venyce or otherwise called the Iewe of Venyce', and the 1600 Quarto title page allows Shylock his name only to blacken it, promising as it does a portrayal of 'the extreame crueltie of *Shylocke* the Iewe'.[7] Here, it should be noted, is no hint of the effortlessly discountable Shylock, replete with the marks of all his tribe, but on the contrary a disturbing alien presence.[8]

Venice in *The Merchant of Venice* derives from both myth and, more specifically, an Elizabethan ideology about the exotic fringes of Christian civilization. Far from separate discourses, *The Merchant*'s depiction of Shylock and Venice is apposite and shares references both to a wider, more gracious world, while at the same time it taps a reservoir of less reassuring notions of *laissez-faire* capitalism that reflects London preoccupations with its cost and effect on older manners.[9] Venice faced east as well as west, and had developed tolerant immigration policies to facilitate a broad trading base.[10] Since 1397 Jews had been obliged to occupy Mestre, where the moneylender lived in *Il Pecorone*, the most influential source for the play. On visits to the city proper, all Jews were initially obliged to wear a large circular badge and, latterly, a yellow hat. When Shylock claims he has met Antonio's taunts with 'a patient shrug', because 'suff'rance is the badge of all [his] tribe' (I.iii.104–5), he is both conforming to a racial stereotype and translating an outward mark of racial difference to one of inward resolution. Barabas in Marlowe's *The Jew of Malta* (1589; produced 1592) had learnt in Florence

> to kiss [his] hand,
> Heave up [his] shoulders when they called [him] dog,
> And duck as low as any bare-foot friar, . . .
> *(The Jew of Malta*, II.iii.23–5)

For Shylock the 'Jewish gaberdine' (I.iii.109) on which Antonio is supposed to have spat on the Rialto derives more from stage tradition than any known requirement in Venice of the sixteenth century.[11] The main influx of Jews into Venice is likely to have been as refugees from the armies of the League of Cambrai from 1509 onwards. Certainly, by 1516, the Venetian senate had formalized the situation with a decree restricting them to the 'Geto at San Hieronimo', circled with high walls and policed by Christian watchmen. A strict curfew was enforced, 'to prevent the Jews from going about all night, provoking the greatest discontent and the deepest displeasure on the part of

Jesus Christ', in the wording of the decree itself (Chambers and Pullan 1992: 339). Certainly, the threat posed at the Battle of Lepanto by the heathens at the gates in 1571 brought the threat of expulsion, but, by the late 1570s, the flow was in the other direction. The Jews were good for business, especially in lending money to the poor of the city, and Venice had gained a general reputation for tolerance. As McPherson (1990: 51–68) points out, the myth of Venice bears on the play to suggest a recognizable context not only of racial friction, but also of even-handed gentile justice.

This would seem to suggest that the play's Christians should be operating a relatively liberal society. Moreover, unlike the historical Venice, Shylock is allowed to choose to eat at Antonio's, and obviously owns a house giving out on to the public street (an impossibility in Venice itself for a Jew). Even so, Jessica has to swear not to 'thrust [her] head into the public street/To gaze on Christian fools with varnished faces' (II.v.32–3), when it is masquing time. This Venetian detail is crucial. Known for its carnival, Venice was also publicized as a location not just for liberty but also licence (see McPherson 1990: 38–47; Chambers and Pullan 1992: 120–9). Volpone and Nano disguise themselves in a Venetian street in Act II, scene ii of Jonson's play (1605), and provoke Celia, who has not heeded Shylockian advice, to throw down her handkerchief. When Corvino breaks up this display of verbal trickery, the scene is associated with the extremes of *commedia* motivation: a plot of broad humour centring on cuckoldry, as he mentions Flaminio (a specifically Venetian figure), Francisca (the stock maid) and, in reference to himself, Pantalone di Besogniosi, the beslippered lean old man with distinctive black gown, cap and red tunic (II.iii.3–8). Two scenes later, Corvino is planning to board up the window, immolating Celia from all human contact (II.v.50–66). In true *commedia* style, however, this does not hold the world at bay and Volpone inveigles his way to her (in Act III, scene vii).

What Jonson noted about Venetian festivity, he was also to recognize as London alchemy: the protean city life of his *The Alchemist* (1610) celebrates verbal and intellectual wit and yet examines it as meretricious. The disguises and androgyny staged in the Pythagorean 'entertainment' of Act I, scene ii of *Volpone* form an antimasque that suggests perversion as well as play. One reading may stress Shylock as a superannuated Pantalone, yet the structure of feeling here is difficult to assess completely, in that there is a diminished sense of straight moral aversion. Jessica dresses as a boy to leave her father's house;

Portia becomes Balthasar. Graziano comments as Jessica flees, 'Now, by my hood, a gentile and no Jew' (II.vi.51).[12] Transformations can be as fast as lightning in Venice.

This conjunction of disguise and liberality as well as the chasing of desire has recently been examined by Catherine Belsey, who isolates the specific resonances of Venetian love. As she leaves Venice, Jessica also swaps a masculine world of 'market forces and racial tensions' for the more 'feminine, lyrical, aristocratic' Belmont (Belsey 1991: 41).[13] It is surely apposite to be reminded that apparently non-fictional Venice can be, in Lacanian phrase, the cultural Other to Belmont, its dialectical binary twin. Venice is as much a confluence of myths as a mimetic attempt at tapping the wisdom of travellers' tales. The lubricious Venetian courtesans noted by Thomas Coryat and Fynes Moryson were simply seen as the logical extension of political and religious toleration (see McPherson 1990: 44–8), and yet these same commentators were also quick to note the occasional severities of Venetian inquisitorial law. Lovewit excuses Face at the conclusion of *The Alchemist*, yet even *Volpone*'s suspect Avocatori in the Scrutineo deliver swingeing sentences, the most exacting on those who dissemble, Mosca (who had 'abused the court,/ And habit of a gentleman of Venice' (V.xii.110–11)) and Volpone. The first Avocatore is adamant that such judgements 'may not be revoked' (V.xii.146). This stern imposition of justice may seem a distinct alternative to the attempt at a closing harmony in *The Merchant of Venice*, yet its mix of liberty and law, of masque and ghetto and of trade and aristocracy, is more irresolvably symbolic than it is open to historical verification. As Nick Potter points out in relation to both *The Merchant* and *Othello*, 'both law and expediency are dishonest in terms of each other. Law represents a rigidity which denies flexibility, expediency a flexibility which denies the absolute nature of moral values' (Holderness *et al.* 1987: 204). Law, being the corrective to mercurial desire and disguise, is still tempered by mercy. The letter (epistolary as well as literal) can save as well as condemn.

As a proverbial reference, Venice is more often touted as a *città-galante*, but with all the accompanying distrust of polite, yet superficial, manners. To some degree, this is doubtless due to its topographical distinction. In Nuttall's (1983: 121) succinct description, it is 'the landless landlord over all'. This fluidity (puzzling to the landowning English) perhaps helped the transfer of epithets from Venice to the hazard of trade and the deeper fathoms of desire. For the action of *Othello* to move from Venice to the outer edge in Cyprus is simply an intensification of threat and crisis, not its sudden introduction. In his jealous fit Othello can associate Desdemona with her city in dubbing her 'that cunning whore of Venice/That married with Othello' (IV.ii.88–9), but there are more innocent references, too. Holofernes, the pedant of *Love's Labour's Lost*, can communicate his enthusiasm for Mantuan by quoting the traveller's estimate of Venice: '*Venetia, Venetia/Chi non ti vede, non ti pretia*' (IV.ii.95–6) ('Venice, Venice; he that does not see thee cannot value thee'). Don Pedro counsels the confirmed bachelor, Benedick, in *Much Ado About Nothing*, that Cupid may not have 'spent all his quiver in Venice' (I.i.260–1). At the height of her decisiveness to leave her father and her faith, Jessica expresses her anxiety as well as her excitement in her recognition of racial disadvantage and Cupid's influence. Glad that it is night, she is 'ashamed of [her] exchange', a reference both to her boy's disguise and the advisability of the elopement and theft:

> JESSICA: But love is blind, and lovers cannot see
>   The pretty follies that themselves commit;
>   For if they could, Cupid himself would blush
>   To see me thus transformèd to a boy.
> LORENZO: Descend, for you must be my torchbearer.
> JESSICA: What, must I hold a candle to my shames?
>   They in themselves, good sooth, are too too light.
>   Why, 'tis an office of discovery, love,
>   And I should be obscured.
>
>   (*The Merchant of Venice*, II.vi.36–44)

The surface word-play proposes matters of wider significance. 'Lovers cannot see'; her flight, as well as her cross-dressing, needs to be obscured. The candle here does not 'throw his beams' amidst evil, but onto it. Jessica, thereafter, is always the convert, as Gobbo and others remind her, and the duet with Lorenzo that raises the curtain on Act V is a sore test of their security, composed as it is predominantly of instances of star-crossed love from Chaucer's *Legend of Good Women* and *Troilus and Criseyde* as well as Ovid's *Metamorphoses*. The 'unthrift love' Lorenzo mentions at V.i.16 is glossed and its consequences extended by the punning on 'steal':

> LORENZO: In such a night
>   Did Jessica steal from the wealthy Jew
>   And with an unthrift love did run from Venice
>   As far as Belmont.

JESSICA: In such a night
  Did young Lorenzo swear he loved her well,
  Stealing her soul with many vows of faith
  And ne'er a true one.
LORENZO: In such a night
  Did pretty Jessica, like a little shrew,
  Slander her love, and he forgave it her.
JESSICA: I would outnight you, did nobody come.

(V.i.14–23)

– but someone does, with news of Portia's return to take control of Belmont society, accompanied by a deed of gift and significant news for Antonio. Has Lorenzo stolen Jessica's soul or strengthened ('steeled') it?[14] Jessica has only one further line, and it is to proclaim how proof she is to the musical enchantment cast over this last push towards consonance and harmony: 'I am never merry when I hear sweet music' (V.i.69).[15]

This only seems perverse if we have taken the designation of the play as comedy too much on trust – and this does not yet attempt to salvage Shylock as a three-dimensional victim. There is a common notion that the action is circular in form, an 'inclusion of differences – heaven and earth, comic and tragic, darkness and light, male and female, anxiety and joy, division and union – . . . [a] playful movement from love's teasing to love's comedic teaching and harmonious re-bonding' (Holmer 1995: 272–3). As we shall see, this desire to celebrate artistic unity bonds itself with the wish to resolve opposed perceptions of racial and gender difference or social *anomie* – as a condition of art. Joan Ozark Holmer's detailed and carefully argued study of the play explores a wide nexus of myths and traditions, and yet cracks begin to show whenever she dwells on the waywardness of theatrical effect:

> The challenge for the comedian is to keep the teasing laughably in-bounds, as in Portia's mockery of her suitors, so that teasing does not cross the line into outright cruelty . . . In Shakespeare's audience surely some laughed *with* such insensitive mockers but others probably laughed *at* them as well. On the other hand, Lancelot's teasing of his blind father [Act II, scene ii] about his death loses such emotional poignancy because Lancelot is only joking . . .

(Holmer 1995: 273)

but there are jokes and there are yet again other jokes, and to maintain laughter 'in-bounds' is not necessarily to serve the play or its author. As Leggatt (1974: 146) notices, the harmony desired by Lorenzo and Jessica in Act V, scene i 'achieves its confidence only by keeping off the problems of the characters themselves; and the more boisterous, bawdy fun of the ring sequence may seem like a descent to crude realities'. After all, one could claim that it is from exactly this discursive 'descent' that the last word is actually provided.

The possibilities discovered by refusing to identify with the metaphysical claims advanced by some of the voices in the play (usually connected with Belmont) involve a process of *renversement*, which Derrida (1976: 215) identifies as following a 'logic of supplementarity' – the very language in which we express coherence or convergence inevitably possesses an 'unintended' surplus of meaning that works to overturn its avowed sense.[16] Interpretation of this order of attention to fractures and slips almost renders the work of interpretation itself as the posing of a critical story over and against the source 'object' of exegesis – in practice, never static or productive of objective knowledge (see Bloom 1973: 70) – a substitute, not a key. It matters little from this perspective that interpretations are partial. Overtly, the play is a comedy; what that term turns out to signify is not, however, (without argument or some measure of textual blindness) explored by such linguistic pigeon-holing. Derrida reads Rousseau, for example, to discover a logic that is more a property of the text's rhetoric than could ever be usefully or *truthfully* ascribed to an authorial point of origin (see especially Derrida 1976: 239–45). This breaks with 'traditional, normative ideas of textual commentary and critique', as Norris (1987: 109) notes, in that it is 'not so much interested in what the text says – what it is "about" at the express thematic level – as in the organization of its logical resources *despite or against* its manifest drift'. The jokes of comedy – structural as well as strictly linguistic – can threaten the stability that is invoked whenever plays are viewed ('whole') by a process of retrospective tinkering: 'Given the way that the play ends, that must have been how we felt about matters in the fourth act' or 'Because the action is closed so satisfactorily, it must answer all (or most of) the questions in which it invests dramatic capital'. This is hardly a matter for deconstruction alone – nor has it been in the play's critical and theatrical history.

Performance and Context

In broad terms, the critical history of *The Merchant of Venice* has been responsive to two significant factors: how safely comic Shylock could be portrayed and, latterly, how the relationship between Antonio and Bassanio affects the heterosexual union with Portia. While never isolated considerations, these two matters stem from alternative sources which Shakespeare amalgamated to form the play: the vindictive and uncomplicated Jew from *Il Pecorone* and the romantic protagonists of Belmont (with the choice of caskets as complication) from the *Gesta Romanorum*. At the time of Granville-Barker's (1930: 71) oft-quoted remark that these two sub-plots defied dramatic unity – 'The stories, linked in the first scene, will, of themselves, soon part company' – Shylock had become the main centre of dramatic interest. The Elizabethans' view of Shylock is as unplayable now as their unproblematic romantic understanding of Bassanio and Portia. On the other hand, there is little now available to us to help an understanding of precisely how the Lord Chamberlain's Men put the text to work. The 1600 first quarto's title-page proclaims that it had been acted 'divers times', which points to a first season of 1596–7 (see Chambers 1923, 2: 195). As staged by the King's Men (as they were then called), James I saw it at Court on Shrove Sunday (10 February) in 1605, and it was repeated, presumably at his request, on Shrove Tuesday. Shrovetide masquing about to give place to Lenten fare, as Halio (1994: 59–60) reminds us, might well have been an added thematic ingredient of the occasion, with the associated 'suggestions of ritual sacrifice, God's mercy, and the grace of love that dominate both the play and the liturgy of Shrovetide' – sentiments that would 'appeal to the theologically oriented James'. If the appeal was so basically Christian in inspiration, then it is hard to identify a Shylock even as an anti-hero. There were several stage Jews to accompany Shylock, the most notorious being Marlowe's Barabas from *The Jew of Malta*, but the evidence for what we would now realize as simple racialist comment is not definitive. It should not be forgotten that Barabas shows up the hypocrisies of Christians as well as his own basic amorality (see Bulman 1991: 6–22).[17]

There then follows a silence in the play's theatre history, for which the likeliest explanation would seem to be that it had initially tapped such a contemporary taste for debates on usury or the law and supplied such an acceptably romantic gloss on them that it simply failed to retain hold of the popular imagination once these concerns were no longer seen as quite so crucial. Even with the renewed interest in Shakespeare fostered in the Restoration, *The Merchant* is not on record as a favourite, this despite a continuing interest in stage Jews during the Caroline period (see, for example, Thomas Heywood's *A Challenge for Beauty* (1636) and James Shirley's *The Gentleman of Venice* (1639)).

With George Granville's *The Jew of Venice* (1701) as competition, Shakespeare's text fell out of the repertory. This may now seem unthinkable, but Granville's adaptation (almost a completely different play) provided simplified emotional appeal. The main casualty was the part of Shylock, which exploited the broad comic talents of Thomas Doggett. In streamlining the play around the themes of love and friendship (no Gobbos, Morocco or Arragon), Granville avoided the temptation to find dramatic interest in any conflict between the two. In a completely new scene (Act II, scene ii), Antonio toasts Friendship, Bassanio Love and Shylock Money:

> SHYLOCK: I have a Mistress, that out-shines 'em all –
> Commanding yours – and yours tho' the whole sex:
> O may her Charms encrease and multiply;
> My Money is my Mistress! Here's to
> Interest upon Interest.
> (II.ii.27–31; Spencer 1965: 364)

There immediately followed a masque of Peleus and Thetis, 'Set to MUSICK', where the couple are freed from Jupiter's wrath by the aid offered by the prophesy of Peleus's friend, Prometheus. Even the latter is liberated (stage direction: 'The Vulture drops dead at the Feet of *Prometheus*, His Chains fall off, and he is borne up to Heaven' (Masque, s.d. 128; Spencer 1965: 370) – see Schneider 1993). Shylock, in Doggett's hands, is an unproblematic 'Stock-Jobbing Jew', who deserves punishment ('Prologue', 1.29; Spencer 1965: 348). Not every spectator was happy with this version. Nicholas Rowe admitted in 1709 that it was likely that the play was regarded as a comedy, and he was taken with the 'Great, Generous and Tender' friendship between Antonio and Bassanio, yet there was also such a 'deadly Spirit of Revenge, such a savage Fierceness and Fellness, and such a bloody designation of Cruelty and Mischief' that it was surely an atypical one (*Some Account of the Life etc. of Mr William Shakespeare* in Vickers 1974–81, 2: 196). As Dobson (1992: 121–4) has recently traced, there is a purifying impulse in *The Jew*, evidenced in the 'Prologue's' abhorrence of miscegenation and homosexuality and also the reduction of Shylock's threat to one merely of low-grade financial misdemeanour (see Wilson 1934).

It was with a deep sense of exploration and novelty that Charles Macklin persuaded the Drury Lane management to back a full-text Shakespeare version in 1741. Macklin had made his name as a comic actor, having recently taken the parts of Touchstone (*As You Like It*). Osric (*Hamlet*) and Trinculo (*The Tempest*) with great success. His Shylock, however, went thrillingly against type. Keeping his intentions secret throughout the rehearsal period, Macklin burst on to the stage on the first night with a tempestuous portrayal which suggested
• a deep sense of wrong as well as a deep capacity to wrong others•(see Gross 1992: 94–9). This tactic caught others by surprise, especially those who had hoped to salvage a little from what they fully expected to be a resounding flop by cameo comic turns. Kitty Clive's Portia went through a spectrum of farcical impressions of eminent legal figures during the trial scene, while Macklin apparently spat out malice and involvement. The net effect was anti-Semitic, but, at least, Shylock was no comic walk-on, and it proved seminal. Belmont began to pale in comparison. David Garrick chose the Macklin *Merchant* to open the 1747 season at Drury Lane – and thus inaugurate his own term as co-manager. For Samuel Johnson, in his note to IV.i.90 in his 1765 edition ('You have among you many a purchas'd slave'), Shylock's view was 'conclusive', and he used it as ammunition trained on eighteenth-century slaving (Johnson 1986: 95).

The rehabilitation of Shylock can now be regarded as part of the renewed interest in character and its capacity to excite a spectator's powers of empathy. Shylock did not need to enjoin impeccable sentiments to be comprehensible.[18] Charles Lamb's distinction between Marlowe's Barabas ('a mere monster brought in with a large painted nose to please the rabble') and Shylock discovered 'something human' in the latter (*Specimen of English Dramatic Poets* (1808), in Bate 1992: 456). Macklin's rediscovery of the uncomic play was finally canonized in 1814 by Edmund Kean at Drury Lane. It was not only Kean's talent that unlocked more mercurial possibilities for Shylock, but also one member of the audience on its first night (26 January): William Hazlitt. Three years later, in his *Characters of Shakespeare's Plays*, he was to record the shock he received that night. Expecting 'a decrepid old man, bent with age and ugly with mental deformity' (Hazlitt 1930–4, 4: 323), Kean served up an intellectually and physically supple performance – see the account in Brown (1961). Shylock had shed years, and rejoined the human race. Though bowed down by prejudice, his own acquired variety as well as that shown him by others, Kean's Jew never lost 'his elasticity and presence of mind' (Review for *The*

Chronicle, 6 March 1816; Hazlitt 1930–4, 5: 296). He was more sinned against than even Macklin's creation, but it is likely that the most striking effect was visual: Kean had discarded the traditional (and alienating) red wig and appliqué hooked nose for a more modest head of black hair and beard.

For Hazlitt, the portrayal of character was a test of the creative reach of an artist. When lecturing on both Shakespeare and Milton in 1818 he discovered an aesthetic freedom in the poetic genius that was enshrined in the 'generic quality' of the imagination: 'its power of communication with all other minds' that derived from 'no one peculiar bias, or exclusive excellence' (*Lectures on the English Poets*; Hazlitt 1930–4, 5: 47). Shylock was, uncomfortably perhaps, a portion of ourselves (see Bate 1989: 180–1). For both William Charles Macready (1847, Drury Lane) and Edwin Booth (1867, New York) Shylock was actually part of a more unified and global dramatic experience. Macready's loving recreation of Venice and a painstaking reliance on historical detail was not literal-minded, but did detract from Shylock's powerful centrality. Similarly, Booth's gloriously appointed Winter Garden designs dwelt almost lovingly on a tourist's Venice: in John Gross's words, 'San Marco served as a backdrop in the street scene; the walls of the senate-chamber were hung with Tintorettos' (Gross 1992: 123; Lelyveld 1960: 63–77). What Booth had done was contrast the hatred of the outsider with the gaiety of those who had already joined the club.[19]

There is plenty of evidence that the nineteenth century saw Shylock as a dark character study whose presence in Venice was part of a larger statement about human subjectivity. As the century progressed, comment on the play found its dual plot curiously intermingled on several levels. Various perspectives on the same set of actions partook of Hazlitt's 'no one peculiar bias'. It is unsurprising that at the same time Victorian productions immersed the audience in spectacle and the exotic. For Henry Irving's *Merchant* (1879) at the Lyceum, the Venetian colours of carnival, the prelude to the elopement scene, ended with the curtain dropped to break the action before the stark dusk and moonlight of the same scene broken only by the gleams of Shylock's lantern on his return to what he was about to learn was an empty house. There was a further addition that has appeared on further occasions as well. On Shylock's painful exit from the trial he was pursued by a knot of Jews, but just as many Christians, baying for blood. Irving's Jew had developed a pride in his self-possession – up to this moment when he dwindled into a study of pathos, the same sudden degeneration that awaited Laurence Olivier's Shylock in Jonathan Miller's National Theatre production of 1970. An all but assimiliated late Victorian businessman, Olivier displayed Shylock as perfectly capable of riding this particular storm out until his final stumble off-stage and last howl of almost bestial anguish (see Bulman 1991: 95; Gross 1992: 301–4).

In a very significant sense this call for renewed attention to the way in which racial variety only appears to be disguised in a world of commercial transactions runs counter to more mythical or even psychanalytic readings of the play. In Richard G. Moulton's *Shakespeare as a Dramatic Artist* (1885) Shylock, for example, becomes simply a nemesis figure out of the story of the Jew, a function of the plot to illustrate how 'Antonio's excess of moral confidence suffers a nemesis of reaction in his humiliation, and [how] Shylock's sin of judicial murder finds a nemesis of retribution in his ruin by process of law' (Moulton 1906: 47). In Sigmund Freud's essay on 'The Theme of the Three Caskets' (1953–74, 12: 291–301) Shylock is not mentioned. This more holistic approach to the action has helped cast a colder eye on Venice and a more indulgent one on the value of friendship. E.E. Stoll refused to find Shylock's humanity entirely without dross in his *Shakespeare Studies* essay from 1927. The pathos is always held at bay, 'so hedged about is it with prejudice, beginning on a note of thwarted avarice and of revengefulness, and ending on one of rivalry in revenge' (Stoll 1960: 324). This reversal of the Romantic critical tide that had carried Shylock right to the centre of the play's mystery gave rein to those who were Venetians at heart. Harley Granville-Barker was so taken with Venice that he constructed his 'Preface' to the play around a contrast between 'sordid Shylock and Tubal and our magnificent young gentlemen, superfine still of speech and manner, but not above a little Jew-baiting' (Granville-Barker 1930: 346–7). The tone is generally ironic here – but the point is still carried. There is a fairy-tale here, the spirit of Belmont and the task assigned to Bassanio, and Shylock gets in the way.

At the same time as this spirit of revision was taking hold, there were bold attempts to dispense with the glamour and detail that the Victorian stage had introduced. Perhaps the most celebrated (or notorious) was the 1932 Stratford-upon-Avon Festival production, directed by the Russian Theodore Komisarjevsky, which dispensed with recognizable locations and bathed the whole acting space in shades of green and crimson. Morocco and Arragon were reduced to the level of comic butts, as was a hapless Duke, all at sea in the trial scene. Portia wore over-sized spectacles, and Antonio came near to being a sensualist, his melancholy merely a surfeit of pleasures. Against this effete backdrop, Shylock's glowering mendacity and sense of upright principle protested rather too much. Moreover, the effect on the Belmont plot was not in its favour. The events of the 1940s soon determined that *The Merchant* could no longer be about matters either merely entertaining or universally abstract.

With increasing archival illustration, many recent commentators have isolated not just racial distinctions but also those derived from gender or capitalism or both. For E.C Pettet, the problem of usury (from his essay of 1945) was an Elizabethan one, and his rediscovery of Thomas Wilson's *Discourse upon Usury* (1572) plus R.H Tawney's 'Introduction' to the 1925 edition provided a bridge to more contemporary anxieties. As Elizabethan usurers were not Jews, but City of London merchants, the play provided a covert thesis on the fatal necessity of the money market. Since 1571 the activity had become legal, but, in tracts such as Miles Mosse's *Arraignment and Conviction of Usury* (1595) and Wilson's, the Real World of negotiation and compromise was regarded as eroding the hitherto steadfast interpretations of Holy Writ. By emphasizing the Jewishness of the activity, the moneyed interest came over as 'something alien to the national and traditional way of life' (Wilders 1969: 107). This same ambiguity about the excesses of hazard and investment is now a contemporary issue, as David Thacker's 1993 Royal Shakespeare Company production demonstrated, set in a geographically imprecise City of stocks, shares and VDUs. Thanks to the exacting ultra-modern set, the tubular chrome office framework had to double as a Belmont orchard.

Just as surely as there are those who find the play a comment on completely free enterprise, this perspective is challenged by a Belmontian emphasis on 'love's wealth', as John Russell Brown had it in his 1957 essay on the play, in his *Shakespeare and his Comedies* (1962). Brown strives to keep Shylock within bounds, as a negative example, to be contrasted with 'a purposefully contrasted generosity in love as portrayed by Antonio, Portia, Bassanio, and others' (Brown 1962: 73). C.L Barber, whose deservedly influential *Shakespeare's Festive Comedy* (1959) challenged a generation of character analysers, was more concerned to identify Shylock's function in the general plan of the play: 'Shylock is the opposite of what the Venetians are; but at the same time he is an embodied irony, troublingly like them'. In terms that recall Moulton's concern with the nemesis figure, Barber finds Shylock a Scapegoat: 'a figure in whom the evils potential in a social organization are embodied, recognized and enjoyed during a period of licence, and then in due course abused, ridiculed and expelled' (Barber 1959: 168). Anthony Sher's portrayal in the 1987 RSC version (directed by Bill Alexander) tapped some of this fascinated regard for the exotic outsider. Obviously a Levantine Jew, Sher was vengeful, yet amidst gentile prejudice of a high order. As he himself put it in his interview for *Drama*, the temptation to find the play just about 'anti-Semitism' was not a contemporary preoccupation, as it attacked racism in general (Sher 1987). For Barber, the closing scenes gave us a community that had found its *raison d'être* – even if it existed in an ideal and abstract sense. Sher found the audience reaction to the production a high-risk option, especially in the reversal of the trial scene, which still provoked 'a roar of delighted applause' (Sher 1987: 29; see Bulman 1991: 117–42). The potential for a homosexual relationship between Bassanio and Antonio (a kiss of more than platonic companionableness in Act I, scene i) also left the closing harmony rather less than enhanced in Barber's terms. For W.H. Auden, in his essay 'Brothers and Others' (from *The Dyer's Hand* (1963)), the fairy-tale motif need not be purely of a heterosexual nature. As a last tableau, Alexander engineered it so that Jessica and Antonio would be alone on stage, and neatly wove together matters of both sexual and racial significance. Having let fall her convert's cross, Jessica prepared to pick it up only to find Antonio had got there first. The lights went out on her hand reaching up (but not grasping) the crucifix, which he held (sardonically?) just out of her reach.

The above debate about Shylock's role would seem to be an all-engrossing matter. To a degree, the play has become Shylock's, yet this collection of readings demonstrates how difficult it has become to isolate individual items. *The Merchant of Venice* refuses, thankfully, to obey most laws of aesthetic unity and also fails to deliver the full Romance of both the *Gesta* and *Il Pecorone*. This might seem to make it a play more for the study and seminar room, yet, however much a theme-hunter's playground, it eventually denies also the validity of an allegorical approach *tout court*, and opens the text to, and helps us recognize, those 'non-discursive forces' that so provide us with norms and expectations that the text is both 'comprehensible' *and* transgressive.

CHAPTER 1

Historical Difference and Venetian Patriarchy

JOHN DRAKAKIS

[John Drakakis's reading of *The Merchant of Venice* draws on several associated perceptions concerning the role of literature (specifically drama) in late sixteenth-century English society. The search for 'historical difference' is not some deliberately divisive strategy with no higher end in view, but rather the basis for all full understanding of the past, as it emphasizes details normally ignored in order to serve the traditional stress on identity ('They were much like us – nothing really changes'). For Bertold Brecht (quoted this essay, pp. 25–6), the reverse should be the case, because the force of drama lies in its 'impermanence'. If the understanding of literature throws up a perspective on the past *and present* as open to significant change, indeed, as always in process, then this cannot help but stress how most texts are basically divided in their aims: emergent ideas war with residual forms and settled notions. We may recognize certain works as 'Tragedies' or 'Comedies', but these transhistorical generic categories actually inform us little about the dramatic conflicts contained within the movement towards their prescribed conclusions.

For Roland Barthes, in his *Mythologies* (1973), there is a constant tendency (which must be resisted) to efface this 'difference' by relying on 'myths', that is, narratives that are taken to derive from basic human concerns and so capable of communicating truths. Myths are, however, stories with certain agendas and propose a world-view in the guise of merely recording human responses. No matter how much the form appears to be identical with the 'truth' communicated, the one underpinning the other, for Barthes they are perpetually involved in an elusive alternation of focus, not direct contradiction (see Barthes 1973: 123–4). The narrative is at once just a story gradually unfolding in time and winning our empathetic involvement, yet it is also a global statement which motivates (perhaps unconsciously) all stages of its development:

> We reach here the very principle of myth: it transforms history into nature. We can understand why, *in the eyes of the myth-consumer*, the intention, the adhomination of the concept can remain manifest without however appearing to have an interest in the matter: what causes mythical speech to be uttered is perfectly explicit, but it is immediately frozen into something natural; it is not read as a motive, but as a reason.
>
> (Barthes 1973: 129)

Thus, Shylock can be simultaneously the stage Jew, part of a theatrical tradition, and also a specific cultural reference to the late Elizabethan understanding of the alien 'other'.

In these latter terms, he is a significant part of the process by which this society defines itself, as non-usuring, familiar, subscribing to the *agape* of the New Testament, and understanding what spirit means in terms of manners and apparent equity. Unfortunately, this cannot help but entail a further set of hidden assumptions – not part of the mythic narrative directly, but available due to critical and so 'perverse' assessments of the play: that Antonio needs Jewish help in order that Bassanio's pursuit of Portia might come to fruition, that the 'familiar' is actually Venice, not London, that 'spirit' only proves itself endorsed in the trial scene by subscribing to an unexpectedly literal reading of the bond, and that this eventual, dextrous use of law eerily supports *Shylock's* reliance on its even-handedness.

These fissures in the structure of the play cannot, and should not, be ignored simply because we think we 'really' knew what Shakespeare had in mind: a totally unified artefact, built around a describable Aristotelian 'action'. As Drakakis illustrates, building on the perceptions of both Jonathan Dollimore and Michel Pêcheux, the binary opposition of superiority (Christian patriarchy) and subjection (Jewish reaction) suggest each other, and the relation is a critical one. Unlike generations of commentators on the play, however, this relation allows two-way traffic.

For further comment on the use here of Marxist concepts, see the headnote to the essay by Graham Holderness, pp. 57–60.]

Nigel Wood

I

In his 'Introduction' to the Penguin edition of *The Merchant of Venice*, Moelwyn Merchant (1967: 8) rejects Harley Granville-Barker's dismissive account of the play as a 'fairy-tale' on the grounds that

It is usually unsafe to mistake Shakespeare's lightness of touch for levity, or assume that an illogical fantasy, as early as *The Merchant of Venice* or as late as *The Tempest*, is a mere tale, a moment of relaxation.

But he goes on to assert that although the play 'is much preoccupied with two matters of Elizabethan concern: Jewry and usury', there are dangers in the assumption that 'the play is "about" race and greed' (Merchant 1967: 9). Throughout, Merchant is aware of a Shakespearian even-handedness in his opposing of the different economic practices of Antonio and Shylock in the play, the dramatist allegedly refusing, and by implication, choosing not, to take sides, and as a result evincing a moral tone which is neither indignant of usury, nor expedient (Merchant 1967: 16). Clearly, Merchant is troubled by the play, but his unease – which extends to a comprehensive critique of the ways in which the play manipulates the niceties of the Elizabethan judicial system – is compromised by an overwhelming concern to find an order which vindicates Shakespeare's superior artistry, while at the same time asserting that the play ends unequivocally in concord: 'The "concord" has been hard-won in *The Merchant of Venice* but it is achieved with a gracious dignity and with wit' (Merchant 1967: 60).

What plays across Merchant's very sensitive essay is a simultaneous awareness of the *difference* which a text such as *The Merchant of Venice* generates between its own historically specific concerns and those of the modern world, and of its *sameness* in so far as those historical differences can be collapsed into a timeless presence. It is to this notion of a 'timeless presence' that a materialist account of a text such as *The Merchant of Venice* addresses itself. Moreover, this location of 'sameness' is part of a general process to which Bertold Brecht objected in his *A Short Organum for the Theatre*, where he advocated a redefinition of theatrical practice in 'historically relative terms'. His argument is of direct relevance to a play such as this in which complex and problematical historical factors are often filtered out through the cognate processes of reading and theatrical representation (see Bulman 1991: 28–101; Brown 1966: 71–90); indeed, what he demanded of the analysis and representation of social structures in general is *a fortiori* true of the critical mediations of literary productions of the past. Brecht (1977: 190) insists that:

we must drop our habit of taking the different social structures of past periods, then stripping them of everything that makes them different; so that they all look more or less like our own, which then acquire from this process a certain air of having been there all along, in other words of permanence pure and simple. Instead we must leave them their distinguishing marks and keep their impermanence always before our eyes, that our own period can be seen to be impermanent too.

This emphasis upon historical 'process', and 'change', this regarding 'of nothing as existing except insofar as it changes, in other words is in disharmony with itself' (Brecht 1977: 193), directs our attention away from questions of aesthetic coherence, and of the finished work as the proper object of an allegedly disinterested critical contemplation, and towards the historically specific conditions of its production and subsequent reception. These conditions are necessarily inscribed within a dialectic of *difference* which only a politically involved and theoretically aware reading can properly recover. To locate 'change' in the past is to affirm the possibility of change in the present, and to detect the process working imaginatively through the tensions, structural discontinuities, and contradictions negotiated through any text, is to observe the manner in which such change might be articulated, perceived and possibly secured. It should also be emphasized that this fundamentally political trajectory is simultaneously a product of *reading* as much as it is the property of any text. In other words, it is the reception of a text by subsequent generations of readers (and in the case of a theatrical text, spectators) that will determine the cultural use that is made of it. Texts themselves do not usually or systematically *resist*, although there are exceptions such as Laurence Sterne's novel *Tristram Shandy* (1759–67), Trevor Griffiths's play *Comedians* (1976), or, indeed, many of the plays of Brecht, whereas reading always identifies interests in a particular text which it frequently ascribes to an authorial intention. To resist the dynamics of this process is no less political in its determination to establish 'sameness', continuity, or the primacy of 'ideas' over material cultural practice, though its politics, unselfconscious and divested of a theoretical rigour, are displaced into the sphere of aesthetics and invariably ascribed to the text itself. Merchant's account of the variability of the play's language presupposes an existing formal 'pattern':

When Shakespeare, then, came to write *The Merchant of Venice* he had at his command a range of dramatic verse and prose to express every modulation which the play's pattern demanded. In the transitions from the trial scene of the fourth Act to the closing tones of Belmont this range was tested to its furthest point in Shakespeare's early maturity.

(Merchant 1967: 44)

But we may juxtapose against this Theodor Adorno's insistence that 'I have no wish to soften the saying that to write lyric poetry after Auschwitz is barbaric; it expresses in negative form the impulse which inspires committed literature' (Adorno, 'Commitment' (1965) in Taylor 1980: 188),[1] except that, perhaps, the truly barbaric activity might consist in the self-apologetic emotional response to lyric poetry which in certain circumstances the text of The Merchant of Venice might elicit from a modern reader.[2] The question, therefore, for us, is not whether as modern readers we should refrain from reading a text such as The Merchant of Venice, a form of readerly cynicism which might parallel the negative valuation of writing and accept Adorno's verdict, rather it is a question of how we might read it, given the inescapable modern conditions of the text's reception. It also raises fundamental questions about the role and function of 'art' both in Elizabethan society, and in our own.

II

In his book The Stranger in Shakespeare (1973), Leslie Fiedler argues that Shakespeare's The Merchant of Venice is 'undeniably, among other things, a play about a Jew'. Following a number of commentators, he suggests that the occasion of the play may have been the scandal of Elizabeth I's Portuguese Jewish physician, Roderigo Lopez, who was executed for treason, and that this incident was still in the minds of theatre audiences who 'having scarcely any other Jews on whom to vent their wrath, demanded on stage symbolic scapegoats' (Fiedler 1973: 86).[3] In addition, Fiedler locates a further tension in the play arising out of the conflict between Judaism and Christianity, a conflict deeply implicated in the structures of patriarchy, whereby figures such as Antonio represent those 'Christian sons, who, in seeking to destroy Judaism, have turned against the father of Jews and Christians alike, the patriarch Abraham' (Fiedler 1973: 111). Fiedler's argument proceeds from there to the proposition that the play embodies a range of 'myths' and 'archetypes' within whose framework the fate of a figure such as Shylock represents an attempt to translate into mythological form the dogmatic compromise by which Christianity managed to make the New Testament its Scripture without surrendering the Old, and in the course of doing so, worked out ways of regarding the Jews simultaneously as the ultimate enemy, the killers of Christ, and the chosen people, with whom God made the covenant, the bond (this is the meaning of 'testament'), under which all who believe in Jesus the Christ are saved.

(Fiedler 1973: 117–18)

A little later, in a provocative comment in his chapter on *Othello*, Fiedler goes on to argue, in relation to the maid Emilia's defence of female infidelity as 'woman's sole weapon in what she takes to be the endless battle of the sexes' (Fiedler 1973: 166), that 'Exploited outsiders tend to resemble each other strangely, so that women and Jews fall together not only in Shakespeare but in the imagination of the Western world as a whole' (Fiedler 1973: 167).

Fiedler's general approach, which moves swiftly from the demands of 'history' to those of 'myth', finally falls prey to precisely that 'operational movement' whereby, as Barthes (1973: 142) observed, concrete social relations emerge through the process of mythologizing as 'a harmonious display of essences'. Thus Fiedler's displacement of the historically specific concerns of a play such as *The Merchant of Venice* to the level of 'myth' enacts a process of essentializing, analogous to that of the text itself, which, Barthes (1973: 143) argues, 'embodies a defaulting' upon the representation of 'the whole of human relations in their real, social structure, in their power of making the world'.

A critical raising of the text to the level of 'myth' is, however, a slightly different proposition from the process of mythologizing that might be detected at work in the text itself, as a material practice. Here we come up against questions of historical context which extend beyond the kind of stimulus to which I have already referred, to encompass the role and status of theatrical art in Elizabethan society, and the extent to which it may or may not be complicit with cultural myths. If, as Adorno has observed, 'Art is the negative knowledge of the actual world' (Adorno, 'Reconciliation under Duress' (1961) in Taylor 1980: 160), then the historical question that we need to ask of this problematical text is, to what extent does it succeed in achieving an internal distance from the cultural material with which it deals? The answer to that question is closely tied up with the actual social positioning of the Elizabethan theatre as institution, not one based on a model of capitalist consumption, but one based on a tense opposition between 'work' and 'pleasure', as opposed to the development of a leisure industry, and an exchange involving the simultaneous representation *and* critical mediation of communal values and assumptions. Or, to put it another way, the Elizabethan theatre stood in a relation of *difference* to the values and norms of Elizabethan culture, and as such could not but be sensitive to the differentially constructed relationships which constituted that culture. Being in a position of 'otherness' itself, that is to say, existing *outwith* the boundaries of official ideology, but at the same time being symbolically central to its definition, it could recuperate for its practices those images of the dominant order, at times simply representing them, at others inverting them, but always rendering them 'open': at times reinforcing their ideological power, while at others exposing the inadequacies of ideology to contain contradiction. It would be wrong to regard the theatre as existing wholly in an ironic relationship to culture, but it had available to it a variety of different positions, all of which could be represented within a single text. This is not to restate the proposition that Shakespearian texts were characterized by their stylistic and linguistic plenitude, rather that the variety of modes of articulation could produce discordant effects within the text itself, and thus render the demand for generic conformity inoperable. I want to argue that *The Merchant of Venice* is just such a text.

III

In her recent book, *Strangers to Ourselves*, Kristeva (1991: 1) observes:

> Strangely, the foreigner lives within us: he is the hidden face of our identity, the space that wrecks our abode, the time in which understanding and affinity founder. By recognizing him within ourselves, we are spared detesting him in himself.

Later she goes on to suggest that 'The foreigner who imagines himself to be free of borders, by the same token challenges any sexual limit' (Kristeva 1991: 31), and she further suggests that the foreigner 'can only be defined in negative fashion'; he is 'the other of the family, the clan, the tribe' (Kristeva 1991: 95). If we apply this to the figure of Shylock in *The Merchant of Venice*, then it will be clear that he stands in a negative relation of 'otherness' to Venetian society. But, as a number of commentators on the play have observed, Venetian society is not presented uncritically. So there is a sense in which Shylock represents an externalization, and a demonization of a force that Venice finds necessary in order for it to conduct its daily commercial activity, but which it cannot acknowledge as such. Indeed, we may say, provisionally, along with Greenblatt (1990: 43), that in this play 'the Jew seems to embody the abstract principle of *difference* itself' which, in the trial scene in Act IV, resolves itself into the negative pole of the opposition between 'reason' and 'madness'. If this were simply the case, then the difference between the two radically opposed mercantile activities in Venice would achieve a sinister clarity in its reinforcement of that anti-Semitism which was known to have been rife in Elizabethan society. Shylock is certainly the victim of judicial violence in the play, and Venice certainly depicts him negatively. But unless we are to think along certain oversimplified new historicist lines that Shylock is merely an effect of Venetian power which requires to be contained, then we are forced to recognize that there is much more at stake in this conflict. In this more complex version, Shylock is not primarily a realistic representation, not a 'Jew' in the strictly ethnological sense of the term, but both a subject position *and* a rhetorical means of prising open a dominant Christian ideology no longer able to smooth over its own internal contradictions, and therefore a challenge and a threat. But the nature of this threat is rendered in a combination of theatrical and sociological terms in the play. We know that the figure of the 'Jew' was a theatrical type, and as such identified with the theatre itself, but in the play Shylock is depicted as a repressive puritan who presents a challenge to the orthodoxies of restraint and pleasure to which the theatre itself would claim allegiance. Shylock's own pronouncement on Venetian masques issues an implicit challenge to the play-world as he instructs Jessica:

> Clamber not you up to the casements then,
> Nor thrust your head into the public street
> To gaze on Christian fools with varnished faces;
> But stop my house's ears – I mean my casements:
> Let not the sound of shallow fopp'ry enter
> My sober house.

> (II.v.31–6)

Later, when his daughter has eloped with Lorenzo, he confronts Salerio and Solanio. The latter identifying him as 'the devil' (III. i.19) and proceeding to play bawdily upon the alleged sexual effects of puritanical repression; to Shylock's expostulation: 'My own flesh and blood to rebel!', Solanio retorts: 'Out upon it, old carrion, rebels it at these years?' (III. i.132–4). Here the challenge to Shylock's patriarchy, which, as we shall see later, the play takes very seriously, is turned back upon him as an allegation of sexual deviation, aligning corrupt venality with the faint suggestion of incest. Sexual rebellion is posited as the transgressive 'other' of those romantic rituals and property relations which, elsewhere in the play, are venerated as necessary for the sustenance of Venetian society. Interestingly, Shylock's patriarchal law has no force in relation to Jessica, unlike that 'will of a dead father' (I.ii.24) which restrains the 'blood' and living will of Portia.

But let us return for a moment to the question of 'realism' in relation to the figure of Shylock, and particularly to Stephen Greenblatt's brief remarks on *The Merchant of Venice* as a prologue to his reading of Marlowe's *The Jew of Malta* through Marx's early essay 'On the Jewish Question'. It is Greenblatt's contention that Marx's essay 'represents the nineteenth-century development of a late sixteenth-century idea or, more accurately, a late sixteenth-century trope'. He continues:

> Marlowe and Marx seize upon the Jew as a kind of powerful rhetorical device, a way of marshaling deep popular hatred and clarifying its object. The Jew is charged not with racial deviance or religious impiety but with economic and social crime, crime that is not only committed *against* the dominant Christian society but, in less 'pure' form, by that society. Both writers hope to focus attention upon activity that is seen as at once alien and yet central to the life of the community and to direct against the activity the anti-Semitic feeling of the audience. The Jews themselves in their real historical situation are finally incidental in these works, Marx's as well as Marlowe's, except insofar as they excite the fear and loathing of the great mass of Christians.
>
> (Greenblatt 1990: 41)

Greenblatt concludes that the difference between Marx and Marlowe is that where 'Marx can finally envisage the liberation of mankind from what he inexcusably calls "Judaism" Marlowe cannot'. For Marlowe's Barabas, a radical commitment to 'the anarchic, playful discharge of his energy' functions to divest him of 'hope' and leads to his ultimate self-destruction (Greenblatt 1990: 55), whereas for Marx 'there is the principle of hope without the will to play (Greenblatt 1990: 56). By contrast, in the more evenly dialectical world of *The Merchant of Venice*, Shylock both is and is not the alienated essence of Christian society; indeed, his appeal to what Greenblatt calls 'moments of sameness' which run 'like a dark current through the play, intimating secret bonds that no one, not even the audience, can fully acknowledge', can often compel them to transform 'into a reassuring perception of difference' (Greenblatt 1990: 43). Greenblatt insists that Shylock represents the point of convergence of a series of constitutive structural oppositions in the text, but what traditional criticism has come to regard as a fullness of characterization, here becomes a substantive *subject position* which the phrase 'rhetorical device' only partly encompasses. This is not so much the construction of the figure of Shylock as an *effect* of linguistic difference, rather it represents that convergence of a multiplicity of identities in the figure of Shylock *against* which Venetian identity defines itself. This does not so much rule out 'history' as an effect of discourse; on the contrary, it marks that complex point of entry of a range of discrete 'histories' as 'absent causes', into discourse, showing how textual forms make accessible to audiences and readers that which resists reduction to the status of 'text' (see Jameson 1981: 34).[4] What Shylock represents in *The Merchant of Venice* is what Barthes would describe as a transformation of history 'into nature', at the same time as the 'myth' which he embodies 'is a type of speech chosen by history' (Barthes 1973: 110).

The process that we see operating through the text of *The Merchant of Venice* is one which, with the benefit of hindsight, can be shown to constitute a systematic 'forgetting', effected through the conversion of Shylock, and the formal shift into the genre of comedy as a means of effecting closure. Whereas in tragedy what we experience is the *isolation* of the protagonist, in comedy the closure is usually one which incorporates participants into an inclusive definition of 'society'. But the play also, uncomfortable with its own formal means of resolution, testifies to a history which Lyotard (1990: 22) outlines in his statement that

> 'The jews', never at home where they are, cannot be integrated, converted, or expelled. They are also always away from home when they are at home, in their so-called own tradition, because it includes exodus as its beginning, excision, impropriety, and respect for the forgotten.

As we shall see, the language of 'forgetting' paradoxically carries its own intractable history with it, which the formal mechanisms of comedy cannot successfully bring to full closure.

From a purely historical perspective *The Merchant of Venice* is a play which, as has often been recognized, appears to confront economic questions directly. Some fifty years ago (1945), E.C. Pettet observed that it 'contains one of Shakespeare's rare considerations of a major socio-economic problem of his time', that of usury ('*The Merchant of Venice* and the Problem of Usury', in Wilders 1969: 100); although, in what is arguably the best materialist account of the play to date, Cohen (1985: 199) has pointed out that the bond between Antonio and Shylock is not usurious in the strict sense of the term at all. Indeed, Cohen goes on to suggest that the play's conflict is 'a special instance of the struggle, widespread in Europe, between Jewish quasi-feudal fiscalism and native bourgeois mercantilism, in which the indigenous forces usually prevailed', and in this context Shylock is conceived as 'an old man with obsolete values trying to arrest the course of history' (Cohen 1985: 202). Cohen's argument, quite different from Pettet's or indeed from R.H. Tawney's which inscribes the response to a generalized conception of usury within the framework of medieval ideology, 'as part of a hierarchy of values, embracing all interests and activities, of which the apex was religion' (Tawney 1947: 158), derives its emphasis directly from Marx's chapter on 'Pre-capitalist Relations' in *Capital* Volume 3. Here it is argued that 'usury centralizes monetary wealth. It does not change the mode of production, but clings to it like a parasite and impoverishes it'; thus, Marx continues, 'In place of the old exploiter, whose exploitation was more or less patriarchal, since it was largely a means of political power, we have a hard money-grubbing upstart. But the mode of production remains unaltered' (Marx 1981: 731). Indeed, we may deduce from this that although the position of the usurer was clearly, in moral and ethical terms, on the margins of the social order, the political effect of his activity was symbolically central to its operation and to its self-definition. In other words, the usurer stood in a relation of *difference* to the dominant order, he was its 'other', having no independent existence or self-definition. But at another level usurious capital fulfilled a potentially revolutionary function, since, aligned with 'mercantile wealth', it helped to 'bring about the formation of a monetary wealth independent of landed property' (Marx 1981: 732–3). In the play this notion of the landless usurer is given an added historical piquancy in its emphasis upon the inverted and 'devilish' household attributed to Shylock, compared with the fully integrated and legitimized household of Belmont. For Marx usury is conservative in that it reinforces an already extant mode of production, but makes it 'more wretched' (Marx 1981: 745), at the same time, as we saw earlier in relation to Leslie Fiedler, that is, it is associated with a particular form of patriarchal control; but it is also potentially subversive in that it accelerates the erosion of the very means through which patriarchal power and authority realize themselves fully: landed property.

If we bear this in mind, then the proliferation of treatises on the subject of usury, from the time of Martin Luther onwards, takes on a slightly different complexion from its usual designation as 'background' material. Indeed, they may be said to constitute a web of discourses into which the text of *The Merchant of Venice* intervenes. For Luther (1962, 2: 297), usury 'lays burdens upon all lands, cities, lords, and people, sucks them dry, and brings them to ruin', and eliminates the influence of God in human affairs. Sir Thomas Wilson, in his *A Discourse Upon Usurye* (1572) argues that the practice is 'against nature' (Wilson 1572: sig*3ᵛ), and destructive of the entire social fabric of society. Perhaps one of the most interesting alignments of usurious practice with femininity occurs in Philip Caesar's *A General Discourse Against The Damnable Sect of Usurie* (1578), where it is conceived as a form of self-deception analogous to an unruliness associated with the figure of the biblical Eve: 'For thei whiche painte their couetousnesse vnder this colour, beeyng deceiued by their domesticall *Eve*, their corrupt Nature whiche was misreablie seduced by Sathan, wilfully destroy them selues, and by their owne sophistrie are deceiued' (Caesar 1578: sig. N2ᵛ). This strategic feminizing of usury is also augmented with images which abound in tracts, and later plays, concerned with rapaciousness and sterility. The tracing through of these images as part of a series of discursive strategies lays down a radical challenge to traditional hierarchical methods of delineating 'source' material for a play such as *The Merchant of Venice*, and functions to suggest a recontextualization of its concerns way beyond those of a formal textual nature.

IV

In a provocative essay on *The Merchant of Venice*, W.H. Auden detected a series of disharmonies in the play. Like other commentators, he characterized Shylock as a marginalized figure, and a threat to the order of Venice: 'a professional usurer who, like a prostitute, has a social function but is an outcast from the community' (Auden 1963: 227). He saw this fundamental division echoed first in the character of Antonio, excluded from the pattern of marriage relationships at the end of the play because, 'though his conduct may be chaste [it] is concentrated upon a member of his own sex' (Auden 1963: 231), and finally in the opposition between Venice and Belmont – although they are related spheres of activity, 'their existences are not really compatible with each other' (Auden 1963: 234).

At a deep structural level there is less opposition between Venice and Belmont than at first seems to be the case, but the division that Auden identifies operates both at an external level in the opposition between 'Christian' and 'Jew', and at an internal level in the self-division of individual characters torn between romance and money, although the hidden motivation may be more complex than Auden himself believed.

To take the external division between 'Christian' and 'Jew' first: ostensibly, this would appear to be a straightforward conflict between two mutually hostile cultures, expressed in terms of religious and economic difference. To this extent Shylock may be said to represent both a challenge to the ethos of Venice, while at the same time providing the differential means through which that ethos achieves its own ideologically inflected self-definition. But it is worth recalling that although formulated as an external conflict between 'Christian' and 'Jew' – the position which in one sense Marx accedes to, as we have seen – many of the objections to usury levelled by English commentators at the time were expressly against *Christians* who practised it: 'I do not knowe', lamented Sir Thomas Wilson, 'anye place in Christendome, so much subiect to thys foule synne of usurie, as the whole realme of Englande ys at thys present, and hathe bene of late yeares' (Wilson 1572: sig D4ʳ). To this extent the Venetians in the play project onto Shylock a hatred which stems from their recognition of the need of his money to sustain their own society, but they refuse to acknowledge that his means of aquisition, which are in effect a practical necessity, can have either a religious or an ethical validation. In this sense, Shylock is the object upon whom Venetian society vents its own hatred of itself, and in this respect his own dramatic characterization is made to incorporate those negative social forces, such as puritanism, which challenge the norms of Venetian/Elizabethan society. It is within this complex web of significations, both as an *effect* of Venetian self-hatred, and as the representative of a historically ostracized ethnic group, that Shylock is forced to eke out a precarious existence, marginal, yet symbolically central to Venice's own perception of itself, tolerated, yet repressed.

Dollimore (1986: 59) has recently reminded us that in Marlowe's *Doctor Faustus*, 'Faustus violates Christianity in the name and image of Christ', and in so doing demonstrates how repressed energies return, 'via the very images, structures, and mechanisms of repression itself'. At one level, of course, it would appear that the dominant order *produces* its 'other' and prescribes, in order to limit, the resistance to which the latter has access. If we push this argument a little further we might say that Faustus's resistance is, therefore, *contained*. But, as Dollimore goes on to argue, this imitation of 'the dominant from below' results in a 'transgressive mimesis' whereby the repressed, 'even as it imitates, reproducing itself in terms of its exclusion, also demystifies, producing a knowledge of the dominant which excludes it, this being a knowledge which the dominant has to suppress in order to dominate' (Dollimore 1986: 61). Michel Pêcheux articulates this problem in terms of an opposition between the 'good subject', who adopts a position in which his/her subjection is 'freely consented to', and the 'bad subject' who takes up a position of 'separation (distantiation, doubt, interrogation, challenge, revolt . . .)' in relation to the reality to which he/she is expected to give consent; the result is 'a struggle against ideological evidentness on the terrain of that evidentness with a negative sign, reversed in its own terrain' (Pêcheux 1983: 156–7). Thus, the 'bad subject' is involved in what Pêcheux calls a counter-identification with the dominant discourse through which resistance to its ideological imperatives is made possible. In *The Merchant of Venice* this is a position which Shylock sustains for much of the play, and in doing so he is the instrument through which Venetian values are exposed, stripped of their ideological efficacy.

Significantly, Shylock's first appearance in the play occasions a dispute concerned with the reading of Scripture. The difference between Antonio and Shylock is a religious difference, but it extends into an area of juridical and social practice which sharpens the distinction between the two adversaries. The moment of Shylock's acceptance of Antonio's 'bond' is carefully juxtaposed against his refusal of Bassanio's invitation to dine with them: 'I will buy with you, sell with you, talk with you, walk with you, and so following; but I will not eat with you, drink with you, nor pray with you' (I.iii.33–5). The legality of Shylock's transaction – which is, in effect the only means he has of protecting himself – is, however, glossed on the occasion of Antonio's entry by a soliloquy which functions dramatically as a means of providing a motivation for the hatred that each bears to the other. Shylock's hatred of Antonio is reciprocal:

I hate him for he is a Christian,
But more for that in low simplicity

He lends out money gratis and brings down
The rate of usance here with us in Venice.
If I can catch him once upon the hip,
I will feed fat the ancient grudge I bear him.
He hates our sacred nation, and he rails,
Even there where merchants most do congregate,
On me, my bargains, and my well-won thrift,
Which he calls interest Cursèd be my tribe
If I forgive him.

(I.iii.39–49)

The difference between them is that Shylock's own violation of the decorum of dialogue serves simultaneously as a justification of his hatred, at the same time as it edges his characterization towards the position of the demonic. Moreover, Antonio, who for what will become clear *scriptural* reasons firmly resists Shylock's philosophy, begins by acknowledging the need for a practice that he despises:

Shylock, albeit I neither lend nor borrow
By taking nor by giving of excess,
Yet to supply the ripe wants of my friend
I'll break a custom.

(I.iii. 58–61)

It is difficult to gauge precisely how disingenuous this claim is, since Venice needs Shylock even though it despises him. But what this exchange does do is initiate a process of gradual exposure of the way in which Venice articulates Shylock. The latter's scriptural justification of his usurious practices is not challenged simply on the grounds of interpretation, but on those of a much deeper motivation – 'Mark you this, Bassanio,/The devil can cite Scripture for his purpose' (I.iii. 94–5) – and it is one for which some evidence earlier on in the scene has already been forthcoming. Thus, when after pointing up the contradictions in Christian practice, Shylock formulates his 'merry bond' (I.iii.170), its carnivalistic excess smacks of the subversive who operates from within the very discourse of demonization that Venice ascribes to him. Bassanio's 'I like not fair terms and a villain's mind' (I.iii.176) crystallizes that process of counter-identification through which Shylock evinces a familiar kind of behaviour, while at the same time exposing those contradictions in which Antonio and Bassanio are now caught, and against which their ideologically loaded responses can offer them no real protection.

In this context Shylock's rejection of Venetian social rituals represents a rejection of courtesies which are not contingent upon the latter's economic practices, but rather are constitutive of them. It is clear that dining, and male friendship, as well as romantic entanglement, are the socially constituted means through which Venice conducts both its interpersonal *and* public economic life. From the very outset the 'friendship' between Antonio and Bassanio effectively subsumes money into its aegis: 'My purse, my person, my extremest means,/Lie all unlocked to your occasions' (I.i.138–9); for him his 'person' is an extension of his 'purse', yet this is underwritten by an already extant friendship, and serves, in effect, to contain, while at the same time shadowing, a bawdy, carnivalesque meaning.[5] It is worth contrasting this utterance with Solanio's later account of Shylock's response to Jessica's elopement with Lorenzo where essentially the same formulation is made to produce a different, far more reductive effect, even though what is clearly at issue is the crucial question of patriarchal authority, that is in essence no different from that exercised by Portia's father, and accepted reluctantly by her. Here it is the *contents* of Shylock's 'purse' with which he is preoccupied, rather than with the purse as a facilitation of the practice of human multiplication:

> I never heard a passion so confused,
> So strange, outrageous, and so variable,
> As the dog Jew did utter in the streets:
> 'My daughter! O my ducats! O my daughter!
> Fled with a Christian! O my Christian ducats!
> Justice! The law! My ducats and my daughter! . . .'
>
> (II.viii.12–17)

Parody here functions to expose Shylock's behaviour as the practice of the 'bad subject', hinting at sexual excess as opposed to the legitimized sexual practices of Venetian society, and as such it augments Antonio's ascription of demonic tendencies to his adversary. Conversely, Shylock's parody of Venetian practices functions to expose the extent to which they are not so much essentially natural and hence humane, but rather irreducibly social constructions invested with powers of exclusion.

The vehemence of Antonio's response to Shylock's semitic identity – 'A goodly apple rotten at the heart./O, what a goodly outside falsehood hath!' (I.iii.98–9) – which is sustained throughout the play, is one of its most disturbing features. The image which Antonio produces of Shylock (which the latter's behaviour does little to invalidate), augmented with a cumulative rhetorical force, is that of the infernal patriarch whose very existence threatens to deconstruct the faith and practice of Venice. That in the play Shylock is given a 'family' of his own, that its own internal interpersonal, psychic, and emotional relations are directly represented, and that it is shown to be a divided unit – 'My own flesh and blood to rebel!' (III.i.32) – articulates in dramatic terms precisely that 'transgressive mimesis' which demystifies even as it imitates, and which is positioned in Venetian discourse as a demonic form, a challenge from below, a 'family' in the devil's name, so to speak. Let us pursue this question of patriarchy a little further in the play.

The debate between Antonio and Shylock about usury follows immediately upon the scene between Portia and Nerissa, set in Belmont. Here the emphasis is upon Portia's acceptance of the constraints imposed upon her by patriarchal law, but it is clear that this prescriptive restraint is a rational masculine response to the subversive potential of an irrational, feminized 'blood':

> I can easier teach twenty what were good to be done than to be one of the twenty to follow mine own teaching. The brain may devise laws for the blood, but a hot temper leaps o'er a cold decree: such a hare is madness, the youth, to skip o'er the meshes of good counsel, the cripple. But this reasoning is not in the fashion to choose me a husband. O me, the word 'choose'! I may neither choose who I would, nor refuse who I dislike; so is the will of a living daughter curbed by the will of a dead father. Is it not hard, Nerissa, that I cannot choose one nor refuse none?
>
> (I.ii.15–26)

Portia is here caught in a double bind, accepting the rationale for control, but agonizing over the uncertainty of its consequences. The whole issue is handled more circumspectly in the case of Jessica, where some justification for her rebellion is cautiously provided, but where the emotional effects upon her 'father', though contextualized parodically, as we have seen, imitate the frustrations consequent upon the loss of patriarchal authority. Nerissa's response to Portia's question illuminates for us the hermeneutic significance of the episode with the caskets as one involving the choice of one from a determinate number of 'meanings' – a domestic, gender-specific analogue of the discussion

between Antonio and Shylock in the following scene – which reinforces the patriarchal notion of authority which prevails throughout
the play; Nerissa responds:

> Your father was ever virtuous, and holy men at their death have
> good inspirations; therefore the lott'ry that he hath devised in
> these three chests of gold, silver, and lead, *whereof who chooses
> his meaning chooses you*, will no doubt never be chosen by any
> rightly but one which you shall rightly love.
>
> (I.ii.27–32; emphasis added)

In both cases the challenge to the dominant patriarchal order from
below, characterized in Portia's case as a rebellion of the (female)
'blood', and in Shylock's case literally as a rebellion of his 'own flesh
and blood', which Solanio mocks as a demonically Judaic excess – 'Out
upon it, old carrion! rebels it at these years?' (III.i.33–4) – threatens
a division in the ideology of patriarchy, and proposes that in certain
circumstances rebellion is justifiable.

Shylock's repression of his own 'flesh and blood', augmented with
the evidence in the play by the escape from captivity of Lancelot
Gobbo, becomes for the mocking Solanio the site of a hermeneutical
conflict: 'There is more difference between thy flesh and hers than between jet and ivory' (III.i.36–7). But by this point in the play Shylock
has accumulated a number of identities; what is now an infernally
hermaphroditic Shylock, who is both 'the dam' and the devilish instrument through which Jessica will, 'if the devil may be her judge"
(III.i.31), receive her damnation, is also puritanically anti-festive in his
disposition, a combination which marginalizes him theologically *and*
historically as the protean embodiment of all that is symbolically central to the play's dominant ideology.

The 'will' or law of Portia' s dead father represents a secret meaning
which it is the task of her prospective suitors to prise from the caskets;
this practice is underwritten by patriarchal goodness and virtue which
resists the temptation to align itself with shows of material wealth.
In a play where gold in its material guise figures prominently, the
housing of secret meanings in a leaden casket affirms ideologically the
non-material claims of Christian patriarchy. By contrast, Shylock's
patriarchy is shown to be not one of provision, but rather one of
tyranny and restraint. After his earlier refusal in Act I, scene iii, to
eat with Antonio and Bassanio, Shylock accepts an invitation to
supper, but goes 'in hate, to feed upon/The prodigal Christian'
(II.v.14–15). Moreover, his exhortation to Jessica to 'stop my house's

ears – I mean my casements:/Let not the sound of shallow fopp'ry enter/My sober house' (II.v.34–6) augments that initial counter-identification with a refusal to acknowledge that productive excess through which contractual obligations are celebrated in Venice.

In the case of Shylock, it is precisely the *failure* of this patriarchal power of constraint, embodied in Jessica's rebellion, which is empha-sized. But this creates an additional problem in that Shylock feels her rebellion as a father; and the language in which he articulates his own agony is one which imitates the ethos of Christian humanism, even though that position is not sustained, and the project to which it becomes allied is one which directly challenges Christian judicial practice:

> I am a Jew. Hath not a Jew eyes? Hath not a Jew hands, organs, dimensions, senses, affections, passions; fed with the same food, hurt with the same weapons, subject to the same diseases, healed by the same means, warmed and cooled by the same winter and summer, as a Christian is? If you prick us, do we not bleed? If you tickle us, do we not laugh? If you poison us, do we not die? And if you wrong us, shall we not revenge? If we are like you in the rest, we will resemble you in that. If a Jew wrong a Christian, what is his humility? Revenge. If a Christian wrong a Jew, what should his sufferance be by Christian example? Why, revenge. The villainy you teach me I will execute, and it shall go hard but I will better the instruction.
>
> (III.i.55–69)

In what is a superb example of resistance through counter-identification, Shylock's simultaneous alignment with, and exposure of, the essentially violent underpinnings of Venetian humanism, exposes some of the ways in which he is himself constructed as a 'sub-ject' in this social formation. If, as Barber (1959: 179) has perceptively observed, Shylock 'can be a drastic ironist because he carries to extremes what is present, whether acknowledged or not' by the values of a 'silken' Venetian world, then it has to be said that the irony is double-edged.

What draws Portia and Shylock together as particular foci of resistance is that they are both possessed of material wealth which Venice needs. What distinguishes them from each other in structural terms is that, while in Portia's case the institution already exists for making that wealth available, and constitutes a legitimate form of acquisition articulated through the discourses of romance and marriage, the stark necessity of Shylock's role in Venetian economic life can only be expressed negatively. Because he is engaged in an 'unnatural' and therefore unchristian practice, the sterile activity of making money breed, Venice can only admit him as a demonization of its own social and economic practices, and as an obstacle, in the sphere of aesthetics, to comic closure. Only when he is coerced fully into the life of Venice by being forced to become a Christian, does he become a reconstituted subject who can then play a full patriarchal role in its affairs, transferring his wealth legitimately to his heirs, and replenishing the coffers of the state. To this extent the play historicizes a key element of the genre, the obstructive father, by effecting what is actually a problematic transformation of its content. The transition for Shylock is, however, not an easy one; we should recall that, after being forced to accept Christian values, to be 'christened', in effect, he asks leave to depart the court of justice: 'I pray you, give me leave to go from hence./I am not well' (IV.i.391–2). Instead of succeeding in his quest to deprive Antonio of 'an equal pound/Of your fair flesh to be cut off and taken/In what part of your body pleaseth me' (I.iii.146–8) – itself, as James Shapiro has argued, a form of circumcision, and hence an attempt at conversion (Shapiro 1992: 14–15) Shylock is himself 'converted' and with that conversion comes an anxiety which he now shares with his adversary Antonio.

V

This moment marks the entry of Shylock into the Christian state, a process which enacts through its deployment of the metaphor of death and rebirth the history of Christianity itself:

> You take my house when you do take the prop
> That doth sustain my house; you take my life
> When you do take the means whereby I live.
>
> (IV.i.371–3)

Prevented from owning land, all Shylock has is his money; his life is synonymous with the means by which he lives. He is, however, coerced into Christian patriarchy, and his entry into this religion also involves his entry into the institutions in and through which it sustains itself; as Machiavelli observed, 'every religion has the basis of its life rooted in some one of its main institutions', at the same time as it inculcates a belief in the abrogation of the responsibility for human action now displaced on to a superhuman force: 'the god who can predict your future, be it good or evil, could also bring it about' (Machiavelli 1970: 143). Significantly, part of Shylock's accumulated wealth is to pass on his death, 'Unto his son Lorenzo and his daughter' (IV.i.386), betokening a shift from what Freud, in *Moses and Monotheism* (1938), called 'the religion of the father' to 'a religion of the son' (Freud 1953–74, 23: 88). If we were to extend this into a full-blown Freudian reading of this moment then we might connect the symbolic 'killing' of Shylock's Semitic identity with what Freud called, in *Civilization and Its Discontents* (1930), 'the killing of the primal father' (Freud 1953–74, 21: 132). Antonio's self-definition as 'a tainted wether of the flock,/Meetest for death' (IV.i.113–14) brings him into alignment with the emasculated Shylock whose identity at the end of the scene is reconstituted but under duress. For Antonio money 'breeds' in the sense that it permits him a vicarious pleasure in the amorous success of his friend, and yet there remains a vaguely articulated residue of guilt. With the 'conversion' of Shylock that guilt is given a much sharper focus; the symbolic 'killing' of 'the religion of the father' produces a psychic disability which is 'an expression of the conflict due to ambivalence, of the eternal struggle between Eros and the instinct of destruction or death'; for Freud, of course, this conflict is initiated when human beings form communities, and he goes on to insist that 'So long as the community assumes no other form than that of the family, the conflict is bound to express itself in the Oedipus complex' (Freud 1953–74, 21: 132). It is around the institution of the family, and the dispositions of power within its framework, that images of money, civilization and psychic disability circulate in this play. But I want to draw back from a full-blown Freudian reading, and to seek to identify the psychic energies in play at such moments in the text of *The Merchant of Venice* as symptoms of historical rather than universal and timeless phenomena.

It is only to this extent that it is possible to see Shylock as Cohen (1985: 202) sees him: 'a figure from the past – medieval, marginal, diabolical, irrational, anarchic'. He is, of course, both the focus of Christian history, and that part of it that requires to be repressed and marginalized in order for Venice to continue to function economically. To this extent he represents that *real* history which Venetian representations overlay with social and cultural forms designed to displace their own anxieties. Indeed, the 'discontent' which Shylock feels as he enters the domain of Christian patriarchy is a registering of that political repression upon which a form of national unity is predicated. Shylock is part of Venice' s own unconscious that it can only deal with either by repression, or by transformation into what we might call the Christian imaginary – that set of images and institutions in and through which Venice recognizes its own cultural identity. Here a form of anarchy, positioned in the play's dominant discourse as a 'damned' patriarchy, is repressed through the very mechanisms of sacrifice and salvation upon whose structures and images its ideologically dominant 'other' depends for its own identity. Thus, Shylock's 'transgressive mimesis' turns out to be the means whereby Venice recognizes itself and *experiences*, as Foucault would say, 'its positive truth in its downward fall' (Foucault 1977: 34). That process, however, decentres the human subject, splits him and forces him to live in the world, as it counsels him to disregard worldly practice: forced to accept a normative ethic of wealth accumulation whose operations are attributed to the determining force of a divinely motivated 'Nature', but committed by practical desire to secular intervention. By a subtle manoeuvre, the play first demystifies usury, and then discloses the mechanisms whereby it can be remystified again, transformed into a theatrical practice and dispersed through a series of symbolic representations which aligns the theatre itself with the non-theatrical production of cultural forms. But that mystification, once dismantled, is not easily reinstated. Shylock's 'illness' is the direct consequence of his entry into what is now a deeply decentred Christian patriarchy. His illness becomes, as it were, a form of self-hatred which can only be expressed in terms of a mechanism of displacement.

If Shylock's 'illness' is the condition of his entry into the patriarchal order of Venice, then Antonio's 'sadness' is a condition of his existence within it. The homily 'Of the Miseries of Man' counsels the open confession of 'our state of imperfection' (*Book of Homilies*, 1594: sig. B3^v), and ends with the exhortation: 'In the meane season, yea and at all times, let us learne to knowe our selves, our frailtie and weakenesse without any craking or boasting of our owne good deedes and merrites' (*Book of Homilies*, 1594: sig. B6^v). Antonio, we may recall, is committed to accepting a causal link between mercantile success and divine providence, where the operations of God are articulated as the 'risk' which the Christian merchant must always undertake. Antonio suffers also from a 'sadness' which is inexplicable: 'And such a want-wit sadness makes of me/That I have much ado to know myself' (I.i.6–7); in other words, his unease produces in him a failure to recognize himself, and as a consequence, his own identity is unsettled.

Criticism has generally been receptive to W.H. Auden's reading of the cause of Antonio's 'sadness': the consequence of frustrated homosexual desire for Bassanio. Certainly the sublimated metaphors of sexuality would, as we have already seen, lend some support to this view. In an attempt almost to equate the sterile breeding of money with homosexuality, Marilyn French somewhat confusingly asserts that in this instance 'erotic love of man for man is repudiated because it cannot breed naturally' (French 1982: 114). But at no level in the play is it possible to read such a negative image of male friendship. If the problem revolves around Antonio's 'friendship' with Bassanio, then it is important to understand what that relationship actually involves. Here friendship is deeply implicated in the process of wealth accumulation and distribution whose operations are subject to the vagaries of 'Nature', but whose practices can easily be displaced into the sphere of romantic pursuit. Bassanio plans to get rich by marrying Portia:

> if you please
> To shoot another arrow that self way
> Which you did shoot the first, I do not doubt,
> As I will watch the aim or to find both,
> Or bring your latter hazard back again
> And thankfully rest debtor for the first.

> (I.i.147–52)

For Antonio, this is not a matter of economics but 'honour', an honour that conflates, as we have seen, Antonio's 'purse' with his 'person', his identity with a capacity to inseminate. This is Shylock's 'Christian courtesy' (III.i.46), which he imitates himself when his daughter absconds with his wealth.

Antonio rejects the suggestion that his 'merchandise' should make him sad, since he has taken all human precaution against the vicissitudes of Nature:

> My ventures are not in one bottom trusted,
> Nor to one place; nor is my whole estate
> Upon the fortune of this present year:
> Therefore my merchandise makes me not sad.

> (I.i.42–5)

There is a sense in which Antonio as a Venetian 'subject' cannot admit *directly* to the need for money credit as a safeguard against failure. What Portia is later made to feel as a consequence of patriarchal constraint, Antonio anticipates as an experience which is unaccountably *in excess* of his own capacity to explain. That 'excess' is always present and threatens to undo those discursive formations through which Venice articulates its own mercantile practice; Venetian institutions convert the real mechanisms of financial exchange into a series of symbolic practices, such as the patriarchal bond between man and man, and the relationship between man and woman, where the two are not conflictual but complementary.[6] Any departure from that complex discursive formation of 'Christian courtesy' can only be admitted in textualized form as a demonic force. Shylock, therefore, comes to occupy that space in which Christian patriarchy seeks to efface through ideology the contradictions in its own practice of wealth accumulation. As Braudel (1982, 2: 166) observes of the Jews in the Renaissance generally: 'if they had not existed, it would surely have been necessary to invent them'. In reality the presence of Shylock as a composite figure who challenges Venetian mercantile practice at the same time as he represents, within the genre in which the play is nominally cast, an anti-comic force, signals a practical need which cannot be openly acknowledged without radically transforming the ethical basis of Christian patriarchal ideology altogether. In this way commercial activity is never quite represented in the play as itself, and is forced to repress, not homosexual desire, but the reality of its own operations in the world. The result is precisely that 'alienation' or loss of identity which Antonio laments, and which Marx identifies in the 'Christian state' which has yet to become fully secularized:

> In the so-called Christian state it is alienation [*Entfremdung*] that is important, and not man himself. The man who is important, the king, is being specifically differentiated from other men (which is in itself a religious conception), who is in direct contact with heaven and God. The relationships which prevail are still relationships of faith. This means that the religious spirit is not yet truly secularized.
>
> (Marx 1977: 50)

There are no monarchs in *The Merchant of Venice*, but this is the 'state' which the cross-dressed Portia invokes when, disguised as a man, she lectures Shylock on 'mercy'. Indeed, the Duke arrogates to himself all of those patriarchal powers that elsewhere in Shakespeare are associated with monarchy.[7] Here in the most ironical of contexts, a Christian 'mimesis' is proposed that will supersede the dependency upon the letter of the law which Shylock invokes to protect his interests:

It blesseth him that gives and him that takes.
'Tis mightiest in the mightiest. It becomes
The thronèd monarch better than his crown.
His sceptre shows the force of temporal power,
The attribute to awe and majesty,
Wherein doth sit the dread and fear of kings;
But mercy is above this sceptred sway.
It is enthronèd in the hearts of kings;
It is an attribute to God himself,
And earthly power doth then show likest God's
When mercy seasons justice.

(IV.i.184–94)

From the outset, therefore, Antonio's 'sadness'; and his lack of self-knowledge are, to a very considerable extent, the *subject* of *The Merchant of Venice*, although the play cannot speak its concerns directly except in terms of an intolerant, deeply nationalistic fear.

VI

Thus far our concern has been to situate the figure of Shylock in the aesthetic and historical structures of the text of *The Merchant of Venice*, to demonstrate the threat which he poses to the society which needs his services but marginalizes him for providing them. He represents that part of Venice's experience that it habitually represses, although when that experience surfaces it challenges the stability of identity itself. Our discussion, therefore, has moved away from 'character', and from the presumption of a deep structural similarity between antagonistic forces in the play, to those *differentially* constructed mechanisms whose operations are disclosed at moments of disturbance in the text. Very often what is read in this text as 'sameness' turns out to be inflected very differently; when Shylock repeats Christian values, he does so at a distance from them, and the result is a kind of parody which serves to expose their investment in ideology. In this way the text can be read in such a way as to disclose those fault-lines in ideology which the play's own aesthetic emphases attempt to resolve. Here the theatre itself, charged with imitating ideology, also exposes its workings, and can thus be said to function as the 'mirror' of Elizabethan culture in so far as its function is mimetic, but also as the means whereby the ideological underpinnings of that culture are displayed.

In other words, the theatre *represents*, but also exposes the constitutive features of representation itself.

Shylock's marginal position in the play, and the final recuperation of his subversive energies for the dominant discourse of Christian patriarchy, *presents* what was for Elizabethan society an 'insurmountable contradiction' (see E. Balibar and P. Macherey, 'On Literature as an Ideological Form' (1978), in Young 1981). This contradiction, involving Christian participation in usurious practice, receives its inscription in *The Merchant of Venice* in the form of what Macherey and Balibar would call 'a special language, a language of "compromise", realizing in advance the fiction of a forthcoming conciliation' (Young 1981: 88). That conciliation is achieved aesthetically in the play through the presentation of Belmont as Venice's saviour; or to put the matter a little more tendentiously, what happens in Belmont ultimately guarantees the continuation of a Christian patriarchy which articulates its practices through a discourse of romance, friendship and human ideals. If Shylock is the agency through which Venetian institutions are demystified, then Belmont is the place where an attempt is made to reverse that process. Bassanio's success in winning Portia guarantees racial purity and opposes an essential moral worth against the deceptive surfaces of worldly show. But the process is itself contradictory, since the 'Gifts of rich value' (II.ix.90) that he deploys are part of a rhetoric of persuasion which he later denies in his choice between 'caskets' and 'meanings':

> In religion,
> What damnèd error but some sober brow
> Will bless it and approve it with a text,
> Hiding the grossness with fair ornament?
> There is no vice so simple but assumes
> Some mark of virtue on his outward parts.
>
> (III.ii.77–82)

It is not surprising, therefore, that Bassanio should deny the representational value of 'gold' and 'silver': 'The seeming truth which cunning times put on/To entrap the wisest' (III.ii.100–1), and, 'thou pale and common drudge/'Tween man and man' (III.ii.103–4). Here in the form of a game, is an attempt to construct a 'centre', a 'meaning', but also a recognition that it can never be, as Derrida puts it, 'absolutely present outside a system of differences' (Derrida 1981a: 280).

The object of Bassanio's quest is herself a 'meaning' inscribed within the law of Christian patriarchy *and* Venetian fiscal practice, but presented as a 'knowledge' secreted at the heart of the linguistic sign. The issue is rendered even more problematical by the fact that theatrical practice demanded that the role of Portia be played by a male actor, thus problematizing even further the mimetic possibility that the character should be present to her/himself. Fixed thus ideologically, it is significant that while Bassanio chooses, Portia articulates in an 'aside' those very feelings of 'excess' which it is the function of the law of her dead father to constrain:

> O love, be moderate! Allay thy ecstasy,
> In measure rain thy joy, scant this excess!
> I feel too much thy blessing. Make it less,
> For fear I surfeit.

> (III.ii.111–14)

At a purely psychological level, Portia's 'fear' here is, surely the patriarchal fear of 'excess' internalized by the female subject as part of the mechanism of social and emotional regulation. Spoken by a male actor, its parodic potential is foregrounded to the point where it can be made to reinforce patriarchal constraint. To this extent both Portia and her more unruly counterpart, Jessica, are central to an understanding of the normative, regulatory practices of Christian patriarchy as the play represents them.

Both Portia and Jessica violate the constraints imposed upon their own gender by dressing as males. Portia and her maid Nerissa do so in order to reinforce the very laws that hold them in position as gendered subjects, and when Portia finally submits to Bassanio she does so as a subject who, as Althusser would say, works by herself; that is to say, she accepts her position and her identity. In the case of Portia, her cross-dressing is both a form of empowerment, *and* a disempowerment, where she freely consents to the assigning over of her power to her 'husband'. By contrast, Jessica's cross-dressing represents an act of usurpation of patriarchal authority; she seeks marriage with a Christian, but she takes responsibility upon herself for effecting it. Jessica's systematic *undoing* of a network of domestic power relations is both a challenge *and* an enabling strategy in that it contributes ultimately to the Christianizing of Shylock, but at the same time it aligns the father momentarily with those very emotional structures which support the order of which his own example is, as we have seen, a 'transgressive mimesis'. Why, otherwise, should Shylock be given so powerfully emotional a voice at the moment when he is told of his daughter's prodigality:

Out upon her! thou torturest me, Tubal. It was my turquoise.
I had it of Leah when I was a bachelor. I would not have given
it for a wilderness of monkeys.

(III.i.113–16)

Shylock's ring, the symbol of his marriage, is exchanged by the
iconoclastic Jessica for 'a monkey'. By contrast, Portia recuperates in
her own gesture Shylock's domestic ritual for an act of Christian
betrothal, one which, as we suggested, simultaneously asserts both her
social superiority and her gender inferiority as she yields to Bassanio's
masculine authority. Here, unlike in Jessica's case, patriarchal authority
passes through the willing female subject from father to husband:

Myself and what is mine to you and yours
Is now converted. But now I was the lord
Of this fair mansion, master of my servants,
Queen o'er myself; and even now, but now,
This house, these servants, and this same myself
Are yours, my lord's. I give them with this ring,
Which when you part from, lose, or give away,
Let it presage the ruin of your love
And be my vantage to exclaim on you.

(III.ii.166–74)

If the power which this gives Bassanio is considerable – 'But when this
ring/Parts from this finger, then parts life from hence' (III.ii.183–4) –
it is also conditional. But the threat of female power which it contains
is carefully circumscribed by the fact that Portia's 'self' is itself a social
construct: she fulfils a series of roles, and they facilitate her willing
'conversion' from daughter to wife. By contrast, Jessica's status as an
unruly woman, contradictory though it is in that she wants to marry
Lorenzo, requires a different handling since the problem here is not
the threat of female 'excess', but the identity of her father. Within
patriarchy, if the daughter is an 'effect' of her father, and if her father
inhabits a problematical identity, then it is *his* identity that requires
to be changed. Shylock as infernal patriarch and comic obstacle
becomes, therefore, the point at which the generic features of comedy
are made to intersect with a determinate social history.

It is this troubled and complex history which virtually dictates the
transformation of the 'insurmountable contradictions' involving fiscal
'excess' into a discursive terrain such as comedy, and female sexuality,
where the possibilities of negotiation, if not containment, seem more

promising. In Act V of the play it is left initially to Lorenzo, the Venetian 'son' through whom both Jessica and Shylock are recuperated for the integrated structures of Christian patriarchy, to refurbish masculine identity. He does so through a movement into the sphere of aesthetics, as a way of effecting a closure designed to produce an imaginary resolution to the various problems which have been raised in the play. The wealth which 'gilded' Jessica's subversive act of elopement at a purely materialistic level, is now aestheticized as a transcendent ideal: 'Sit Jessica. Look how the floor of heaven/Is thick inlaid with patens of bright gold' (V.i.58–9). What was earlier, for Bassanio 'The seeming truth which cunning times put on/To entrap the wisest' (III.ii.100–1), now becomes, through the pun on 'paten', a necessary alliance between 'wealth' and 'religion'. The 'paten' as the silver or golden dish upon which the Christian host is placed in the ritual of transubstantiation, heralds a victory for Christianity, but the attempt at transformation is beset by a history, that of Acts I–IV which can never expunge completely the dubious rhetoric of its construction. Faced with the problem that historical example, both theatrical and non-theatrical, foregrounds, the text is forced into the reiteration of a distinction between the material transience of life itself, moralized as Lorenzo's 'this muddy vesture of decay' (V.i.64), and the immortality of the soul whose musical pattern is heaven's inscription in human psychology of a safeguard against political subversion:

The man that hath no music in himself,
Nor is not moved with the concord of sweet sounds,
Is fit for treasons, stratagems, and spoils;
The motions of his spirit are dull as night,
And his affections dark as Erebus.
Let no such man be trusted. Mark the music.

(V.i.83–8)

What has intervened in the space between Lorenzo and Jessica's alignment of their action with those of Troilus and Cressida, and Dido, and Lorenzo's metaphysical pronouncement is, of course, ideology. Indeed, it is as though having raised an issue for which, as yet, there exists no clear historical solution, the text makes a detour onto that terrain for which there already exists a range of formal resolutions already legitimized and authorized by the dominant ideology of patriarchy.

Thus, at the end of the play, and after all obstacles and doubts have been overcome, 'Nature' – in the form of a Christian providence – speaks to Venice, transforming Antonio from his role as 'th' unhappy subject of these quarrels' (V.i.238) into the happy recipient of 'life' from Portia: 'Sweet Lady, you have given me life and living,/For here I read for certain that my ships/Are safely come to road.' (V.i.286–8). Here 'purse' and 'person', 'life and living', receive their composite inscription within the complementary economies of homo-social and heterosexual friendship in Venice. Neutralized within the joint practices of aesthetics and ideology, the 'fear' which interest as 'excess' generates, can be displaced onto an area of *difference* for which solutions exist socially, generically, and theatrically. But yet, even here something of a problem remains. Portia's fulsome confidence: 'Let us go in,/And charge us there upon inter'gatories,/And we will answer all things faithfully.' (V.i.297–9), is shown to rest upon the mystified inter-relationship of patriarchal authority, and the real mechanisms of wealth accumulation. Shylock's ring, which was a ritualized mark of posses-sion and affection, is given a more specific inflection in the 'rings' which are the marks of fidelity and truth in Venice. Bassanio's parting with his token of fidelity to a disguised Portia, and Graziano's to a disguised Nerissa, draws the language of promises irreversibly into the domain of material signification. The removal of Portia's and Nerissa's rings from the fingers of Bassanio and Graziano respectively threatens to undermine sexual possession, and to introduce obliquely one of the persistent fears of masculine authority. Displaced on to the axis of gender ideology, the comic positioning of that 'fear' by the husband of Portia's social inferior, fails absolutely fully to contain the range of competing meanings which it releases: 'Well, while I live I'll fear no other thing/So sore as keeping safe Nerissa's ring (V.i.306–7). The effect of this is to return the text to its own deeply flawed rhetoric.

The venality that the ritualized closure of marriage is designed to contain is shown here submitting to the aristocratic example of Portia and Bassanio. This resolution of the awkwardness which follows directly from the forsaking of gender roles is, however, not simply a reflection of 'historical reality', so much as an ideological product of it (see Macherey 1978: 129). The ending of the play questions even the apparent fixity of gender identities since Graziano's bawdy couplet is delivered, in part, to a male actor *impersonating* a female character. All of this suggests that we should reject absolutely John Russell Brown's defensive suggestion that we should merely submit ourselves to the 'experience' of the play: 'Perhaps when the dance is in progress, it is undesirable to look too closely for a pattern' (Brown 1964: viii). To abrogate this critical responsibility is to propose a complicity with texts such as *The Merchant of Venice* which lays the critic open to the charge of disseminating its prejudices. To discharge that responsibility is to acknowledge that such prejudices are the products of a determinate history whose partial and horrifying solutions cannot, and should never be allowed to, exert a permanent claim on our own historically constituted sensibilities.

SUPPLEMENT

NIGEL WOOD: Most considerations of patriarchy identify it as much more of a gender-specific matter than you have done. Could you identify patriarchy as different from the state or just simply the status quo?

JOHN DRAKAKIS: This question raises a number of complex issues concerned with the definition of patriarchy. In radical feminist thinking the concept has been used to designate various forms of exploitation and oppression of women over and above the level of the economic. I want to locate patriarchy in *The Merchant of Venice* as a means of structuring household relationships, and as such it works both at a sociological level *and* at a psychic level, both as a set of property relations *and* as a set of psychic relations. I do not simply want to argue that psychic relations in the play are an unproblematical expression of what, in another context, Annette Kuhn has called 'the symbolic operation of social and property relations' ('Structures of Patriarchy and Capital in the Family', in Kuhn and Wolpe 1978: 52). My argument in relation to this play challenges the purely functionalist notion of the operations of ideology as an unproblematical set of existing representations which have a unity and a coherence of their own and which are then imposed on the gendered human 'subject'. The play challenges this notion of ideology on a number of fronts, hence we see characters like Portia *negotiating* their space in the play. The tension that is set up involves a challenge to ideology articulated in the various discontinuities in the play itself, and in the unsatisfactory nature of its formal closure, where ideology as a kind of 'false consciousness' is exposed as being unable to produce a satisfactory coherence. I am aware that I am using terms such as 'ideology' and 'false consciousness' that would not have been available to Elizabethan commentators. These are analytical terms used to describe some of the problems and pecularities of this text, and do not in any way undermine the essentially *historical* argument that I am proposing.

NW: You note a crucial distinction on p. 28 between the text's own mythologizing and the 'myths' that are visited on it by its critical reception. How can the play be said, in terms of the subsequent history of its reception, to satisfy a contemporary need for it to be a certain kind of experience?

JD: I am alluding here, of course, to the analysis of the language of 'myth' as offered in Barthes (1973). For Barthes 'myth' is a way of talking about history; the Elizabethans had their way of talking about history and so do we. Phenomena which they considered 'natural' were historically produced. The issue becomes more problematical when what we are discussing is a racial question, and one which since the Second World War involves a recognition of the atrocities committed by one nation upon those whom it has designated as scapegoats. But the other problem that we face in relation to *The Merchant of Venice* is that it is by Shakespeare. How can the National Bard even be suspected of being implicated in anti-Semitism? Up to the Romantics this does not seem to have been a problem, but thereafter, as James C. Bulman has pointed out in his book on the history of performances of *The Merchant of Venice*, the figure of Shylock became a vehicle for tragic emotion and he effectively became the centre of the play (Bulman 1991: 25–7). This 'humanizing' of the figure of Shylock, which begins in the Enlightenment, has been extended, with one or two notable exceptions, into the twentieth century, and is used as testimony to the essential humanism that is allegedly ingrained in Shakespeare's texts. To locate this humanism *objectively*, so to speak, in the text, is to satisfy a need to regard the National Bard as a model of English tolerance, at the same time as it insists that Shakespeare is able to see the issue from all angles – the transcendent poet.

NW: In his *Shakespeare and The Problem of Meaning* (1981), Norman Rabkin regards Shakespeare's work as a challenge to most forms of critical appropriation because its significance will always exceed ascertainable meaning, an 'art ultimately irreducible to explanatory schema'. His aim is to bypass the need for accounts based on 'meaning' to account for 'the end of a play, the sense of unverbalizable coherence, lucidity, and unity that makes us know we have been through a single, significant, and shared experience' (Rabkin 1981: 27). The point to this exposition here is that Rabkin seems to espouse a critical view diametrically opposed to yours. What do you make of his position?

JD: My first response is to agree, his view is radically opposed to mine, and my second to say that I don't make very much of his position. Rabkin's view of meaning is a familiar referential one: we have the text, which is the final repository of all meaning, and we have literary criticism which is parasitic on the text and which sometimes gets the meanings 'right', but which can never recover the text's *full* meaning. I want to argue that meaning is *produced* by a reader's engagement with the text. To formulate the matter succinctly, let me quote from Terence Hawkes's recent book, *Meaning by Shakespeare* (1992: 7–8) in which he argues the following:

> What passes amongst some literary critics for a text's 'real' meaning can only be a temporary pause in this otherwise healthy process.

And it seems harsh, in its name, to deny to subsequent audiences and readers what Shakespeare's plays apparently freely grant to those – from the Prince of Denmark to Bottom the Weaver – who set themselves to 'mean by' texts within them. A text is surely better served if it is perceived not as the embodiment of some frozen, definitive significance, but as a kind of intersection or confluence which is continually traversed, a no-man's land, an arena, in which different and opposed readings, urged from different and opposed political positions, compete in history for ideological power: the power, that is, to determine cultural meaning – to say what the world is and should be like.

Rabkin's argument, reduced to its crudest level, simply wants us to 'feel good' at the end of an 'experience' of a Shakespeare play. His notion of 'unverbalizable coherence, lucidity, and unity that makes us know we have been through a single, significant and shared experience' (Rabkin 1981: 27) is simply a mystifying of the text. Each of his categories is challenged by any attentive reading of the text of The Merchant of Venice. We *can* produce coherence from this text; my point is that if we do then there is much that we have to suppress. In short, Rabkin's referential model of language just won't work here, and my location of the text of the play within a series of larger, historically specific discourses represents an attempt to demonstrate that just as we 'make meanings' through our engagement with texts and with histories, so the play makes meanings through *its* engagement with other texts *and* with histories.

NW: I'm interested by your closing comments about the necessary difference between the historical formation of a text (and its author) and 'our own historically constituted sensibilities' (p. 53). How can we be made aware (or be aware) of how 'our own' History affects our literary receptivity? Without some inkling of this it's not at all easy to observe the text's history as challenging and alternative.

JD: First of all, let me dispel the idea that we are dealing with a monolithic conception of 'History' here. We have 'histories' which are the sum total of our experiences and of our theoretical analysis of them. We become fully conscious of our own historicity the moment we confront something that is unfamiliar to us or inimical to our knowledge of our own historically constituted sensibilities. Interestingly, postmodernism, with its emphasis upon the irreducibility of 'representation', functions to efface the past. To be aware of one's own history is, of course, to cross a number of what we normally think of as disciplinary boundaries. For example, to engage with a text which is preoccupied with mercantilism – that is, the pre-history of capitalism – we need really to understand where *we* are within the operations of a late capitalist culture. We don't *identify* with the figures in The Merchant of Venice, even though the affective power of the text may move us to positions of sympathy, antipathy and so on. I want to analyse the *disruptions* in such a text, the moment where the text gapes to reveal the conditions of its own construction. I want to resist submitting to its alleged 'power' since in order to do that I have to make a series of assumptions, and I have to engage in a series of suppressions. By trying to analyse the various ways in which I think this text operates – and bear in mind that that analysis is dependent upon my own positionality as a gendered human subject, a professional academic working within one of those institutions which function as an agency within our own society – I open up a whole series of *differences* between late sixteenth-century culture and my own. I engage late sixteenth-century culture through a recognition of a series of problems that lead me to a series of historical speculations about how a representation such as *The Merchant of Venice* might have operated within late Elizabethan culture, and also about what role and status the institution of the public theatre itself might have occupied. These investigations lead me to formulate a series of *differences* between the cultural forms prevalent in the late 1590s and those prevalent now.

CHAPTER 2

Shakespeare on Marx

GRAHAM HOLDERNESS

[When Graham Holderness brings the writings of Karl Marx into a close critical relation with The *Merchant of Venice*, he is not claiming that Shakespeare wrote with proto-Marxist principles in mind. Those who may wish to investigate factors of intention behind literary texts try to establish origins or sources and so construct horizons of meaning, what was likely to have 'been there' in the beginning. In striving to pull the work of interpretation away from our own culture to that surrounding the text in question (and so erect walls of legitimation around the process of reading) such commentators are actually cloaking the political nature of their own work. If we regard our responses as inevitably subservient to the past, then that is a proposition smuggled in about life in general: we should always consult how we ought to fit into present arrangements, as if the present distribution of power and knowledge were part of the 'nature of things'. Any objection to this is not at the same time the rejection of a search for information about the past. The crucial task is what to do with such archival traces, when found. How critical should we be of them? How creative should we be in supplying the links that are inevitably missing from such accounts? Are these records all to be considered as consistently even-handed in their representation of past reality? Or do they have hidden agendas of their own, all the more insidious (or skilful) for their appearance as neutral or passive reportage? The freedom to be critical is hard-won, given the processes that package notions of History and Literature for us, and a renewed urgency to this creative criticism is one of Marx's most significant contributions to cultural debate.

Marxist theories of literature are varied in detail, but stem more or less directly from the view that, while art may seem to be produced just by individuals, we might learn much more about their work if we identify, first, the artist's 'ideology', which is to say, not a set of codified beliefs, but rather an unphilosophical reflection of how individuals see their roles in class-society and the values, symbols and ideas that help explain that role to such individuals and which therefore ties them all the more securely to their inherited context; and second, the basic conditions under which such art can be produced (for example, conditions of patronage, growth of the mass market, availability of new technologies of production) and which establish inexorable limits to the apparent freedoms of artistic activity.

Marx's (and Engels's) terms still provide the original inspiration for Marxist interpretation. In Marx and Engels's *The German Ideology* (1845–6) the 'production of ideas, of conceptions, of consciousness is at first directly interwoven with the material activity and the material intercourse of men'. Thus, thought is the 'direct efflux' of this 'material behaviour', and individuals must be brought to realize that they, in fact, have a hand in the production of their own conceptions, 'real, active men, as they are conditioned by a definite development of their productive forces'. The conclusion is inescapable that 'life is not determined by consciousness, but consciousness by life' (Marx 1977: 164). This is given more specific focus in the 'Preface' to *A Critique of Political Economy* (1859), where it is held as a condition of the 'social production' of one's own life that one enters 'into definite relations that are indispensable and independent of [one's] will, relations of production which correspond to a definite stage of development of [one's] material productive forces'. This forms 'the economic structure of society, *economic* the real foundation, on which rises a legal and political superstructure and *mode* to which correspond definite forms of social consciousness' (Marx 1977: 389). This model seems particularly deterministic, and most recent Marxist analysis regards this 'base–superstructure' divide as a preliminary move, one which, if carried through without extra sophistication, reduces all art to its modes of production, a position that makes it particularly difficult to account for individual variations (see especially Raymond Williams's 'Base and Superstructure in Marxist Cultural Theory' [1973], in Williams 1980: 31–49).

The 'definite forms of social consciousness' group themselves in analysis as *ideology*. In order to render such awareness as narrow and partisan (that is, stemming from a class identity, not 'nature' or 'common sense'), there is a need to compare it with some greater entity or notion that proceeds from a more 'scientific' grasp of the total system of social relationships. 'Ideology' was often, then, equated with 'false consciousness'. More recently, 'ideology' has come to be associated with *all* forms of social perception, without which we could not function as members of society. In the work of Louis Althusser the role assigned to art is a major one, for he claims that it is only through the depiction of a process of thought in literary form that the work of ideology can be inspected with sufficient detachment. In his essay 'Ideology and Ideological State Apparatuses' (1969), Althusser finds ideology integral to *all* thought processes. It supplies a focus for definitions, even if actually based on biased premises. The state apparatuses (Church, political party, university and the legal system) 'interpellate' us (encourage us to believe) that we are free individuals, and therein lies their attraction and power (see Althusser 1977: 123–73).

This tendency to differentiate literary from non-literary expression is obviously fraught with the difficulty of defining just what the 'literary' might be, but it also creates a system of evaluation as well as of analysis. For Pierre Macherey, in *A Theory of Literary Production*, literary form was capable of showing up the internal incoherences and multiple contradictions of ideology. The apparent coherence of ideology can only be maintained by a process of repression and economies with the truth. By dwelling on the 'silences' that come to be implied by the work of art Macherey reveals the way that ideology operates and, implicitly, how we can question its hold over us (see especially Macherey 1978: 61–101; and Eagleton 1991: 136–51).

Holderness recognizes the dangers of anachronism by reading *The Merchant of Venice* through the lens of Marx's early essay, 'On the Jewish Question' (1843), yet also points out that this contrast between different cultural assumptions, 'then' as opposed to 'now', far from blending the past with the present, actually sharpens the perception of how alternative societies operate and thus how literature might reflect that. Marx wrote his essay in the form of a review in the *Deutsch-französische Jahrbücher* of some recent work by Bruno Bauer, who had asserted that Jews and Christians could only coexist if religious differences were laid aside. The enemy was a state religion, because that established those outside the norms of the state, and so those who were outsider figures. Marx considers this as not radical enough. The idea that an abolition of the forms of religious organization would lead to emancipation is inaccurate, because religion itself was present because of some deeper social ill – a disorder that would still persist because not addressed by this 'reformation'. The basic problem lay in the split forced on members of any state between the calls of bourgeois self-interest (that of civil society) and those of fellow-feeling and brotherhood (that of the universal state). This latter Marx terms the 'species' essence of man which is obscured by the needs of the state to perpetuate its own divisive order. The answer lay in the recognition that man could serve other interests than his own.

The choice of this Marx essay is apt, in that it is part of Marx's movement towards the depiction of economic alienation in his *Economic-Philosophical Manuscripts* (1844). He there chooses to illustrate the barren power of 'gold' by quoting at length a Shakespearian passage (see the commentary on money at Marx 1977: 109–11), Timon's desperate monologue outside the walls of Athens, when he is at his most disappointed by the lack of aid forthcoming from his erstwhile friends (*Timon of Athens*, Act IV, scene iii).

Timon is a near-neighbour to Antonio, in that he too lends to one who does not repay (Ventidius), and ends up alienated from all society. In Act IV, scene iii, he digs for gold, and finds it 'Yellow, glittering' (IV.iii.26), yet apt to make slaves and

> ... knit and break religions, bless th'accursed,
> Make the hoar leprosy adored, place thieves
> And give them title, knee, and approbation...
>
> (IV.iii.35–7).

This forms part of Marx's analysis of civil society (see Demetz 1967: 152–9), and Holderness employs its guiding principles to help lay bare how Shakespeare can question Venice's *mores* and economic structure.]

NIGEL WOOD

[In Timon of Athens*] Shakespeare portrays admirably the nature of* money.

(Karl Marx, 'Economic and Philosophic Manuscripts' (1844),
in Marx 1963: 191)

Though conclusive evidence is hard to come by, it is difficult to read Shakespeare without feeling that he was almost certainly familiar with the writings of ... Marx.

(Eagleton 1986: ix)

Marx certainly read Shakespeare; but did Shakespeare read Marx? Terry Eagleton's provocative question is not merely a whimsical fantasy. Marx found in Shakespeare's verse an artistic confirmation of his own economic arguments about the nature of money. Renaissance artist and modern economist observed analogous social conditions and came to similar conclusions.

Eagleton's Marxist approach is quite different from Marx's. Marx was present in Shakespeare, not because Shakespeare had access to his writing in the way Marx had access to Shakespeare (an absurdity): but because Marx, together with other formative modern thinkers, is indelibly present in the mind of the reader who by reading Shakespeare's writings, brings them into being in a context of contemporary thought. If 'Shakespeare' exists only in terms of such present contemporary readings, then the voice of the Bard is indistinguishable from the voice of the critic, the meanings of 'Shakespeare' are *ab initio* permeated by modern thought, and Shakespeare cannot possibly pretend, by appeal to mere anachronism, that he had not read and been profoundly influenced by Freud, Derrida, Marx ...

This essay can be thought of as an exercise in a two-way process: reading Shakespeare through Marx, and reading Marx through Shakespeare.

I

The particular focus for a context of Marxist theory against which to read *The Merchant of Venice* is provided here by Marx's early essay 'On the Jewish Question', first published in 1843. The essay thus belongs to Marx's 'early writings', and therefore to an intellectual context in which a critical engagement with contemporary philosophy, particularly the ideas of Hegel, was shaping the style of radical debate. On the other hand, although Marx's development of new modes of economic and historical enquiry lay in the future, this early essay is focused very sharply on materialist questions of commerce, finance, wealth, the rule of money. These economic themes are closely intertwined with political questions – the nature of the state, religion, political emancipation – and above all with psychological considerations, particularly the celebrated concept of 'alienation', which appears here related to religion, politics and economics. Philosophical conceptions such as religion as the self-alienation of humanity, and political conceptions of the state as man's alienated 'species-life' (communal nature), coexist with a linking of alienation to the rule of money that anticipates Marx's later development of such crucial economic theories as 'the fetishism of commodities' (Marx, *Capital* (1867), Vol. 1, in Marx 1977: 435–43).

The occasion of 'On the Jewish Question' was the publication of a treatise by Bruno Bauer, arguing against religious emancipation for the Jews (Bauer 1843). Jews should not be demanding a privileged status for their religion, Bauer argued, for two reasons: first, religious equality between Jews and Christians would only bring Jews to the same political level as Christians, that is, the status of slaves. Second, all religion, both Judaism and Christianity, should be regarded as an obstacle rather than a means to real emancipation. Jews should relinquish their claim to religious difference and join with Christians in the movement for general human emancipation.

Marx quarrels first with Bauer's view of the relation between religion and the state. If the state, in Bauer's argument, abolished all religious privileges, and religion became a purely private matter of personal conviction, then the state would begin to express (as it had already begun to express in the American states, with their republican constitutions based on principles of the Enlightenment) the values of universal political equality. But the root cause of religion, Marx argues, whether public or private, is the nature of the state itself: the basic religious idea, the duplication of the human world into a real earthly world and a heavenly community, arises from the self-division and contradiction of actual society (see Thesis IV, 'Theses on Feuerbach' (1845) in Marx 1977: 157). This can be seen most clearly in precisely those societies, such as France and the American states, which embody in political and constitutional forms values of universal equality that are contradicted by the actual inequalities of civil society. The abolition for an electorate of the property qualification, for instance, does not abolish private property, and may even constitute a means of protecting it.

The concept of 'civil society', and the attendant distinction between 'civil' and 'political' societies, are crucial terms in Marx's exposition. 'Civil society' is the real material world of economic inequality, class division, and the isolation of the individual to promote a naked egoism of commercial competition. Separated from this reality stands the 'political state', which can be characterized by assumptions of universal equality, organic community and the inalienable rights of man. The opposition between the two arises, in the same way as religion, from the alienation and self-contradiction of civil society itself:

The perfected political state is by its nature the species-life of man in opposition to his material life. All the presuppositions of this egoistic life continue to exist in civil society outside the sphere of the state, but as proper to civil society. When the political state has achieved its true completion, man leads a double life, a heavenly one and an earthly one, not only in thought and consciousness but in reality, in life. He has a life both in the political community, where he is valued as a communal being, and in civil society, where he is active as a private individual, treats other men as means, degrades himself to a means, and becomes the plaything of alien powers. The political state has just as spiritual an attitude to civil society as heaven has to earth. It stands in the same opposition to civil society and overcomes it in the same manner as religion overcomes the limitations of the profane world ... Man in the reality that is nearest to him, civil society, is a profane being. Here where he counts for himself and others as a real individual, he is an illusory phenomenon. In the state, on the other hand, where man counts as a species-being, he is an imaginary participant in an imaginary sovereignty, he is robbed of his real life and filled with an unreal universality.

('On the Jewish Question', in Marx 1977: 45–6)

Where religion has been separated from the state and turned into a matter of private belief, religion has simply become a further expression of civil society:

Religion is no longer the spirit of the state where man behaves, as a species-being in community with other men albeit in a limited manner and in a particular form and a particular sphere: religion has become the spirit of civil society, the sphere of egoism, the *bellum omnium contra omnes* [war of all against all]. Its essence is no longer in community but in difference.

(Marx 1977: 47)

In the Christian state the political alienation of individual from community and the religious alienation of man from himself are ratified and confirmed. At the centre of the Christian state stands the conception of man as a sovereign being. But in reality that image of 'man' is an embodiment of alienation: it is man with his freedom given over to the political state, and his communal life alienated in religion; man as he really is in civil society, alone, dispossessed from community, at war with his fellows:

What makes the members of the political state religious is the dualism between their individual life and their species-life, between life in civil society and political life, their belief that life in the state is the true life even though it leaves untouched their individuality. Religion is here the spirit of civil society, the expression of separation and distance of man from man. What makes a political democracy Christian is the fact that in it man, not only a single man but every man, counts as a sovereign being; but it is man as he appears uncultivated and unsocial, man in his accidental existence, man as he comes and goes, man as he is corrupted by the whole organization of our society, lost to himself, sold, given over to the domination of inhuman conditions and elements – in a word, man, who is no longer a real species-being. The fantasy, dream, and postulate of Christianity, the sovereignty of man, but of man as an alien being separate from actual man, is present in democracy as a tangible reality and is its secular motto.

(Marx 1977: 50)

It is on this theoretical basis that Marx then approaches the 'Jewish question'. The true social meaning of Judaism lies not in the Jewish religion, with its emphasis on cultural difference, but rather in the practical significance of Jewish commercial activity, which is actually indistinguishable from the practical values of Christian civil society.

> The Jew has emancipated himself in a Jewish manner, not only by annexing the power of money but also because through him and also apart from him money has become a world power and the practical spirit of the Jew has become the practical spirit of the Christian people. The Jews have emancipated themselves in so far as the Christians have become Jews.
>
> (Marx 1977: 59)

The practical commercial spirit of Judaism is therefore the true essence of Christian society, that *bellum omnium contra omnes* in which hostile individuals relate to one another only through commercial exchange, and worship the alienated divinity of money:

> Money is the jealous god of Israel before whom no other god may stand. Money debases all the gods of man and turns them into commodities. Money is the universal, self-constituted value of all things. It has therefore robbed the whole world, both human as well as natural, of its own values. Money is the alienated essence of man's work and being, this alien essence dominates him and he adores it.
>
> (Marx 1977: 60)

Thus Marx sees Judaism, both in terms of the privatized Jewish religion and the economic practice of the Jews, as the essential spirit of bourgeois society, and as the true meaning of the Christian state: 'Christianity had its origin in Judaism. It has dissolved itself back into Judaism' (Marx 1977: 61). It follows that real emancipation – the restoration of man to himself as a social and communal being, the overcoming of alienation – must necessarily involve the disappearance of both Christianity and Judaism; but that elimination of religion can only occur by a resolution of those contradictions in civil society that produce both religion and the illusory political state. Only when 'practical need' has become *humanized*, rather than – as in civil society – alienated, will 'the conflict of man's individual, material existence with his species-existence [have been] superseded' (Marx 1977: 62).

II

To read *The Merchant of Venice* in the light of a nineteenth-century philosophical treatise is to raise key questions about the relationship of literature to criticism, of past culture to present interpretation. It can be argued that in *The Merchant of Venice* we have a work which is essentially 'historical', in the sense of being strictly confined within the ideological framework, the belief systems, the prejudices of the age in which it was produced; and that the qualities of difficulty, ambivalence, internal conflict discovered in the text by modern criticism are symptomatic not of the character of the play itself, but only of the extent to which since its composition certain attitudes have changed. Thus if it is assumed that the play embodies, from a modern point of view, an extraordinarily casual view of anti-Semitism, that is explained by the prevalance of anti-Semitic prejudices in its surrounding historical context. Or an application of Marx's theoretical terms to Shakespeare's play could be regarded as an anachronistic distortion of original historical meaning. Marx's basic terms – civil society, the state, alienation – would have been quite unintelligible to the sixteenth century; and his startling reversal of fundamental assumptions about ethnic and religious differences, whereby the distinction between Christianity and Judaism is collapsed, and the Jew is placed at the very centre of the Christian economy and society, could not have been understood by a Christian age which acknowledged such differences as that between Christian and Jew as natural and ineradicable.[1]

Modern interpreters can in turn adopt two different approaches towards this historicist reading: that the proper responsibility of critical interpretation is to reproduce an appropriate context for the expression of that strictly limited, historically circumscribed character (in short, to don intellectual doublet and hose and read the play as if we were Elizabethans); or that criticism should acknowledge the deep divergences between the ideologies of the past and the culture of the present, and read the play as a document of its time. Differences of interpretation would then arise not from any inherent complexity of the dramatic text, but from the subsequent evolution of cultural differences. Dramatists, readers and playgoers of the 1590s may have shared a basic, unreflective anti-Semitism; but a reader of the later twentieth century, whose views are inevitably coloured by the horrors of the Holocaust, would find it impossible to overlook such a presence within the text of an ideology that has proved in very recent history the source of immense cruelty and suffering.

In that type of reading the ideology of the text is regarded as basically simple, historically conditioned and firmly located in the past. All the complexity, contradiction and ambivalence of modern criticism is produced in retrospective accounts by the facts of historical change. In one school of criticism, which could be called a traditional historicist approach, we should attempt imaginatively to re-enter that past ideology, in order fully to appreciate the drama of that lost culture (as with Tillyard 1950). In another, typical of certain kinds of post-structuralist criticism such as new historicism, our responsibility as readers is quite the opposite: we should recognize the past as an enemy, and mobilize our own critical methods in order to force the past's attention towards those questions and problems which we consider to be of paramount importance, although – perhaps even because – the past chose to ignore or minimize their significance.[2] In a traditional historicist reading, we should paradoxically forget the historical specificity of Shylock's racial hatred, and acknowledge his villainy as universal, since the 'Jewish' dimension of the Elizabethan play was only a convenient costume for dramatizing larger ethical concerns about friendship and enmity, justice and mercy. In a new historicist interpretation, the crudity and prejudice of the play need to be highlighted and exposed by a critical method attuned more closely to the concerns of contemporary theory than to the detail of a vanished history. If the play were anti-Semitic, then that should be recognized in a critical account that foregrounds the past and continuing dominance of repressive and exploitative ideologies. We should face up to the anti-Semitism of *The Merchant of Venice* precisely because of an imperative need to identify and combat anti-Semitism and all other forms of racial prejudice in our own contemporary world.[3]

The alternative method of interpretation is to propose that all the complexities discovered by modern criticism were from the outset embodied within, or implicitly potential within, the Elizabethan text. It is always difficult to argue for a simplistic imputation of ideological uniformity to a cultural form like drama, which is by its very nature 'dialogic' (composed by the juxtaposition of different and divergent voices) rather than 'monologic' (expressive of a single authoritative voice enclosing a single ideological perspective). The Elizabethan drama was particularly remarkable for such 'polyphonic' ('multiple-voiced') discourse because of its generic heterogeneity: where a single play can contain and synthesize the conventions of comedy, romance, tragedy and even history, it is unlikely to offer itself for simplistic, single-minded readings. If the same dramatic narrative can be experienced as comedy by one individual character or group of characters, romance by another and tragedy by a third, then where is the play's ideological centre? If generic diversity suggests discontinuous fortunes for the characters, would that not be likely to produce divergent reactions from members of an audience, disparate interpretations from different readers?

We have no choice but to read the literature of the past in the light of our own contemporary ideology: but this can be done either naïvely (using the past as a mirror which obediently reflects back to us our own assumptions and convictions) or self-consciously (where we identify our own ideological context, and recognize to what extent that context modifies our reading of the past). We need to read both contemporaneously and historically at the same time. When we bring the fiction of the past into present consideration, it becomes assimilated to the conditions of contemporary culture. But the past is also another country, where they do things differently: to read historically is often to acknowledge the cultural difference of the past, its strangeness, the discontinuities that separate 'their' experience from 'ours'. To read a play in the light of a later theoretical text is an effective means of foregrounding this complex relationship between past and present, ancient writing and modern interpretation. Do we find in Shakespeare prophetic observations that Marx, and Marxist readers, were able later to rediscover? Or are we simply putting into 'Shakespeare' some of the theoretical and interpretative luggage we carry with us on any journey back into the past? Are we enlisting the aid of Marx in a retrospective reading of Shakespeare; or facilitating, by the intertextualizing of Shakespeare and Marx, the release of meanings silently present in Shakespeare, and disclosed by a 'Marxist' reading? Is this essay a Marxist reading of Shakespeare, or a Shakespearian reading of Marx?

III

In its own consciousness the Christian state is an ideal whose realization is unattainable. It can only convince itself of its own existence by lies and so remains for ever an object of self-doubt, an insufficient, problematic object. . . . In the so-called Christian state, it is alienation that is important, not man himself.

> (Marx, 'On the Jewish Question', in Marx 1977: 49–50)

The entire action of *The Merchant of Venice* is imagined as taking place in one of two locations: the commercial and financial republic of Venice, a historical place; and the ancestral country seat of Portia's family, Belmont, a fantasy of aristocratic romance. Venice is a real, modern world, dominated by trading and dealing, by commercial and financial transactions; Belmont is a fantasy world, dominated by the past, characterized by the conventions of fairy-tale and legend.

In Venice the conversation is always of money, trade, entrepreneurial adventure; of ships and cargoes, silks and spices; of debt and credit, risk and fortune, the course of law and the state of justice. At its centre are the Rialto, the 'exchange' where commercial dealings are conducted; and the Duke's court where the trial of Antonio takes place. The play opens with the character of Antonio, the 'merchant' of the play's title, and within a few lines the audience is treated to an elaborate imaginative sketch of his 'merchandise' in its traffic across the oceans: the silks, spices and other luxury goods that Antonio buys from the Far East and ships to Venice and elsewhere to be sold on the market. Although, however, the language of 'merchandise' is a poetry of distance and traffic, of commercial activity and the international circulation of commodities, the character of the 'merchant' is as remote as could be imagined from the pragmatic acumen, entrepreneurial decisiveness and business confidence that could be expected to stand at the centre of such a financial operation. Antonio is not a sharp opportunistic capitalist, but a gentle figure of melancholy and sadness; not thrustingly entrepreneurial, but shy and withdrawn; not a repository of trustworthy commercial confidence, but an individual deeply inhibited by a condition of extreme anxiety.

Antonio's opening words express nothing of his 'merchantly' status: but speak only of the dissipating and distracting effects of melancholy sadness, the weariness of depression, and a curious sense of self-alienation.

> In sooth, I know not why I am so sad.
> It wearies me, you say it wearies you;
> . . .
> And such a want-wit sadness makes of me
> That I have much ado to know myself.

> (I.i.1–2, 6–7)

We are thus introduced to this great financial and commercial centre of Venice via a merchant who is preoccupied with anything but his merchandise. At the heart of the Venetian trading empire stands a shy, diffident, anxious individual, who is deeply preoccupied with private thoughts, naïvely reliant on his own economic security, and suffering from a deep crisis of identity: 'I have much ado to know myself' (I.i.7). In Marx's terms, Shakespeare's Venice is very clearly a representation of 'civil society': a society based on economic exchange and commercial transaction, in which the individual leads a double life – in reality alienated from himself and isolated from his communal nature; in abstraction, in fantasy, a member of a community ('Venice') whose egalitarian constitution as a modern state purports to overcome all such alienation and isolation. Whatever the particular reasons, alleged or surmised, within the drama for Antonio's acute sense of self-alienation, his inability, in his own words, to 'know himself', the explanation is in Marx's terms self-evident. The individual as he is in civil society, 'lost to himself', appears in political society to exist as a sovereign individual integrated into an organic community. But that self-division of the individual into a 'civil' and a 'political' identity, a real and a fantasy existence, constitutes the true alienation of man within modern society, and results in those experiences of deep emotional hungering, of nostalgia for that which is irrecoverably lost, and yearning for that which continually eludes the grasp, that Marx acutely identified as the root of religion. Antonio cannot 'know himself', just as man in Marx's analysis is estranged from himself, as a consequence of the deep and wounding contradictions in civil society.

Antonio's only positive relationship is with his friend Bassanio: and since the subject of their conversation is the prospect of an immediate parting and severance of friendship, that relationship is clearly fraught with many difficulties:

> Well, tell me now what lady is the same
> To whom you swore a secret pilgrimage,
> That you today promised to tell me of.

> (I.i.119–21)

Antonio poses his question to Bassanio in the language of courtly love, with its familiar religious overtones: Bassanio proposes a 'pilgrimage', a sacred passage to a holy site, as the nature of his quest to win Portia; then shifts the metaphor into the nostalgic glamour of ancient mythology, identifying Portia as the golden fleece and her suitors as so many Argonauts:

> In Belmont is a lady richly left,
>
> . . .
>
> Her name is Portia, nothing undervalued

> To Cato's daughter, Brutus' Portia;
> Nor is the wide world ignorant of her worth,
> For the four winds blow in from every coast
> Renownèd suitors, and her sunny locks
> Hang on her temples like a golden fleece,
> Which makes her seat of Belmont Colchis' strand,
> And many Jasons come in quest of her.
>
> (I.i.161, 165–72)

Portia is both the holy shrine of a religious pilgrimage, and the legendary object of a mythical quest. The obvious difference between pilgrimage and quest is, however, that the latter, with its image of the golden fleece, draws attention to Portia's wealth as a primary focus of Bassanio's attention, and opens to the reader the possibility of interpreting his pursuit as an exercise in fortune-hunting as well as a pilgrimage of love. Terms such as 'nothing undervalued' and 'worth' seem more like moral celebrations than economic valuations; but 'richly left' can only mean that Portia is the heiress to a large fortune.

Bassanio approaches the question of Portia through a financial assessment of his creditworthiness, as if his initial consideration is not to gain a beautiful, loving and virtuous wife, but to settle all his debts by acquiring her fortune.

> 'Tis not unknown to you, Antonio,
> How much I have disabled mine estate
> By something showing a more swelling port
> Than my faint means would grant continuance.
> Nor do I now make moan to be abridged
> From such a noble rate; but my chief care
> Is to come fairly off from the great debts
> Wherein my time something too prodigal
> Hath left me gaged. To you, Antonio,
> I owe the most in money and in love,
> And from your love I have a warranty
> To unburden all my plots and purposes
> How to get clear of all the debts I owe.
>
> (I.i.122–34)

Bassanio has accumulated debts, mainly from Antonio, in the course of sustaining a lifestyle of conspicuous consumption and display which he could not afford – 'showing a more swelling port/Than my faint means would grant continuance' (I.i.124–5). His behaviour has been 'prodigal' both in the sense that he has sought to establish a social and economic status through borrowed money, and that so far he has failed to hit the kind of jackpot which would justify the investment of his financial backers. What Bassanio describes to Antonio here is not so much a courtship suit as a business plan. Given this prior context of financial analysis, it becomes impossible to read Bassanio's language of romantic quest in the innocent manner proposed by the conventions of romance:

> O my Antonio, had I but the *means*
> To hold a *rival place* with one of them,
> I have a mind presages me such *thrift*
> That I should questionless be *fortunate*.

> (I.i.173–6, emphasis added)

All the key words in this speech can be read within the discourse of romantic courtship: 'means' being the basic minimum requirement for mounting the enterprise; 'rival place' signifying a place among the rival suitors; 'thrift' usually in Elizabethan English meant simply 'success', what happens when you 'thrive'; and 'fortunate' could suggest 'in receipt of the gifts of fortune' in a very general way, 'happy and blessed' rather than merely 'successful'. The context already discussed requires, however, that we also read those words in their economic sense: where 'means' simply signifies financial credit; 'rival place' suggests commercial competition; 'thrift' indicates not success but sound financial management; and 'fortunate' can be understood quite literally as 'in receipt of a fortune'.

The ambivalence of Bassanio's language corresponds exactly to Marx's differentiation of civil from political society, and of religion from its basis in the contradictions of social life. At the level of fantasy Bassanio's project is integrated within the abstract glamour of romance, and is figured as a heroic and romantic quest in pursuit of an unattainable satisfaction. At the level of reality, the enterprise is envisaged as an adroit negotiation of conditions on the marriage market: a careful weighing of obstacles and opportunities, the strengths and weaknesses of the initiative; and an extrapolation of success as the appropriate reward of financial acumen and commercial judgement. The two levels are incompatible and incommensurable, and correspond exactly to Marx's distinction between the real world of economic competition and the illusory world of human community. But the two dimensions are encountered by the individual as a single dimension, a single continuum of experience: 'man leads a double life ... not only in thought and consciousness, but in reality, in life' (Marx 1977: 46).

IV

Money is the alienated essence of man's work and being; this alien essence dominates him and he adores it.

(Marx 1977: 60)

As the play's location shifts from one place to another (Act I, scene ii in modern editions) the immediate effect is one of contrast. We move from a world occupied entirely by men (Shylock's daughter Jessica is the only female inhabitant of Shakespeare's Venice) to one dominated by women. Although Portia speaks here of her dependence on masculine power, operating through the conditions of her father's will, she is also literally 'lord' and 'master' of her own house, estate, property and wealth (see III.ii. 167–8). In terms of the play's overall narrative structure, this situation of female power lies in a temporary limbo between Portia's subservience to her father when alive, and her eventual renunciation of authority to the man she is destined to marry; and since even during that temporary respite from the direct pressures of masculine powers she has to adhere to her father's prescriptions governing the method of her marital choice, it could be argued that Portia is never truly free:

> O me, the word 'choose'! I may neither choose who I would, nor refuse who I dislike; so is the will of a living daughter curbed by the will of a dead father.
>
> (I.ii.22–4)

Parental authority bears upon the child even after the individual occupants of that authority have died. In Belmont experience of the present is framed within that strong responsibility to the past: the language of present conversation echoes the presence of those who are no longer here. Nevertheless, despite Portia's awareness of the strength of her own 'will' (desire, inclination, independence), her acceptance of the conditions of her father's 'will' (last will and testament) indicates a spirit of obedience to the past, to family, to the law, to parental and masculine authority.

Already the geographical distance between Venice and Belmont seems to have its counterpart in sharp cultural difference. In Venice most of the characters do not even seem to have fathers, or at least never mention them: the lives of Antonio, Bassanio and the Venetian gallants operate in a world of nuclear individuals free from any family dependence or obligation. The virtual absence of an older generation strengthens the impression that Venice is a world without a past: one in which present experience and future aspiration flourish in a rootless, dislocated medium of perpetual contemporaneity: people live between the immediate security of what they have already gained, and the optimistic hyperreality of what they hope to acquire in the future. This virtual imprisonment of consciousness within the immediate moment is clearly exemplified in the trial scene, where the ruling élite of Venice seems incapable of remembering any law enacted earlier than the day before yesterday. Why does it take the intervention of Portia to recall the statute about conspiracy on the part of aliens? Apparently because Venice has literally forgotten its own past: the state has invested everything in the constitutional liberties of a modern commercial republic, and forgotten older and cruder codes of political self-defence without which its freedom cannot survive.

On the other hand, the comparison of Belmont and Venice begins to yield suggestions of similarity. Portia's opening words actually echo directly the words of Antonio with which the play opens:

PORTIA: By my troth, Nerissa, my little body is *aweary* of this great *world*.

NERISSA: You would be, sweet madam, if your miseries were in the same abundance as your good *fortunes* are; and yet, for aught I see, they are as sick that surfeit with too much as they that starve with nothing.

(I.ii.1–6; emphasis added)

We inevitably recall Antonio's 'it wearies me', and 'I hold the world but as the world, Graziano' (I.i.2, 77). Nerissa's dramatic function of cheering up her melancholy mistress parallels the role performed by Salerio and Solanio: they suggest that Antonio's imperilled fortune gives him every reason to be sad; Nerissa suggests that Portia ought to be cheered by the thought of her own good fortune.

That initial hint to the effect that Venice and Belmont may be considered as analogous societies, contingent rather than contrary moral worlds, perhaps even separate territories of the same realm, is intensified by a system of parallels and similarities, often lying slightly beneath the surface of the play's language. Antonio describes himself as a figure of stable and secure economic confidence, in control of his own destiny, while Portia protests against her lack of freedom to choose. And yet, as the action of the play makes clear, Antonio's confidence is illusory, and his destiny subject to the same arbitrary chances as Portia's. But the most significant parallel between Venice and Belmont lies in the concepts of 'risk' and 'hazard', which are continually identified and cross-referenced across the two locations by the use of a common language. The 'lottery' by which Portia's husband is to be chosen is a game of 'hazard', in which both the suitor (who will either win or lose all hope of future marriage) and Portia take an enormous risk. Despite Nerissa's assurance that the casket choice is guaranteed to reconcile accident and design, some element of risk must enter into the dramatic emotions of the play. Suppose the wrong suitor chooses rightly? Suppose someone were to cheat? Thus life in Belmont is governed by 'hazard', in exactly the same way that life in Venice is dominated by 'risk' (the perils of financial disaster entailed in Antonio's merchant ventures), and the dangerous prodigality of the type of personal relationship (such as that between Antonio and Bassanio) in which one partner is prepared to risk everything for the sake of the other. The same moral affirmation of the virtue of 'prodigality' is, of course, inscribed on to the lead casket which contains Portia's portrait. The other two caskets, gold and silver, with their respective slogans – 'Who chooseth me shall gain what many men desire', and 'Who chooseth me shall get as much as he deserves' (II.vii.5, 7) – are calculated to tempt the chooser with an ethic of acquisition and self-interest: where the leaden casket invites compliance with the morality of risk, in which the player hazards everything on the chance of a single throw. Bassanio's ritual meditation before making his choice establishes a correct system of relationship between the apparent and the real, show and substance, physical beauty and moral worth; and his final election of the slogan on the lead casket – 'Who chooseth me must give and hazard all he hath' (II.vii.9) – enfolds the romantic idealism of Belmont with the personal and economic risk-taking of Christian Venice. At this point Venice and Belmont cease to look like two separate worlds, appearing rather as linked departments of the same enterprise, united by a common morality.

Our comparison of Venice and Belmont has suggested that the two locations are not after all counterpoised in antagonism, but more deeply interlinked into a common social and ideological structure. In most respects Venice and Belmont are represented as contiguous or analogous rather than radically distinguished places. There are much bigger gaps of culture, race, religion, business ethics, language, between Venetian Jews and Christians, than any barrier that separates Christian Venice from Belmont. Bassanio, despite his relative poverty, is never considered as less than an appropriate suitor for Portia's hand: and since Portia is in any case in love with him, the barrier between them is composed purely of inherited obligations and responsibilities to paternal authority. 'O, these naughty times' says Portia 'Puts bars between the owners and their rights' (III.ii.18–19). But all she means is that since Bassanio already 'owns' her by virtue of her love for him – 'One half of me is yours, the other half yours' (III.ii.16) – it seems unjust that their union should be prevented by the barriers of an inhospitable age. At the end of the play all the Christian characters confidently take possession of Belmont, now Bassanio's house, as if it were little more than their country retreat, awaiting the owners' arrival at the end of a social season. This is not the conquest or acquisition of an alien place, but simple occupation of what has always been rightfully 'ours'.

Just as Venice contains both Marx's civil and political societies, the competitive system of commercial exchange and the illusory fantasy of human community, so Belmont and Venice stand in precisely the same relation one to another as Marx's explanation of religion and its root cause in social self-division. Belmont offers to reconcile in a fantasy synthesis – past and present vertically integrated, chance and destiny providentially interfused – the self-evident contradiction between society (Venice) as a 'war of all against all' and religion as a realization (Belmont) of human community; between the individual as a naked ego in confrontation with its fellows (Antonio) and the person who has recovered his own 'species-life', resolved his differences with his kind, and joined the human community (Portia).

V

What is the secular basis of Judaism? Practical need, selfishness.
What is the secular cult of the Jew? Haggling. What is his secular god? Money.

(Marx, 'On the Jewish Question', in Marx 1977: 58)

When Shylock first appears, his language is initially all of money, the terms and conditions of loans, Antonio's creditworthiness. When Shylock refers to Antonio as 'a good man',[4] Bassanio interprets the remark as a slight – 'Have you heard any imputation to the contrary?'

(I.iii.12–13). Shylock's riposte – 'My meaning in saying he is a good man is to have you understand me that he is sufficient' (I.iii.15–16) – proposes the indicator of financial 'sufficiency' as a measure of goodness. Shylock's adherence to the morality of what Thomas Carlyle later called the 'cash-nexus' ('bond of cash' – men bound to one another only by bonds of money and exchange (Carlyle 1829: 442)) is demonstrated by his careful calculation of Antonio's resources, an elaborate indication that for him the matter is purely a question of money. Under pressure from the eager Bassanio, who invites him to dinner, Shylock drops his guard and voices a language of racial exclusiveness:

> Yes, to smell pork; to eat of the habitation which your prophet
> the Nazarite conjured the devil into. I will buy with you, sell
> with you, talk with you, walk with you, and so following; but
> I will not eat with you, drink with you, nor pray with you.
>
> (I.iii.31–5)

That manifesto of cultural difference prepares the way for Antonio's entrance, and Shylock's first major speech, marked by a shift from prose to verse, in which he expresses the complex interrelations of race, religion and economics:

> How like a fawning publican he looks.
> I hate him for he is a Christian,
> But more for that in low simplicity
> He lends out money gratis and brings down
> The rate of usance here with us in Venice.
> If I can catch him once upon the hip,
> I will feed fat the ancient grudge I bear him.
> He hates our sacred nation, and he rails,
> Even there where merchants most do congregate,
> On me, my bargains, and my well-won thrift,
> Which he calls interest. Cursèd be my tribe
> If I forgive him.
>
> (I.iii.38–49)

Here, then, within the first few pages or minutes of Shylock's appearance in text or on stage, he has exhibited all the characteristics attributed to his race and profession by the many hostile witnesses represented in the play. Shylock is preoccupied by money; he sees his relations with other human beings exclusively in terms of the cash-nexus; he adopts an attitude of exclusiveness in his social and domestic life, shunning contact with those regarded as 'unclean' by his religion; he hates all Christians, and particularly Antonio, from a mixture of cultural and economic animosities. The vindictive malice which comes to the surface on Antonio's entrance – 'If I can catch him once upon the hip,/ I will feed fat the ancient grudge I bear him' (I.iii.43–4) – can easily be assumed as implicit in all Shylock's words and actions. It can be read both as referring backwards, explaining his careful calculations of Antonio's 'sufficiency' (perhaps Shylock is not searching Antonio's creditworthiness, but looking for an advantage over him), and forwards, to the implicit malevolence of the 'merry bond'. It is even possible, tracing a series of buried metaphors through Shylock's speech, to find the plot of the flesh bond almost fully formed in Shylock's imagination. Though he refuses to share food with the Christians (I.iii.31), he cherishes the idea of 'feed[ing] fat' (I.iii.44) his appetite for revenge. When the flesh bond is proposed, Shylock actually compares the relative market values of human and animal meat:

> A pound of man's flesh taken from a man
> Is not so estimable, profitable neither,
> As flesh of muttons, beeves, or goats.
>
> (I.iii.162–4)

Piecing these images together produces an alarming sub-text which makes Shylock's initial greeting of Antonio with the odd phrase 'Your worship was the last man in our mouths' (I.iii.57) seem positively cannibalistic in implication.

VI

From its own bowels civil society constantly begets Judaism.
(Marx, 'On the Jewish Question', in Marx 1977: 60)

But here we need to 'tarry a little', to adapt Portia's famous phrase from the trial scene. The Shylock I have just described is certainly there in the text. But there is another Shylock there, too, equally implicit in the dramatic context, narrative action and poetic language of the scene. Shylock's first words are of money because Bassanio is seeking to borrow money from him: Shylock is here being constituted by others as the calculating usurer, rather than spontaneously defining himself in that role. Bassanio's irritability springs, we know, from his impatience to fund his project rather than from any high-principled economic or racial animosity. He is borrowing to satisfy his own needs, but it is Antonio who 'shall become bound' – all the responsibilities and penalties of the bond attach to him, all the benefits to Bassanio. It is true that Bassanio is in this respect complying exactly with Antonio's instruction to 'Try what my credit can in Venice do' (I.i.180); but given Antonio's highly public moral stand against usury, Bassanio, by approaching Shylock, is surely dragging his friend into a delicate ethical compromise. His credit, Antonio urges, may be 'racked, even to the uttermost' (I.i.181) to acquire what Bassanio needs; but that image of torture asks to be applied uncomfortably to Antonio's body as well as to his credit balance.

This context of Christian self-interest and even hypocrisy – it is morally inconsistent to take advantage of a financial service you regard as morally pernicious – colours the depiction of Shylock differently. When Shylock declares his credit-search of Antonio's means to be adequate for the purpose – 'I think I may take his bond' (I.iii.26) – Bassanio responds indignantly: 'Be assured you may' (I.iii.27). 'Be assured' here is a mere device of rhetorical insistence, suggesting that Shylock is being insolent to question Antonio's financial competence. Shylock's reply is exact: 'I will be assured I may' (I.iii.28) – that is to say, he has a perfect right to establish the security of the proposed loan, since it needs to be 'assured' (cf. modern 'insured') against the possibility of loss. In this reading, the exchange between the two men is beginning to look less like Christian civility and enthusiasm pitted against Jewish calculation and malice; and more like the dignified resistance of a persecuted minority to the high-handed hypocrisy of those who wish both to despise and make use of their services. Even Shylock's punctilious definition of religious exclusiveness as applicable to certain private activities ('I will not eat with you' (I.iii.34–5)) and not to other more public ones ('I will buy with you' (I.iii.33)) is perfectly in line with the multicultural constitution of Venice, which permits independent private belief and custom in the context of an open involvement in and compliance with the general conditions of social life.

Already the play has begun to problematize that fundamental distinction upon which its ideological infrastructure rests: the difference between Jew and Christian. The Christian sees the Jew as an outsider: intolerant, exclusive, antisocial, refusing integration – antipathetic in every way to the Christian conception of social life as consisting in free exchange, harmonious community, generosity and friendship. Yet the play, like Marx's essay, entertains the possibility of a reversal, in which Jew and Christian exchange places. The Christian becomes alienated, like Antonio, from himself and from his own community; the Jew assumes the dignity and authority of a central place within the economy of exchange, a place guaranteed by the egalitarian constitution of the Venetian republic. The stigma of racial exclusiveness, historically ascribed to the Jews, passes from them and contaminates the Christians in the form of racial hatred; the principles of free economic competition are espoused by the Jew, while the Christians unfairly rig the market; and Shylock's faith in the liberty and tolerance of modern Venice seems highly sophisticated by comparison with the barbaric prejudices of the Christians.

VII

> *Judaism has maintained itself alongside Christianity not only as a religious critique of Christianity, not only as an incarnate doubt about the religious provenance of Christianity, but just as much because the practical Jewish spirit, Judaism or commerce, has maintained itself, and even reached its highest development, in Christian society. The Jew who is a particular member of civil society is only the particular appearance of the Judaism of civil society.*
>
> (Marx, 'On the Jewish Question', in Marx 1977: 60)

Shylock's hatred of Antonio is exposed in personal, economic, racial and religious terms. Shylock's inveterate hatred of Christianity envelops Antonio into a history of persecution and resistance: it is because Antonio 'hates our sacred nation' that Shylock hates him as a racial and religious duty: 'Cursèd be my tribe/If I forgive him' (I.iii.48–9). This fundamental conflict between religions also has a history of Christian aggression in its economic aspect: since Antonio does not restrict his hostility to verbal and physical abuse, but extends it into business dealing: 'He lends out money gratis and brings down/The rate of usance here with us in Venice' (I.iii.41–2).[5] And although Shylock has already shown himself vigilant for any advantage he can secure over Antonio, it is the latter who first introduces the idea of a financial transaction sealed in enmity rather than friendship:

> If thou wilt lend this money, lend it not
> As to thy friends, for when did friendship take
> A breed for barren metal of his friend?

But lend it rather to thine enemy
Who, if he break, thou mayst with better face
Exact the penalty.

I.iii.128–33

A clear distinction is drawn in *The Merchant of Venice* between the respective commercial activities of Shylock and Antonio; and underlying that distinction is a clear moral separation, in sixteenth-century thought, between different kinds of business dealing which in the modern capitalist economy would be very difficult to separate. This apparently absolute moral distinction rests on a sharp contrast between the two characters, which in a paradoxical way draws them together into a certain relationship of affinity. Although Antonio clearly belongs to the Christian community, he and Shylock tend to face each other as individuals with a common identity.

It is commonly assumed by readers of the play that Shylock's fault is to charge 'excessive' interest on loans. This misapprehension rests on an understandable misreading of the word 'excess' (I.iii.59), which actually means, simply, what we mean by 'interest'. Shylock himself, however, rejects that particular term – he speaks of his 'bargains' and his 'well-won thrift', which Antonio calls 'interest' (I.iii.47–8). Shylock lends money at interest and on security of property, land or person. Antonio does not object to Shylock because he charges too much interest: he objects to the idea that interest can be charged, as it would be today, from the moment of the loan. He does not object, however, to the adding of interest to the principal (the sum borrowed) after the repayment date has passed; which is why he is able to reconcile himself to Shylock's bond, which operates on this latter system rather than on the basis of 'usury'.

The difference is similar to that between a bank loan, on which you pay interest from the moment the agreement is signed, and borrowing on a credit card, where interest becomes payable only after the repayment date has passed, after the 'interest-free' period has expired. This distinction between different methods of lending money and collecting interest was a key issue in the anti-usury propaganda of the early modern period: though clearly it seems a very fine distinction to us (for more on this, see Cohen 1982; and E.C. Pettet, 'The Merchant of Venice and the Problem of Usury', in Wilders 1969: 100–13). The distinction is further blurred for us because in the ethics governing the kind of modern economy to which we are accustomed there is no such moral distinction between 'usury' and speculation, between what would now be called finance and venture capital. To think ourselves into this moral climate we would have to imagine a society in which financiers, and bank and building society managers, were hated and reviled, while company shareholders and speculators were regarded as irreproachably beneficial members of society. It is entirely possible comprehensively to admire or dislike all of these functionaries, but their activities are far too deeply intertwined in the modern capitalist economy to permit any clear ethical distinction between them (see Cohen 1982; E.C. Pettet, 'The Merchant of Venice and the Problem of Usury' in Wilders 1969; and W.H. Auden, 'Brothers and Others', in Auden 1963: 218-37).

Even in the play, these apparent opposites are linked in a deeper affinity. Both Shylock and Antonio are isolated from the remainder of the cast. Although the play, as the title indicates, is all about commerce, trade, financial dealing and exchange, only two of the leading characters appear in fact to be directly involved in business. In this way Shylock and Antonio are differentiated from the other characters, and placed (in different but related ways) outside the play's central community. They represent two opposed business ethics and two opposed moralities within the world of Venetian commerce. They are business rivals and competitors, enemies in trade and financial dealing. And in some strange way, they are very much alike.

Antonio is clearly from the outset isolated from the community of Christians, of which Bassanio is a natural member. His melancholy, his loneliness, his sense of difference and isolation, all link him to his mighty opposite, Shylock. The play opens with Antonio's supposedly mysterious and inexplicable melancholy. The reason for this sadness is in fact perfectly obvious: he loves Bassanio – 'only loves the world for him' (II.viii.50). He is not a lover of women, indignantly rejecting suggestions that he may be in love with one; and he is pointedly left out of the otherwise universal celebrations of marriage at the play's conclusion. His melancholy, then, is a response to the frustration of an unrequited love (homosexual, though not necessarily entailing a physical relationship) for Bassanio. When in the opening scene all the other characters leave the two men alone together, Antonio offers himself to Bassanio in naked though equivocal language: 'My purse, my person, my extremest means,/Lie all unlocked to your occasions' (I.i.138-9). 'Purse' and 'person' are linked in a very suggestive metaphor, as Antonio offers the 'extremities' of both fortune and body to his friend. Thus by virtue of his sexual difference as an isolated homosexual man, Antonio stands out from the norms of Venetian society just as sharply as Shylock is contradistinguished against the norms of Christian Venice.

In two important passages of reported action, closely juxtaposed within a single scene (Act II, scene viii), these two characters are polarized into a dialectical relationship of identity and opposition.

> SOLANIO: I never heard a passion so confused,
> So strange, outrageous, and so variable,
> As the dog Jew did utter in the streets:
> 'My daughter! O my ducats! O my daughter!
> Fled with a Christian! O my Christian ducats!
> Justice! The law! My ducats and my daughter! . . .'
> (II.viii.12–17)

> SALERIO: I saw Bassanio and Antonio part.
> Bassanio told him he would make some speed
> Of his return. He answered, 'Do not so;
> Slubber not business for my sake, Bassanio,
> But stay the very riping of the time; . . .'
> And even there, his eye being big with tears,
> Turning his face, he put his hand behind him,
> And with affection wondrous sensible
> He wrung Bassanio's hand; and so they parted.
> (II.viii.36–40, 46–9)

The loss, in each case, of wealth and of affection, is identical: having eloped with a Christian, Jessica is lost to her father, and a share of his wealth with her; Antonio is assisting Bassanio towards a relationship which will inevitably introduce some estrangement of their accustomed intimacy, by contributing a substantial part of his fortune to the enterprise. The merchant and the usurer are polarized into a diametrical opposition which suggests both analogy and difference. If we read the comparison in terms of opposition, we find a distinction between a man who puts love on a level with money ('My ducats and my daughter!'), who cannot separate human from material loss; and a man who, having already given, in financial terms, enough to render him vulnerable to bankruptcy and execution, and having yielded up his love to the embraces of a woman, can yet find it possible to give more. There could be no clearer distinction between the man who cannot distinguish money from love, and the man who is prepared to 'give and hazard all he hath'

(II.vii.9) for the sake of a love that can never bring him compensation or restitution.

Yet when inspected more closely, the linking of Shylock and Bassanio yields a dimension of parallelism together with the sense of contrast. The relationship between Antonio and Bassanio, expressing itself through giving and indebtedness, lending and gratitude, is no more free from mercenary considerations than that between Shylock and Jessica. Love and money are just as closely interconnected, though with different emphases corresponding to different commercial moralities: Shylock committed to an ethic of personal and financial possession – in the later scene with Tubal he wishes his daughter 'dead at my foot, and the jewels in her ear! Would she were hearsed at my foot, and the ducats in her coffin!' (III.i.84–5) – and Antonio to a morality of infinite generosity. But this distinction, though real enough, is (like that between usury and merchant capitalism) a comparatively fine distinction within a larger shared compliance with the necessary interpenetration of love and wealth, money and affection. It seems more just to regard the two predicaments as parallel personal tragedies of loss. Both men are isolated, culturally or sexually, in their grief. As Antonio turns his back on Bassanio he decorously hides his unmanly sorrow: yet at the same time places himself in a characteristic posture of homosexual intercourse.

Antonio is perhaps at his most impressive when in the trial scene his language rises to the biblical dignity and tragic intensity of Shylock's:

I am a tainted wether of the flock,
Meetest for death.

(IV.i.113–14)

Since a 'wether' was a castrated sheep, Antonio is again calling attention to his sexual difference, which isolates him as much as his status as victim. The Christian whose ritual persecution of Shylock consistently strove to place the Jew on a level with animals, now finds himself turned into a lamb in a Jewish ceremony of sacrifice. It is not for nothing that the title by which we know the play seems originally to have been interchangeable with another: in the Stationers' Register it is referred to as 'The Marchaunt of Venyce or otherwise called The Iewe of Venyce'.

VIII

> *The imaginary nationality of the Jew is the nationality of the merchant, of the money man in general.*
> *(Marx 'On the Jewish Question', in Marx 1977: 60)*

Out of Shylock's resentment at a recollected history of indignity, abuse and economic warfare, lacerated into particular anger by the personal hurt and humiliation of his daughter's desertion, there evolves a compelling affirmation of human dignity which seems both 'universal', essentially human, and culturally specific:

> I am a Jew. Hath not a Jew eyes? Hath not a Jew hands, organs, dimensions, senses, affections, passions; fed with the same food, hurt with the same weapons, subject to the same diseases, healed by the same means, warmed and cooled by the same winter and summer, as a Christian is? If you prick us, do we not bleed? If you tickle us, do we not laugh? If you poison us, do we not die? And if you wrong us, shall we not revenge? If we are like you in the rest, we will resemble you in that.
>
> (III.i.55–64)

The common humanity to which Shylock lays claim is a simple concept: human beings are biologically virtually identical to one another despite the differences and barriers of race, religion and culture. If all human beings are fundamentally alike, sharing an identical physical nature in the form and operations of the body and its sensory relation to the world, what justification can there be for discrimination between one human being and another on grounds of race or ethnicity?

On the other hand, Shylock is launching his demand for equality of rights and dignity specifically from a position of 'difference'. The statement 'I am a Jew' functions dramatically as a response to the rhetorical questioning of Antonio's motives for his personal enmity, 'and what's his reason?'. Positioned at that point in the dialogue, the statement reads initially as a denial and dismissal of cultural difference – 'Antonio's reason for persecuting me is no stronger than this: I am a Jew'. On the other hand the statement can also be read affirmatively, as a positive proclamation of cultural identity – 'I *am* a Jew, and as such should not be denied the dignity and toleration to which all men are entitled, and which are particularly appropriate to my race and religion'. The claim to equality must, paradoxically, spring from exactly such an experience of cultural subordination: no one pleads to be treated as a human being (a plea which is then inevitably read as an assertion of humanity) unless they are already being treated as less than one (and therefore conscious of being dehumanized by that treatment). I am a Jew: I am human like everyone else. I am a Jew: I am human, but not like everyone else. I am a Jew: I am not treated as a human being. I am a Jew: I should be accorded a basic human dignity.

In the same way the logic of Shylock's speech runs in two quite different directions. Underlying it there is, on the one hand, the utopian ideal of a universal equality: a fundamental biological kinship between all human beings, which should prescribe parallel values of social, cultural and political equality. Running quite counter to this is a contrary idea: a reductive diminution of all human existence to the lowest possible level. All human beings, including Christians, react in precisely the same way to the same external stimuli: tickling produces laughter, a wound provokes the flow of blood. Antonio's past persecution of Shylock can clearly be identified as a sustained campaign of vengeance against an imputed injury – the 'offence' caused to Antonio's Christian sensibility by the active existence within his business community of an alien, Shylock. Antonio's response to this 'provocation' has been to take revenge by persecution. Why, then, should Shylock respond any differently to the injuries he has sustained as the object of that persecution?

Just as Shylock's demand for human treatment flows from his expression of cultural difference, so his utopian pleas for universal equality and religious tolerance are inseparable from a vindictive determination to repay his enemy's injustice in like kind, or better still with 'interest':

> And if you wrong us, shall we not revenge? If we are like you
> in the rest, we will resemble you in that.

IX

> The god of the Jews has been secularized and has become the god of the world. Exchange is the actual god of the Jew. His god is only the illusion of exchange.
>
> (Marx, 'On the Jewish Question', in Marx 1977: 60)

By Act IV Venice and Belmont are polarized against one another in a configuration of extreme opposition. In Venice there is only Shylock,

Antonio and the bond: racial conflict, financial competition, the law. In Belmont are Bassanio, Portia and the rest of the Christian community, now incorporating the defector Jessica: cultural integration, economic success, love. Venice and Belmont also invade one another, however, with the news of Antonio's disasters reaching Belmont immediately after Bassanio has chosen the correct casket (s.d., III.ii.234); and with Portia similarly intervening into the trial scene in Venice (s.d.,IV.i.163). Furthermore, if we examine each of the two polarized dramatic worlds, we find once again that each discloses a common deep structure of language and ideology.

This is nowhere more apparent than in Act III, scene ii, the final casket scene. In her opening speech conducting Bassanio to his ritual of choice, Portia identifies the ordeal as a 'venture' (III.ii.10) and a 'hazard' (III.ii.2), thereby linking the conventions of Belmont romance with the values of Venetian commerce. Bassanio gravitates towards the correct casket via a meditation on the emptiness of appearances which concludes – ironically, in the context of his abundantly stated economic motives – in an ascetic renunciation of the symbolism of wealth, in favour of a commitment to a more fundamental reality, embodied in the casket of lead.

> So may the outward shows be least themselves.
> The world is still deceived with ornament.
> . . .
> Thus ornament is but the guilèd shore
> To a most dangerous sea, the beauteous scarf
> Veiling an Indian beauty; in a word,
> The seeming truth which cunning times put on
> To entrap the wisest. Therefore, thou gaudy gold,
> Hard food for Midas, I will none of thee.
> (*To the silver casket*) Nor none of thee, thou pale and
>   common drudge
> 'Tween man and man.
>
> (III.ii.73–4, 97–104)

Symbolically 'gold' and 'silver' are associated here respectively with superficial ornament and with commercial exchange. By opting for the 'paleness' of 'meagre' lead, Bassanio rhetorically distances himself from the pursuit of gilded, superficial beauty ('ornament') and from the financial bartering in which silver changes hands.

The overt meaning of this ethical critique of 'ornament' is that

Bassanio pursues a deeper truth than superficial beauty, a more substantial reality than mere wealth. The problem is that he is seeking here to separate and distinguish things which have hitherto consistently been integrated into a single world-view, characteristic of all the Venetian Christians. From the outset the quest for Portia and the pursuit of a fortune have been inseparable elements of Bassanio's motivation. Contextually this factor is strongly emphasized throughout the final casket scene, despite Bassanio's efforts to disengage romantic from mercenary, ideal from material considerations. The motto of the lead casket, 'Who chooseth me must give and hazard all he hath', may accord with Bassanio's language of renunciation, but also accentuates the seamless unity of Belmont romance and Venetian commerce. The scroll Bassanio finds inside the casket assures him that his prize consists of wealth as well as love: 'Since this fortune falls to you/Be content and seek no new' (III.ii.133–4), where the 'fortune' ('good luck') is both Portia herself and her 'fortune' ('wealth'). Portia in speaking of herself uses the familiar language of wealth and commercial transaction:

> Though for myself alone
> I would not be ambitious in my wish
> To wish myself much better, yet for you
> I would be trebled twenty times myself,
> A thousand times more fair, ten thousand times more *rich*,
> That only to stand high in your *account*
> I might in virtues, beauties, livings, friends
> *Exceed account.* But the full *sum* of me
> Is *sum* of something which to term in *gross*,
> Is an unlessoned girl . . .
>
> (III.ii.150–9; emphasis added)

There is no dissociation here of virtue and beauty from riches and power. Bassanio and his company continue to regard the entire expedition in the light of a financial venture. Bassanio refers to himself as a man who has won a competition, 'one of two contending in a prize' (III.ii.141).

Finally, it is Graziano who confirms the identification of romance and wealth by employing again the image of the golden fleece:

> How doth that royal merchant, good Antonio?
> I know he will be glad of our success;
> We are the Jasons, we have won the fleece.
>
> (III.ii.237–9)

Bassanio had originally used this metaphor (I.i.169–70) in reference to Portia's person: 'her sunny locks/Hang on her temples like a golden fleece'. But in that context the image clearly functions to identify the romantic pilgrimage with the quest for fortune, the 'worth' of a beautiful and virtuous woman with the 'fortune' she would bring to her husband. By linking, through that same image, the economic context of Venice with their 'success' in Belmont, Graziano confirms the successful romance quest as inseparable from a successful commercial enterprise.

X

In moments of particular self-consciousness political life tries to suppress its presuppositions, civil society and its elements, and to constitute itself as the real, harmonious life of man. However, this is only possible through violent opposition to its own conditions …
(Marx, 'On the Jewish Question', in Marx 1977: 47)

In the trial scene (Act IV, scene i) Shylock and Antonio confront one another for the last decisive combat. When Portia first arrives, she asks the Duke to identify plaintiff and defendant – 'Which is the merchant here, and which the Jew?' (IV.i.171) – as if they were virtually indistinguishable protagonists: though they ought to be immediately distinguishable one from another by their dress. Portia's initial inability to distinguish merchant from Jew does, however, emphasize their nominal equality in the eyes of the law. It it precisely that principle of legal equality, constitutionally guaranteed to all citizens of Venice, that has enabled Shylock to pursue his 'strange' and barbaric suit (which, of course, is quite out of keeping with the liberties of a republican constitution) to such extreme lengths. Salerio reported that Shylock 'doth impeach the freedom of the state/If they deny him justice' (III.ii. 276–7); and Antonio himself has admitted that the reputation of Venetian justice would indeed be discredited if Shylock were seen to receive less favourable treatment under the law than Venetian Christians:

The Duke cannot deny the course of law,
For the commodity that strangers have
With us in Venice, if it be denied,
Will much impeach the justice of the state,
Since that the trade and profit of the city
Consisteth of all nations.

(III.iii.26–31)

This paradox – that the laws of Venetian society permit equally to all individual citizens freedoms which can then be used to deprive other citizens of that same freedom – lies at the heart of the trial, just as it lay at the heart of Shylock's great 'I am a Jew' speech. In that earlier speech Shylock's insistence on a fundamental human equality is also paradoxical: since it is used both to demand equality of human rights, and to justify an equality of privilege in the taking of revenge. The ideology of the Venetian state is as self-contradictory as that of the modern republican state in Marx's treatise:

> ... the so-called rights of man, the rights of man as different from the rights of the citizen, are nothing but the rights of the member of civil society, i.e. egoistic man, man separated from other men and the community. ... It is the right to this separation, the rights of the limited individual who is limited to himself. ... Thus the right of man to property is the right to enjoy his possessions and dispose of the same arbitrarily, without regard for other men, independently from society, the right of selfishness.
>
> (Marx 1977: 52–3)

In line with the values of universal equality embodied in the political state of Venice, the Duke invites Shylock to renounce his self-interest as a 'limited individual', and to enter the moral consensus of Christian Venice. That ethical community is defined in terms of universal values: if Shylock could be 'touched with human gentleness and love' in observing the merchant's losses, he would be prepared not only to 'loose the forfeiture', but also to cancel part of the original debt. By appealing to the apparent universality of the values of 'human gentleness and love', the Duke, however, unwittingly draws attention to Shylock's otherness. Antonio's misfortunes would, the Duke asserts,

> pluck commiseration of his state
> From brassy bosoms and rough hearts of flint,
> From stubborn Turks and Tartars never trained
> To offices of tender courtesy.
>
> (IV.i.29–32)

Even non-Christians would feel sorry for Antonio; would be touched by 'human gentleness and love' although they have had no training in civilized graces of 'courtesy'. Members of other racial groups, Turks and Tartars, do not have the benefit of such training.

Shylock, as an inhabitant of Christian Venice, can participate in the benefits of its civilization. But of course Shylock, being as much an 'infidel' as a Turk or a Tartar, can just as easily be accused of antisocial behaviour rooted in his racial otherness. The sub-text of this speech therefore becomes clear: if Shylock were fully a member of the cultural and ethical community of Venice, he would not be able to press his cruel and vindictive suit: 'human gentleness', 'love' and 'tender courtesy' would prevent him. If Shylock is not merely pretending to pursue the suit to its fatal end, then his motives are those of a hostile alien, akin to those of 'stubborn Turks and Tartars'. The Duke's final line of appeal contains a quite extraordinary pun: 'We all expect a gentle answer, Jew' (IV.i.33) – where 'gentle', juxtaposed to 'Jew' comes close enough to 'gentile' to clinch the argument. 'Are you', the Duke is asking, 'going to drop this case, or proceed with it? are you going to behave like a Christian, or a Jew?'

The problem confronting the Duke and the entire Venetian state is that the legal system of Venice simply does not replicate its own sense of moral order. If in the interests of what we would now call 'free trade' no restriction is placed on the limit to which a commercial contract can be used to threaten the life of one of its signatories, then the appeal to a moral dimension transcending the sphere of legal and financial practice can carry little conviction. Shylock's case rests consistently on his rights in law, guaranteed by the contract freely entered into by Antonio, and protected by the law of Venice. The constitution of the political state guarantees the right to private property as a protection of individual liberty; and yet that same right to private property (Shylock's contractual claim on a part of Antonio's body) when exercised by one individual threatens the liberty of another.

Shylock adheres tenaciously to the one salient point which he thinks will win him the case: if the bond is legal, the court must allow him to exact the legal penalty. When questioned as to motive, Shylock simply refuses to answer:

> You'll ask me why I rather choose to have
> A weight of carrion flesh than to receive
> Three thousand ducats. I'll not answer that,
> But say it is my humour. Is it answered?
> . . .
> So can I give no reason, nor I will not,
> More than a lodged hate, and a certain loathing

I bear Antonio, that I follow thus
A losing suit against him. Are you answered?

(IV.i.39–42, 58–61)

In this way, although admitting to his personal animosity against
Antonio, Shylock suppresses the whole question of motive (and with
it all the associated concerns of race and economics with which the
drama has been largely concerned). Besides, Shylock asserts, he is doing
nothing essentially dissimilar, in claiming his rightful share in Antonio's
flesh, than Venetian slave-owners who accept the buying and selling
of human flesh in the form of slavery (IV.i.88–102).

Above all, Shylock tries to make his suit a test case measuring the
true character of the Venetian constitution. Shylock has sworn

To have the due and forfeit of my bond.
If you deny it, let the danger light
Upon your charter and your city's freedom.
. . .
If you deny me, fie upon your law!
There is no force in the decrees of Venice.
I stand for judgement.

(IV.i.36–8, 100–2)

Again, Shylock's argument is that he, in common with all other
inhabitants of Venice, possesses equal rights, protected by the
republic's constitution. But of course the suit can only be regarded as
a legal test case because Shylock, being an alien, is claiming legal compensation from a Christian citizen: so the demand for universal
individual equality is again launched specifically from a position of
cultural subjugation. Each time Shylock is invited to join the Christian
community and subscribe to its values, the discourse of invitation
reminds him of his unequal cultural status. 'How shalt thou hope for
mercy', asks the Duke, 'rend'ring none?' But 'mercy' is of course the
dominant value of the Duke's Christian religion, not of Shylock's
Judaism: 'What judgement shall I dread' is his reply, 'doing no
wrong?' (IV.i.87–8).

Portia proposes exactly the same solution as the Duke: 'Then must
the Jew be merciful' (IV.i.179). Her eloquent celebration of the virtue
of mercy (IV.i.181–99) is strictly irrelevant, since again it privileges
a specifically Christian set of values:

Therefore, Jew,
Though justice be thy plea, consider this:

That in the course of justice none of us
Should see salvation.

(IV.i.194–7)

As a Jew Shylock could hardly expect, however much mercy he displays in this case (and as Portia's brusque manner of address – 'Then must the Jew . . .', 'Therefore, Jew', 'Tarry, Jew' – may forcefully remind him), ever to see Christian salvation. Portia virtually admits the uncertain relevance of her own rhetoric, since it does nothing to undermine the legal basis of Shylock's case:

> I have spoke thus much
> To mitigate the justice of thy plea,
> Which if thou follow, this strict court of Venice
> Must needs give sentence 'gainst the merchant there.

(IV.i.199–202)

Throughout the first half of the trial Shylock is continually assured that he is an equal in the eyes of the law, and is continually offered the opportunity of renouncing his suit, and embracing the common values of Venetian civilization. But since the offer is always couched in the language and imagery of Christian culture, it never quite succeeds in constituting Shylock as the free and equal citizen of Venice he is theoretically guaranteed by the republic's constitution to be. Rather, as Marx observes of Bauer's offer to the Jews of a share in universal emancipation, the Jew is asked to renounce the inequality of his private faith only to be absorbed into a general condition of secularized inequality for all.[6]

Portia leads Shylock almost to the point of execution with her assurances that his suit is legally unassailable; and then with her famous injunction to pause – 'Tarry a little' (IV.i.302) – produces a devastating dramatic reversal, which sets the action spinning off in a completely opposite direction. The law giving Shylock the right to exact his penalty is still not questioned: but alongside it Portia produces other statutes which render the exaction of the penalty a criminal offence. These laws, unlike the law protecting the cosmopolitan freedom of commercial exchange, are violently totalitarian in character, since they are designed to protect the life and property of Venetian citizens against the harmful actions of racial or cultural outsiders:

> Take then thy bond. Take thou thy pound of flesh,
> But in the cutting it, if thou dost shed
> One drop of Christian blood, thy lands and goods

Are by the laws of Venice confiscate
Unto the state of Venice.

(IV.i.305–9)

The subsequent injunction to cut off no more and no less than 'a just pound' seems to be part of that same law protecting Christian flesh against the non-Christian enemy. To subvert the law that treats all men equally, Portia invokes a law designed explicitly to treat them unequally: if the situation were reversed and Shylock stood in Antonio's danger, the Jew would not be protected against the Christian in the same way as the Christian is protected against the Jew. Finally, Portia reveals her bottom-line defence of Antonio, a conspiracy law again targeted directly at the outsider:

It is enacted in the laws of Venice,
If it be proved against an alien
That by direct or indirect attempts
He seek the life of any citizen,
The party 'gainst the which he doth contrive
Shall seize one half his goods; the other half
Comes to the privy coffer of the state,
And the offender's life lies in the mercy
Of the Duke only . . .

(IV.i.344–52)

Initially, then, Portia attempts to resolve the deadlock by appeal to a universal natural law: she elevates the problem from one of law and finance, where there is no rational appeal beyond the justice of contract (the level of 'civil society'), to one of universal morality, where the dominant value is mercy and forgiveness (the levels of 'political society' and 'religion'). She offers Shylock the opportunity of incorporation into a harmonized political economy where the Jew would rationally forfeit his legal rights in the interests of the public good. Shylock's refusal – a resistance in which the determined fundamentalism of religious faith and the stubborn reality of economic forces are joined – renders this solution impossible. Having failed in her attempt at incorporation, Portia openly proceeds to use the power of Christian nationalism against him. Underlying the superficial egalitarianism and multiculturalism of that cosmopolitan Venetian law in which Shylock wholly believed, lies a judicial structure designed to protect individual private property against the claims of others, and to protect Christian Venetian citizens against aliens. Shylock is finally proven right: despite his obvious centrality to the Venetian economy, he was never, in the last instance, considered by Venice as anything other than an outsider. And yet, as the play's conclusion makes abundantly clear, that fate of alienation could be regarded as the destiny of every man and every woman within Venice's representation of Marx's 'civil society'.

XI

> ... the perfection of the idealism of the state was at the same time the perfection of the materialism of civil society ... Man was therefore not freed from religion; he received freedom of religion. He was not freed from property; he received freedom of property. He was not freed from the egoism of trade; he received freedom to trade.
>
> (Marx 1977: 56)

The Merchant of Venice appears by its ending to be shaped into a dominant pattern of ultimate reconciliation, harmonizing, unifying, balance. The comic pattern concludes by reconciling all contradictions, resolving all disharmonies, drawing all discordant elements into a unitary synthesis and integration. At the end of the play, this pattern is effected by various dramatic and poetic means: the symbolic harmony of marriage; the reconciliation of disagreement; the clarification of deception and misunderstanding, especially the throwing off of disguise; and the symbolic harmony of music.

There are, however, as often in Shakespearian comedy, significant undercurrents of disharmony quietly subverting the effect of achieved reconciliation. The most obvious of these disharmonies is of course the fate of Shylock, condemned by the court to a doom described by Antonio as worse for the businessman than death itself (IV.i.265–9). But there are also discordances other than the repressed memory of Shylock reverberating within this final scene. Another shadow, in some ways a longer and darker one, is cast by the presence of Antonio. Antonio is after all, nominally at least, the central character of the play, the 'merchant' of the title; and we would expect him therefore to be prominent in the dramatic ritual of celebration that closes the play. Antonio, however, appears marginalized in comparison with the other characters, all of whom have a much more definite role to play. He moves from being a shadowy figure at Bassanio's side, to the embarrassed witness of a marital quarrel; and is finally constituted by Portia as the grateful recipient of aristocratic bounty. Finally, there is the striking exclusion of Antonio from the otherwise ubiquitous marital pairings which organize the rest of the cast into couples. Clearly the play has not succeeded in integrating Antonio sufficiently into the 'universal' celebration of harmony for these questions to be readily answered. As Bassanio's devoted friend, perhaps he will find a place of affection between man and wife. As Bassanio's thwarted homosexual lover, perhaps he will not.

To the very end, then, Shylock and Antonio, the 'Jew' and the 'merchant' of the play's interchangeable titles, remain connected to one another in a destiny deeper than the comic resolution of the play. Antonio remains as firmly decentred from the final resolution as he was from the initial romantic action: a bystander, a witness, even in some senses a victim. Both Jew and homosexual merchant are identified in terms of cultural difference, and though their fates are very different – one excluded, the other tolerated – neither has the benefit of full participation in the social life of the community. Perhaps even more surprisingly, the play also offers some significant hints to the effect that another minority within the play finds itself less than wholly satisfied by the comic denouement – the women.

Earlier in the play, when Bassanio has chosen the correct casket, Portia, in a highly formal speech of dedication and submission, gives herself over to him, renouncing her authority as lord of Belmont and subjecting her personality entirely to that of her husband.

> You see me, Lord Bassanio, where I stand,
> Such as I am . . .
>   an unlessoned girl, unschooled, unpractisèd:
> Happy in this, she is not yet so old
> But she may learn; . . .
> Happiest of all is that her gentle spirit
> Commits itself to yours to be directed,
> As from her lord, her governor, her king.
> Myself and what is mine to you and yours
> Is now converted. But now I was the lord
> Of this fair mansion, master of my servants,
> Queen o'er myself; and even now, but now,
> This house, these servants, and this same myself
> Are yours, my lord's. I give them with this ring
>   (III.ii.149–50, 159–61, 163–71)

In the trial scene Portia has, of course, proved herself to be 'lacking' in nothing: to be, indeed, infinitely superior in resourcefulness, intelligence, knowledge and determination to any of the men in question, including her husband. By means of that masculine disguise she is able to reassume some of the power she has relinquished by surrendering her 'lordship' of Belmont to Bassanio. On her return to Belmont, however, she must put off both her disguise and her pretensions to continuing power: Bassanio is the master now. As she approaches her former property, Portia seems suddenly possessed of a deep strain of melancholy, a plangent sense of unappeasable loss:

> That light we see is burning in my hall.
> How far that little candle throws his beams –
> So shines a good deed in a naughty world.
>
> (V.i.89–91)

Still thinking of Belmont as her own house – a phrase which is presently adjusted to 'our house' (V.i.139) – Portia appropriates the candle as a symbol of her own recent action in redeeming Antonio from her husband's debt: she, too, is the 'little candle' (we remember her opening words, 'my little body is aweary of this great world') which shines brightly but alone in an otherwise unrelieved darkness of wickedness and futility. In view of Portia's astounding success, the observation is a surprisingly modest celebration of her achievement. Perhaps it is the weight of responsibility, which like her initial world-weariness would be unintelligible to anyone observing her circumstances from the outside. Or perhaps Portia is simply overwhelmed, as she returns from a scene of triumphant action, to find her house occupied by others, with an inconsolable sense of loss. Nerissa's speech sounds the same melancholy note:

> NERISSA: When the moon shone, we did not see the candle.
> PORTIA: So doth the greater glory dim the less.
>   A substitute shines brightly as a king
>   Until a king be by, and then his state
>   Empties itself as doth an inland brook
>   Into the main of waters.
>
> (V.i.92–7)

Portia's entry into the state of marriage is anticipated as an eclipsing of her powers by the 'king' ('lord' and 'governor') to whom she has entrusted and committed herself and her previous status. As soon as the 'king' arrives, on Bassanio's return, her petty brightness will fade into insignificance, her authority will 'empty itself' as a stream disappears into the sea. Even more discordant than the victimisation of Shylock and the marginalization of Antonio is this melancholy voice of female subjection. (See Nick Potter, 'The Merchant of Venice', in Holderness *et al.* 1987: 160–79).

XII

The correspondences demonstrated in my reading between *The Merchant of Venice* and 'On the Jewish Question' are nothing less than extraordinary. Surely Shakespeare must after all have contrived to read Marx?

And yet the play was written in an immediately post-feudal Europe of absolute monarchies, in a kingdom in which protestant Christianity was by violent coercion imposed as a 'natural' ideology. Protestant Christian values, traditional historicism would advise us, can only in Shakespeare's ideological context have been assumed as a norm, from which other religions (such as Judaism) must have appeared as deviations. It is entirely predictable that the conflict of Christianity and Judaism should at that time have been imagined as a moral struggle between norm and deviation, between good and evil. Shakespeare, it is true, was able to apply to the protagonists of that conflict a disinterested universal humanism, problematizing the crude stereotypes of tradition and bringing his Jew to sensitive and compelling life; but such imaginative even-handedness was strictly moral and aesthetic, offering to Shylock (as does Portia) a dramatic equivalent of universal Christian mercy, and grasping the imaginative possibilities of a man sinned against, though not in proportion to his sinning.

The young Marx was writing, by contrast, in a Europe convulsed by economic change and political revolution, with the absolutist states in perpetual and violent crisis, and the young republics of France and America proferring concrete examples of achievable social transformation. The two and a half centuries of economic development that stand between Shakespeare and Marx, and the rise of secular philosophy, enabled a much clearer economic and philosophical grasp of the nature of modern society than any that could have been available to Shakespeare. All Marx's key terms – civil and political society, the state, alienation – presuppose both a more complex world and more sophisticated methods of interpreting it than those of the sixteenth century.

Nevertheless, the possibilities of extraordinary correspondence persist. Shakespeare's Jew is not a medieval villain, but a modern financier, located in that society, Venice, clearly recognized by the sixteenth century as the prototypical modern constitutional republic. Shakespeare's Venice is characterized by a very Marxist self-division between a civil society of naked individualism and ruthless economic competition, and a political society whose values of universal equality paradoxically protect the rights of individual self-interest. In Venice's civil society Jew and Christian, though mutually polarized in stark antagonism, appear in practice to be equally central and equally alienated: the Christians have become Jews. The split between civil and political societies is then reduplicated by the split between Venice and Belmont, in which an apparent opposition of values masks a deeper affinity. Both the political constitution of Venice and the romance world of Belmont purport to integrate men and women into a human community. Yet neither is in practice capable of overcoming a pervasive alienation. In Shakespeare, as in Marx, men and women lead a double life, doubly lost to themselves in their isolation and mutual hostility, and in the illusory reconciliations of political society and the religion of romance.

Do these correspondences then testify to a preternatural prescience on the part of Shakespeare, whose analysis of the emergent modern state prophetically adumbrated Marx's analysis of its maturity? The reader must judge whether or not my reading of the play is plausible and convincing. If it is, then the miraculous correspondence must be admitted, though not thereby explained. Would an innocent and objective reading of the play be capable of producing the same results? This question cannot be answered, since there is for contemporary criticism no such thing as an innocent reading and no possibility of critical objectivity. I could protest that the broad outlines of my reading, though elaborated here for the first time, were formulated 20 years ago and preceded any direct knowledge of 'On the Jewish Question'. I cannot, however, deny that that early reading was already coloured by a thorough knowledge of Marx's other early writings, particularly 'Towards a Critique of Hegel's *Philosophy of Right*' and the *Economic and Philosophic Manuscripts* of 1844.

In *Flaubert's Parrot* (1984) Julian Barnes recalls the story in which Flaubert, on a visit to Egypt with Maxim du Camp, ascending a pyramid at sunrise, found attached to its summit the business-card of a Rouen French polisher. This quintessentially Flaubertian moment of pure modernist irony seems too perfect, Barnes comments, and too perfectly constructed, to have been accidental. In fact, Flaubert not only placed the card there himself in order to dramatize its discovery, but had taken it to Egypt for that very purpose (Barnes 1984: 68–70). In the same way, as a tourist visiting the past, toiling to the summit of that great cultural colossus, the Shakespeare myth, I have discovered, lying neglected on its bald eminence, a copy of Marx's early writings. I cannot be absolutely certain that I had not dropped it there myself just prior to the moment of discovery; nor, indeed, that I had not taken it with me for that very purpose.

SUPPLEMENT

NIGEL WOOD: At the beginning of your essay you quote Terry Eagleton's coat-trailing observation that there is a lot of Marx in Shakespeare. Wry humour aside, does this not seem like an appropriation of the past according to what is now deemed relevant?

GRAHAM HOLDERNESS: The point of that little fantasy of Terry Eagleton's is, of course, to draw attention to the impossibility of an innocent reading of any document from the past. In any contemporary reading of Shakespeare, there is an interaction between the writing, and the content and structure of the reader's mind. What emerges is not the result of a communication between Shakespeare and the reader, but the effects of an intellectual encounter between an old piece of writing and the modern intellectual substance the reader brings to the exchange. If Marx is part of that substance, then an act of reading produces a reaction between the old and the new discourses. Hence Shakespeare is already influenced by an encounter with Marx; Shakespeare's language has already been through that exchange; Shakespeare must have read Marx.

I think we can go some way in the direction of separating an ancient structure from a modern construction. I think it's possible to argue that The Merchant of Venice collocated its economic, ethnic, cultural and social preoccupations in a way that can be said to resemble Marx's philosophical analyses of Judaism, bourgeois society and alienation. I don't seek to attribute this perspective as a preternaturally prophetic and perspicacious insight to an individual genius; but rather to propose that the cultural apparatus of the early modern theatre was capable of producing such a perspective on its own history – just as, two and a half centuries later, the political and philosophical revolutions of the nineteenth century were capable of voicing in Marx's writings a critique of their own contradictory historical progress.

I can't finally say whether this interpretation discloses the intrinsic character of the past, or indicates the irrepressible influence of the present. I don't finally know whether my interpretation is a Marxist reading of Shakespeare, or a Shakespearian reading of Marx.

NW: Aren't we always confronted by an anti-Semitic document when we read/see *The Merchant of Venice*, as Stephen Greenblatt seems to point out in his essay on 'Marlowe, Marx, and Anti-Semitism' (Greenblatt 1990: 40–58)?

GH: There are a number of ways of approaching this problem. Stephen Greenblatt regards Marx as a renegade Jew, who in the course of an anti-patriarchal rebellion against his own cultural and religious heritage lapses into a vicious and dangerous anti-Semitism. This seems a very remarkable concession on the part of a new historicist to the notion of instrinsic meaning embedded in historical language. If the words 'Jew' and 'Judaism' can only ever mean the same thing, then to employ them in a linguistic strategy that appears to criticize or oppose those meanings is always inevitably to fall into anti-Semitism. The corollary of that view would be a species of 'political correctness' permitting only positive and celebratory usage of the terms. This is indeed a familiar factor in certain dialects of political language, where (for example) even to speak of the rights of the Palestinian people would readily and automatically be understood as an assault on Israel, and by definition (since the state is an ethnic and religious entity) as anti-Jewish.

What Marx was attempting in 'On the Jewish Question' was, ironically, something much more 'post-structuralist'. The essay attempts precisely to defamiliarize historical language, to interrogate terms such as 'Jew' and 'Christian': to destabilize the structure of their historical opposition, and to renegotiate their relations with economic ideas and political practice. Marx explicitly refuses to accept that such words contain fixed meanings, and energetically 'slides their signifiers' in order to revolutionize the language of political, economic and philosophical debate.

Now of course there are political positions, particularly those grouped around the term 'Zionism', that adhere fiercely to the apparently fixed contents of historical language. The Zionist can claim, by deploying terms such as 'Judaism' as potent and irreducible cultural tokens, that any opposition to the state of Israel is essentially anti-Jewish; and in doing so can invoke, to authorize a contemporary political conviction, an ancient and continuous history of Jewish persecution. Political language must surely, however, be able to interrogate its own basic terms, without courting a charge of racism: otherwise it consists more of ideology than of politics.

NW: How much weight should we give to the Folio designation of the play as a Comedy?

GH: The now familiar tripartite division of Shakespeare's plays into comedies, tragedies and histories derives in fact from the posthumously published 'First Folio' – *Mr William Shakespeares Comedies, Histories and Tragedies* – of 1623, and was therefore an editorial rather than an authorial or theatrical strategy. When the plays were originally published, in cheap quarto format through the 1590s and early 1600s, they were by no means so clearly identified and distinguished by genre. The original title-pages would offer a play as a 'comical history', or a 'tragical history', or a 'pleasant conceited tragedy'.

Modern criticism began quite early on to reclassify those plays which would not fit very easily into the standard categories, even inventing new types not found in the Folio, such as the 'problem plays', the 'Roman plays' and the 'late romances'. *The Tempest* and *The Winter's Tale*, now firmly settled as tragi-comic 'late romances', are classified in the Folio as comedies; while their companion piece *Cymbeline* is a tragedy.

The plays were written and produced in a popular culture aware of genre as a set of conventions to be played with and renegotiated. The historical direction of the dominant culture, as reflected, for example, in Hamlet's advice to the players, was towards an acceptance of genre as exclusive and limiting. As a theoretical concept genre has again become important, but again regarded as a set of rules to be bent, twisted, subverted. So we continually reclassify Shakespeare's plays in our own terms, redefining, for example, *Macbeth* as a history play, or *King Lear* as a disappointed romance. *The Merchant of Venice*, originally defined as a comedy, can now be seen to manipulate the conventions of comedy, satire, tragedy, romance. It's certainly, by any standards, a 'problem play'.

CHAPTER 3

Reprise: Gender, Sexuality and Theories of Exchange in *The Merchant of Venice*

KAREN NEWMAN

[Karen Newman's essay builds on an earlier study of the network of social obligations that surrounded Elizabethan marriage rituals (Newman 1987). Women were typically objects of exchange, and were rewarded with glowing approbation if they conformed to this expectation, yet the 'unruly woman', such as Katherine in *The Taming of the Shrew*, or the disobedient daughter, such as Hermia in *A Midsummer Night's Dream*, throws these ritualized patterns into some disarray. By refusing to accept their identity purely according to expected patriarchal assumptions, such voices are not merely seen in relation to, and valued according to their conformity to, men.

Far from a perennial paradigm, the 'exchange' of women in effect merely serves certain forms of male repression, not only as regards women as passive objects (see Hero as opposed to Beatrice in *Much Ado About Nothing*), but also in terms of a limited definition of how a society might be maintained. For Claude Lévi-Strauss, building on the investigations of Marcel Mauss, this female role seemed integral to society as he construed all such organization as based on specifically male bonding, into which structure women could only fit in supporting roles, and not as axes of interest in their own right. Such anthropological scientism actually has a great deal invested in its 'factual' rhetoric, as any reader of Simone de Beauvoir's *The Second Sex* (1988) or Luce Irigaray's *This Sex Which Is Not One* (1985) will discover.

Women must define themselves aside from the snares of being just reflections of how men would require them to be. For de Beauvoir, it was essential to discover that 'no man really is God' (de Beauvoir 1988: 611), and that women are not born as stable reference points but constructed as such. For

Irigaray, the problem is rather to do with the search for a language apart from that uttered within patriarchal terms. In her exploration of gender difference, 'a feminine language' (so often relegated to the margins) works to 'undo the unique meaning, the proper meaning of words, of nouns: which still regulates all discourse'. This inevitably questions the assumption that there is somewhere a primal unity, for all such ordering presupposes description, and possession. For Irigaray, there is 'no feminine meta-language':

> The masculine can partly look at itself, speculate about itself, represent itself and describe itself for what it is, whilst the feminine can try to speak to itself through a new language, but cannot describe itself from outside or in formal terms, except by identifying itself with the masculine, and thus by losing itself.

> (Irigaray 1985: 65)

To this extent, it is *positively* illogical, and the 'unruly' or 'mad' woman (see the language of Ophelia in *Hamlet*, Act IV, scene v, where she is allowed to initiate discourse for the first time) is elusive and consequently disruptive.

For Lawrence Stone, in his massively influential *The Family, Sex and Marriage in England, 1500–1800* (Stone 1977), the available record, assembled according to 'orderly', that is to say, masculinist, premises, confirms femininity as the passive 'Other' to male prerogative and control – an instance where an unsparing empirical account actually colludes in the silences visited on women at that time. Newman's return to the play in the last section of her account attempts to open up its positive disruption of surface order to view, and, in so doing, joins several critics whose accounts of the otherwise mute voices of resistance obey no clear rules or formulae (see Jardine 1983: 68–102; Erickson 1991: 23–30; Berry 1989: 134–65; and Lorraine Helms, 'Acts of Resistance: The Feminist Player', in Callaghan *et al.* 1994: 102–56).]

The Traffic in Women

Across disciplinary boundaries, transhistorically, and in varied media, Western feminists have reproduced the paradigm of woman as object of exchange developed most influentially in anthropology.[1] In the French anthropologist Claude Lévi-Strauss's often cited formulation from *The Elementary Structures of Kinship*:

> The total relationship of exchange which constitutes marriage is not established between a man and a woman ... but between two groups of men, and the woman figures as one of the objects in the exchange, not as one of the partners ...

> (Lévi-Strauss 1969: 115)

The paradigm has been both productive and seductive, made available to many through Gayle Rubin's forceful and influential essay, 'The Traffic in Women: Notes on the "Political Economy" of Sex' (in Reiter 1975: 157–210), which named and analysed the paradigm of woman as object of exchange. The 'traffic in women' is everywhere in feminist cultural analysis: in radical feminism, cultural feminism, Marxist feminisms, post-structuralist feminisms, in history, anthropology, art, literature, political theory, economics.[2]

In his *Essai sur le don* (1925), Marcel Mauss had argued that in primitive societies, exchange – giving, receiving and reciprocating gifts – governed social intercourse. In the cultures Mauss described, 'food, women, children, possessions, charms, land, labour, services, religious offices, rank' circulated in exchange (Mauss 1954: 11–12). Lévi-Strauss reworked Mauss's theory of the gift in the *Elementary Structures* by proposing that marriage is the most fundamental form of gift exchange, and women the most basic of gifts. He argues that incest taboos and other rules prohibiting sexual relations and marriage between family members ensure alliances and relationships among men:

> The prohibition of incest is less a rule prohibiting marriage with the mother, sister, or daughter, than a rule obliging the mother, sister, or daughter to be given to others. It is the supreme rule of the gift . . .
>
> (Lévi-Strauss 1969: 481)

For Lévi-Strauss, social life entails the exchange of women since culture depends upon the male bonds constituted by that traffic. Consequently he authorizes the exchange of women by presenting it rhetorically as decreed, ordained, eternal:

> In the matrimonial dialogue of men, woman is never purely what is spoken about; for if women in general represent a certain category of signs, destined to a certain kind of communication, each woman preserves a particular value arising from her talent, before and after marriage, for taking her part in a duet. In contrast to words, which have wholly become signs, each woman has remained at once a sign and a value. This explains why the relations between the sexes have preserved that affective richness, ardour, and mystery which doubtless originally permeated the entire universe of human communications.
>
> (Lévi-Strauss 1969: 496)

Once upon a time, then, in an anthropological Eden, there was an originary state of happy identity between word and thing; after the fall, words were no longer values as well as signs: 'their signifying function . . . supplanted their character as values, [and] language, along with scientific civilization, has helped to impoverish perception and to strip it of its affective, aesthetic and magical implications' (Lévi-Strauss 1969: 496). Women, however, have somehow managed to preserve their value. They are objects, but something more than objects – *values* is Lévi-Strauss's term. Woman's value, for Lévi-Strauss (1969: 496), arises 'from her talent, before and after marriage, for taking her part in a duet'.

In the late 1940s, in *The Second Sex*, perhaps the earliest example of feminist theory, Simone de Beauvoir demystified Lévi-Strauss's romantic 'duet' by recognizing in his celebration of woman's mystery and magic qualities the production of woman 'as the absolute Other', the eternal feminine, the binary always inferior, lacking, useful primarily in the Hegelian, or dialectical, sense in which subjectivity 'can be posed only in being opposed' (de Beauvoir 1988: 17):

> man defines woman not in herself but as relative to him . . . She is defined and differentiated with reference to man and not he with reference to her; she is the incidental, the inessential as opposed to the essential. He is the Subject, he is the Absolute – she is the other.
>
> (de Beauvoir 1988: 16)

Anthropologists have challenged not the phallocentrism of Lévi-Strauss's claim that exogamous marriage and the exchange of women is a necessary condition for the formation of social groups and ultimately of culture, but his theory of kinship itself. Pierre Bourdieu, for example, adduces instances of parallel cousin marriage from nomadic and gatherer groups which refute the structuralist interpretation of kinship as a rule-governed *system*, arguing instead that kin relationships are social *practices* that produce and reproduce historically specific social relations. In the cultures Bourdieu examines, for example, women often take part in the choice of a spouse for their children: how marriages are made and what they do 'depend on the aims or collective strategies of the group involved' (Bourdieu 1977: 58) and are not constitutive *per se* of male bonds or of culture. But Bourdieu's ungendered social science vocabulary ('the collective strategies of the group involved') glosses over the significant fact that these aims and strategies inevitably allot women secondary status, for it is always the bride, and never the groom, who is an object of exchange among family groups and the means whereby social relations are reproduced. However they may disagree about the reasons for and results of kinship 'rules' or 'practices', in both Lévi-Strauss's structural anthropology and Bourdieu's functionalist analysis, women figure as capital, as objects of exchange among men.

But the 'traffic in women' is neither a universal law on which culture depends, as Lévi-Strauss would have it, nor a means of producing and reproducing generalized 'social relations', as Bourdieu claims, but a strategy for ensuring hierarchical gender relations. Since the pioneering work of de Beauvoir's *The Second Sex*, feminists have criticized the anthropological model by arguing that the exchange of women is neither necessary nor inevitable, but produces and reproduces what Gayle Rubin has termed a 'sex/gender system' in which the traffic in women is only part of an entire system of

> sexual access, genealogical statuses, lineage names and ancestors, rights and *people* – men, women and children – in concrete systems of social relationships . . . 'Exchange of women' is a shorthand for expressing that the social relations of a kinship system specify that men have certain rights over their female kin, and that women do not have the same rights either to themselves or to their male kin.
>
> (Reiter 1975: 177)

The French psychoanalyst Luce Irigaray, in her rereading of Lévi-Strauss, recognizes the risk of reproducing what she seeks to contest. Rather than simply applying the exchange paradigm critically, she disrupts the grammar of the syntax of exchange by representing the anthropological case pushed to its logical end:

> the exchanges which organize patriarchal societies take place, exclusively, between men. Women, signs, goods, currency, pass from man to man or risk – so it is claimed – slipping back into incestuous and exclusively endogamous relations that would paralyze all social and economic intercourse . . . the very possibility of the socio-cultural order would entail homosexuality. Homosexuality would be the law that regulates the socio-cultural economy.
>
> (Irigaray 1985: 189)

Irigaray takes Lévi-Strauss at his word, but 'with a difference' and in doing so distorts his argument so as to force her reader to recognize the logical implications of the anthropological paradigm. She makes that syntax ungrammatical in a culture of compulsory heterosexuality by acknowledging, in Eve Kosovsky Sedgwick's word, the 'homo-social' character of patriarchal exchange. Sedgwick defines the homo-social as 'the whole spectrum of bonds between men, including friendship, mentorship, rivalry, institutional subordination, homosex-ual genitality, and economic exchange – within which the various forms of the traffic in women take place' (Sedgwick 1984: 227).

Feminist literary criticism has demonstrated women's objectification in countless texts from every period in literary history, but the traffic in women has figured with particular prominence in Renaissance studies, in part at least because of the complicity between anthro-pological paradigms and work in social history on women and the family in the early modern period. Lawrence Stone's description of the early modern family has been more often cited by feminist literary critics of Shakespeare than those of any other historian. Here is Stone's version of marriage in early modern England:

> The accepted wisdom of the age was that marriage based on personal selection, and thus inevitably influenced by such ephemeral factors as sexual attraction or romantic love, was if anything less likely to produce lasting happiness than one arranged by more prudent and more mature heads. This view finds confirmation in anthropological studies of the many societies where love has not been regarded as a sound basis for marriage, and where one girl is as good as another, provided that she is a good housekeeper, a breeder and a willing sexual playmate.
>
> (Stone 1977: 128)

Here distanced amusement, authority-claiming generalization, and pseudo-scientific diction work to assert the factual status of Stone's claims. With bemused detachment he describes 'the wisdom of the age', suggesting his gentlemanly recognition that such notions are no longer wise, but nevertheless managing to claim for his argument that such attitudes were widely held – by all sorts of people, and not just in England. His is not merely the argot of social science, but the cant of evolutionary biology – 'personal selection', 'factors', 'sexual attrac-tion' – all of which work to assert an indisputable 'scientific' truth. Finally, there is the astonishing segue from the 'wisdom of the age' concerning arranged marriages in the early modern period, to woman as object, but the woman has become a 'girl', at once maid, bitch and lay. The choice of 'girl' is particularly surprising since social historians, including Stone himself, have shown that the average age at marriage of Englishwomen was far from girlhood – their early twenties.[3] 'Girl' depends on the anthropological context he invokes. Stone moves from describing a hegemonic ideology of élite marriage, in which the sex of the parties involved is appropriately unmarked,[4] to an ideologically suspect anthropology that conjures up visions of native girls paraded before men and chosen for their domestic and erotic talents. One is as good as another, provided she is clean, willing and fertile.

Stone has, of course, been widely criticized by other historians, both for the interpretation of his 'data' and for the claim he makes that his model, though based on evidence left by élite culture, trickled down to the 'plebes' as he calls them. E.P. Thompson and Keith Wrightson have marshalled evidence for an opposing view, more nuanced and open to the vagaries of desire, but feminist critics of Shakespeare have continued to base their analysis of the sexual politics of early modern England on Stone's work. As the most cursory glance at endnotes demonstrates, an introduction or opening chapter describing marriage and the family in early modern England heavily indebted to Stone is almost *de rigeur*.[5] Feminists substitute outrage or lament for Stone's pernicious scientism, but the anthropological model persists unchallenged. Whatever the *value* attributed to the exchange of women by Lévi-Strauss, de Beauvoir, Rubin and the host of others who deploy the paradigm, the structure of exchange itself remains the same whether idealized as in Lévi-Strauss, scientized as in Stone, or debunked as in feminist analyses. Feminists criticize women's status as objects as oppressive and demeaning; they analyse strategies for disrupting the law of exchange; they demonstrate how women's object status precludes subjecthood; but the syntax of exchange itself remains unchallenged. The subject–object dichotomy persists untroubled: woman is property, goods, chattel, objectified, reified.

In an essay published in *Shakespeare Quarterly* in 1987 entitled 'Portia's Ring: Unruly Women and Structures of Exchange in *The Merchant of Venice*', I read Shakespeare's play via feminist rereadings of Lévi-Strauss's paradigm of exchange. In what follows, I want to return to that argument taking into account the critique of the exchange paradigm laid out above and finally, in a brief epilogue, consider the impact of recent work on gender and sexuality for reading Shakespeare's play.

Revisiting Portia's Ring

The Merchant of Venice would seem to offer an exemplary case of Lévi-Strauss's exchange system and its feminist critique. The exchange of Portia from her father via the caskets to Bassanio is the ur-exchange upon which the main bond plot is based: it produces Bassanio's request for money from Antonio and in turn the bond between Antonio and Shylock. Though the disposition of Portia by her father's will, and the financial arrangements between Bassanio and Antonio that permit Bassanio's courtship, lead to heterosexual marriage, the traffic in women paradoxically promotes and secures homosocial relations between men. Read from within such a system, Portia's seeming centrality is a mystification, a pseudo-centre, for woman in this series of transactions, to repeat Lévi-Strauss's phrase, 'figures only as one of the objects in the exchange, not as one of the partners'.[6]

In early modern England, among the élite at least, marriage was primarily a commercial transaction determined by questions of dowry, familial alliances, land ownership and inheritance. Daughters were pawns in the political and social manoeuvres of their families, particularly their male kin (Jardine 1983: 68–102). Marriage contracts and settlements, familiar letters and wills, conduct books and sermons alike recognize in marriage an economic transaction based on the exchange of gifts – women, cash, annuities, rents, land.[7] Divines preached sermons with such titles as 'A Good Wife Gods Gift' and women were explicitly commodified, as in John Wing's exemplary exhortation in his treatise on marriage (*The Crowne Coniugall, or The Spouse Royall* (1620)) that men seek wives not in the devil's place – playhouses, may games, dance matches – but in God's house, since '[a]ll men love in merchandizing for any commodity, to goe as neere as they can, to such as *make the commodities themselves*, and from those hands they *doe originally* come' (Wing 1620: K2ʳ). Wing not only calls women commodities; he also recognizes explicitly the male partnerships that were to be posited in Lévi-Strauss's paradigm.

The exchange of women and gifts that dominated kinship relations dominated power relations as well. Gift-giving was a significant aspect of Elizabethan and Jacobean social intercourse, as demonstrated by royal prestation and patronage, and by the New Year's gift roles, account books, and records of aristocratic families who vie with one another in their generosity to the monarch in quest of favour (see Wallace T. MacCaffrey, 'Place and Patronage in Elizabethan Politics', in Bindoff *et al.* 1961: 97–125; Montrose 1980). Not only the monarch and the aristocracy, but also the gentry and the middling sort – all took part in these systems of exchange. Even the poorest families participated in such exchange systems: observers describe the custom in English villages of placing a basin in the church at weddings, into which guests placed gifts to help to establish the newly formed family in the community (Vaughn 1600: M8ʳ). In the 1620s and 1630s, gift-giving declined and signalled the alienation of the aristocracy, gentry and urban élite from the Court (see Stone 1965: 216, 229–31).

Commercial language describing love relationships common to Elizabethan love poetry and prominent in *The Merchant of Venice* displays not only the economic determinants of marriage in Elizabethan society, but also England's economic climate more generally – its developing capitalist economy characterized by the growth and expansion of urban centres, particularly London; the rise of banking and overseas trade; and industrial growth with its concomitant need for credit and large amounts of capital (see Tawney 1947; Stone 1965; Hill 1982; Wrightson 1982). In *The Merchant of Venice*, Act III, scene ii, Portia offers her love to Bassanio in a speech that epitomizes the Elizabethan sex/gender system and its relation to political economy:

> You see me, Lord Bassanio, where I stand,
> Such as I am. Though for myself alone
> I would not be ambitious in my wish
> To wish myself much better, yet for you
> I would be trebled twenty times myself,
> A thousand times more fair, ten thousand times more rich,
> That only to stand high in your account
> I might in virtues, beauties, livings, friends
> Exceed account. But the full sum of me
> Is sum of something which, to term in gross,
> Is an unlessoned girl, unschooled, unpractisèd;
> Happy in this, she is not yet so old
> But she may learn; happier than this,
> She is not bred so dull but she can learn;
> Happiest of all is that her gentle spirit
> Commits itself to yours to be directed,
> As from her lord, her governor, her king.
> Myself and what is mine to you and yours
> Is now converted. But now I was the lord
> Of this fair mansion, master of my servants,
> Queen o'er myself; and even now, but now,

This house, these servants, and this same myself
Are yours, my lord's. I give them with this ring . . .

(III.ii.149–71)

This speech begins with what we might term an affective paradox. Portia presents herself to Bassanio using the first person in an engagingly personal, if highly rhetorical, manner: 'Such as I am'. But her account of herself, as my own dead metaphor suggests, illustrates the exchange between the erotic and the economic that characterizes the play's representation of human relations. The rhetorical distance created by the mercantile metaphor shifts the speech from her personal commitment to a more formal bond marked by the giving of her ring, and that move is signalled by the shift to the third person ('an unlessoned girl . . . she'). Portia objectifies herself and thereby suppresses her own agency in bestowing herself on Bassanio. The passives are striking – she casts herself grammatically in the role of object 'to be directed'; she and all she owns 'Is . . . converted' to Bassanio by an unstated agent. Perhaps the most marked stylistic feature of these lines is the repeated use of 'now' which signals both temporal shifts and, more importantly, a moment of conversion. The rhetorical balance of line 166 is arrested by the caesura and the 'now' of line 167 which insists on the present moment of commitment to Bassanio. The 'But now' that follows refers back in time, emphasizing Portia's prior role as 'lord' of Belmont, a role that she yields to Bassanio with her vow 'I give them with this ring'; the moment of fealty is underscored by the repeated 'even now, but now' in line 169.

The governing analogy in Portia's speech is the Renaissance political commonplace that figures marriage and the family as a kingdom in small, a microcosm ruled over by the husband.[8] Portia's speech figures woman as microcosm to man's macrocosm and as subject to his sovereignty. Portia ratifies this prenuptial contract with Bassanio by pledging her ring, which here represents the codified, hierarchical relation of men and women in the Elizabethan sex/gender system in which a woman's husband is 'her lord, her governor, her king'.[9] The ring is a visual sign of her vow of love and submission to Bassanio; it is a representation of Portia's acceptance of Elizabethan marriage which was characterized by women's subjection, their loss of legal rights, and their status as goods or chattel. It signifies her place in a rigidly defined hierarchy of male power and privilege; and her declaration of love at first seems to exemplify her acquiescence to woman's place in such a system. But Portia's declaration of love veers away in its final lines from the exchange system the preceding lines affirm. Having moved through past time to the present of Portia's pledge and gift of her ring, the speech ends in the future, with a projected loss and its aftermath, with Portia's 'vantage to exclaim on' Bassanio:

> I give them with this ring,
> Which when you part from, lose, or give away,
> Let it presage the ruin of your love
> And be my vantage to exclaim on you.

> (III.ii.171–4)

Here Portia is the gift-giver; she gives more than Bassanio can ever reciprocate, first to him, then to Antonio, and finally to Venice itself in her actions in the trial which allow the city to preserve both its law and its precious Christian citizen. In giving more than can be reciprocated, Portia short-circuits the system of exchange and the male bonds it creates, winning her husband away from the arms of Antonio.

Contemporary conduct books and advice about choosing a wife illustrate the dangers of marriage to a woman of higher social status or of greater wealth. Though by law such a marriage makes the husband master of his wife and her goods, in practice contemporary sources suggest unequal marriages often resulted in domination by the wife. Some writers and Puritan divines even claimed that women purposely married younger men, men of lower rank or of less wealth, so as to rule them. Marriage handbooks and sermons all exhort women to submit to their husbands, regardless of disparity in rank or fortune, as in this representative example from Daniel Tuvill's *St. Pauls Threefold Cord* (1635):

> Yea, though there were never so great a disproportion betwixt them in state and condition; as say the wife were a Princesse, the husband but a pesant, she must be yet in conjugall respects as a hand-mayd unto him; he must not be as a servant unto her ... And this subjection is so necessary, that without it the world could not long subsist; yea nature herselfe would suddenly be dissolved ...

> (Tuvill 1635: B4ᵛ–B5ᵛ)

The vehemence and fear of chaos and disorder Tuvill betrays are characteristic and imply a growing need in the Stuart period to shore up eroding class and gender hierarchies.

Bassanio's answer to Portia's pledge of love implicitly recognizes such disparity and its effect by metaphorically making her the master:

Madam, you have bereft me of all words.
Only my blood speaks to you in my veins,
And there is such confusion in my powers
As after some oration fairly spoke
By a belovèd prince there doth appear
Among the buzzing pleasèd multitude,
Where every something being blent together
Turns to a wild of nothing save of joy,
Expressed and not expressed. But when this ring
Parts from this finger, then parts life from hence.
O, then be bold to say Bassanio's dead.

(III.ii.175–85)

Bassanio's heavily marked epic simile is anomalous in Shakespearian comedy. It echoes the first and perhaps most famous Virgilian simile of the *Aeneid*, when Neptune's effect in quelling the storm inspired by Juno is compared to that of 'a man remarkable/for righteousness and service' for whom the people 'are silent and stand attentively; and he controls their passion by his words and cools their spirits' (I, 151–3; Virgil 1971: 6, ll. 213–16).[10] Shakespeare translates the Virgilian simile into his own romantic context in which the speaker's words, instead of having a quieting effect on heart and mind, create a Petrarchan paradox: blood that speaks, but a lover silenced. And in keeping with Petrarchan conventions, Bassanio's comparison figures Portia as dominating and distant – that is, as a prince. Renaissance rhetoricians such as Wilson and Puttenham define figurative language as *translation*, 'an inuersion of sence by transport' (Puttenham in Hardison 1967: 177) – a kind of figurative exchange which disturbs normal communication and makes unexpected connections. Poets use tropes so that 'the hearer is ledde by cogitation vppon rehearsall of a Metaphore, and thinketh more by remembraunce of a worde translated, then is there expressely spoken: or els because the whole matter seemeth by a similitude to be opened' (Wilson in Hardison 1967: 42). Bassanio's political simile, with its Virgilian intertextual exchange, 'disguises' Portia as a man and prefigures her masculine role in the trial scene where she ensures the Venetian republic by reconciling the principle of equity with the rigour of the law.

We should also remember that Portia, whom Bassanio earlier describes as 'nothing undervalued/To Cato's daughter, Brutus' Portia'

(I.i.165–6), is named after her classical ancestor who describes herself in *Julius Caesar* as 'A woman well reputed, Cato's daughter./Think you I am no stronger than my sex,/Being so fathered and so husbanded?' (II.i.295–7). That Portia was renowned in antiquity for sharing the political ideals of her father and husband, and Shakespeare represents her commitment to political action by her insistence, as Plutarch had recorded, on knowing of the plot to murder Caesar and by her taking part in the conference of Republicans at Antium. *The Merchant's* Portia resembles her classical namesake and her figural persona ('beloved prince') by entering the male lists of law and politics. Far from simply demonstrating the Elizabethan sex/gender system, *The Merchant* short-circuits the exchange, mocking its authorized social structure and hierarchical gender relations.

For Portia's ring, we should remember, does not remain on Bassanio's finger, and *his* gift of the ring to Balthasar does indeed give Portia 'vantage to exclaim'. The gift of Portia's ring shifts the figurative ground of her speech from synecdoche, a figure in which the part stands for the whole, to metonymy, a figure of association or contiguity. Her lines first figure the ring as a part of her which she gives as a sign of the whole to Bassanio; in the final lines, however, the prefigured loss of the ring signals not substitution, but contiguity, metonymic relations. By following the movements of her ring, we may discover something about how the play both enacts and interrogates Elizabethan structures of figural and sexual exchange. Objects, like words, change their meaning in different contexts; as things pass from hand to hand, they accumulate meanings from the process of exchange itself. Bassanio gives away his ring in payment for services rendered and in doing so transgresses his pledge to Portia. When it begins its metonymic travels from Bassanio to the young doctor, the ring picks up new meanings which contradict its status as a sign of male possession, fidelity, and values; it moves from Bassanio to Balthasar to Portia to Antonio and back to Bassanio again and the very multiplicity of exchanges undermines its prior signification. The ring also makes a figural progress; in Renaissance rhetorical terms it is transmuted, 'which is, when a word hath a proper signification of the [*sic*] owne, and being referred to an other thing, hath an other meaning' (Wilson in Hardison 1967: 45). Portia's ring becomes a sign of hierarchy subverted by establishing contiguities in which the constituent parts have shifting sexual and syntactic positions. By opening out the metonymic chain to include Balthasar, Bassanio opens his marriage to what were for an Elizabethan audience forces of disorder:

gender instability, equality between the sexes, cuckoldry, sodomy, all in opposition to the decorous world of Renaissance marriage represented by the love pledges in Act III, scene ii. Bassanio gives his ring to an 'unruly woman', that is, to a woman who steps outside her role and function as subservient, a woman who dresses like a man, who embarks upon behaviour ill suited to her 'weaker' intellect, a woman who argues the law.

In her fine essay, 'Women on Top: Symbolic Sexual Inversion and Political Disorder in Early Modern Europe', Natalie Zemon Davis details the ways in which women's disorderliness manifested itself in England and Europe during this period. Davis observes that anthropologists generally agree that forms of sexual inversion – switches in sex roles, topsy-turvy, and images of the world turned upside down, 'the topos of the woman on top'

> like other rites and ceremonies of reversal, are ultimately sources of order and stability in hierarchical society. They can clarify the structure by the process of reversing it. They can provide an expression of, and safety valve for, conflicts within the system. They can correct and relieve the system when it has become authoritarian. But, so it is argued, they do not question the basic order of the society itself. They can renew the system, but they cannot change it.
>
> (Davis 1975: 130)

Many feminist critics have agreed with such judgements in their readings of Shakespeare's comedies of sexual inversion. They argue that such play, usually in the service of courtship, is ultimately conservative, leading to conventional gender roles and patriarchal marriage. Portia, we are told, in giving up her disguise and returning Bassanio's ring, returns to 'unthreatening "femininity" ' (Parten 1976: 32). But Davis herself disputes the interpretation of sexual inversion as simply a safety mechanism. She points out first that historians of early modern Europe are likely to find inversion and reversals less in prescribed rites than in popular festivities and carnival. Cultural play with the concept of the unruly woman, she argues, was a multivalent image which could 'undermine as well as reinforce' traditional hierarchical formations (Davis 1975: 131). Davis adduces examples of comic and festive inversion that carried over into political action, that not only provided release, but also represented efforts or provided the means whereby the distribution of power in society was questioned and changed. And, I would add, inversion affects not only the distribution of power but also perhaps structures of exchange themselves that historically have ensured male hegemony and patriarchal power. Sexual inversion and play with the topos of the woman on top offered an alternative mode of conceiving family structure and gender behaviour within that structure.

When Bassanio leaves for Venice to aid his friend, Portia evokes the conventional ideal of a Renaissance lady: she promises 'My maid Nerissa and myself meantime/Will live as maids and widows' (III.ii.307–8); to Lorenzo she claims they will live in a monastery to fulfil a vow 'To live in prayer and contemplation' (III.iv.28), behaviour which conforms to the Renaissance ideal of womanhood: chaste, silent and obedient. Shakespeare evokes here the accepted codes of feminine behaviour in his culture, thereby distancing the action from the codes of dramatic comedy that permit masculine disguise, female dominance, and linguistic power. Portia evokes the ideal of a proper Renaissance lady and then transgresses it; she becomes an unruly woman.

The common remedies for the weaker sex's disorderliness were, even among the humanists such as Vives, Erasmus and More, religious training to make her modest and humble, education of a restricted kind designed not to inflame her imagination but to acquaint her with her moral duty, and honest work of a sort appropriate to female capabilities. Transgression of the traditional expectations for women's behaviour brought down wrath such as John Knox's *The First Blast of the Trumpet Against the Monstrvovs Regiment of Women* (1558):

> the holie ghoste doth manifestlie expresse, saying: I suffer not that woman vsurpe authoritie aboue man: he sayth not, I will not, that woman vsurpe authoritie aboue her husband. [sic] but he nameth man in generall, taking frome her all power and authoritie, to speake, to reason, to interprete, or to teache, but principallie to rule or to iudge in the assemblie of men ... [A] woman promoted to sit in the seate of God, that is, to teache, to iudge, or to reigne aboue man, is a monstre in nature, contumelie to God, and a thing most repugnāt to his will ād ordināce.
>
> (Knox 1558: 16ᵛ–17ʳ)

It might be argued that the excess of Knox's attack, directed specifically against Mary Tudor, reflects his own rather than widely held views. But even humanist writers sympathetic to the cause of women's education assume the propriety of Knox's claims, if not his rhetoric. They exclude women from the public arena and assume the necessity of their silence. Leonardo Bruni, for example, warns that 'rhetoric in all its forms – public discussion, forensic argument, logical fence, and the like – lies absolutely outside the province of women'.[11] When Portia takes off for Venice dressed as a man, she looses her tongue in public talk on subjects ill suited to the ladylike conduct she posits as a model and does exactly those things Knox and others violently attacked. She engages, that is, in productive labour reserved for men, and not insignificantly, in linguistic labour, in a profession the successful practice of which depended on a knowledge of history and precedent, on logic and reasoning, and on rhetoric, all areas of education traditionally denied to women.

Portia's manner of winning her case requires consideration. Her defence depends on a verbal quibble, a characteristic linguistic strategy of Shakespearian clowns which allows them to express ideologically subversive or contradictory attitudes or ideas. Indeed, in *The Merchant of Venice*, Launcelot Gobbo uses the quibble for just such purposes. His wordplay around the command to come to dinner at III.v.48,50, and his earlier play with Jessica on damnation (III.v.4–7), give a double perspective to serious issues in the play, issues of social and Christian hierarchy and the like (Cohen 1982: 210–11; Weimann 1978: 39–48, 120–50). Portia and Launcelot Gobbo, woman and servant, are linked by this shared verbal strategy which allows them seemingly at least to reconcile irreconcilable perspectives and to challenge the play's overall mimetic design. They represent in part marginal groups oppressed under the Elizabethan class/gender system, but whose presence paradoxically is needed to ensure its maintenance. Their playful, quibbling misuse of language veils their subversive linguistic power. Portia's wise quibble saves the Venetian republic by enabling the Duke to follow the letter of the law *and* to save Antonio, to satisfy the opposing viewpoints represented by the Old and New law, by Shylock and Antonio. In another register, as Cohen (1982: 776–83) has pointed out, it unites the bourgeois values of self-interest with those of the traditional landed gentry, an imaginary literary solution to ideological conflicts manifest in late sixteenth-century England. But Portia's linguistic play here and in the final scene, like Launcelot Gobbo's, resists the social, sexual and political system of which she is a part and provides a means for interrogating its distribution of power along gender lines.

The Merchant of Venice does not end with Portia's success in the courtroom; after her winning defence of Antonio, Portia asks Bassanio to return her ring, knowing, as her husband puts it, that 'There's more

depends on this than the value' (IV.i.430). We know this ring sym-
bolizes the bargain of faith in patriarchal marriage Portia and Bassanio
have made in Act III, scene ii. By obeying Antonio's exhortation and
giving his ring to Balthasar, Bassanio affirms homosocial bonds – the
exchange of women, here represented by Portia's ring, sustains
relations between men. But Balthasar is, of course, Portia in disguise
(and Portia, we should not forget, was played by a boy, so that literally
all the love relations in the play are homosocial). When Portia laughs
at the thought of 'old swearing/That they did give the rings away
to men;/But we'll outface them, and outswear them too' (IV.ii.
15–17), she keeps her promise. In losing their rings and breaking their
promises to Portia and Nerissa, Bassanio and Graziano seem paradoxically to lose the male privileges the exchange of women and the rings
ensured. When in Act V Portia returns her ring to her husband via
Antonio, its multiple metonymic travels have changed it. The ring no
longer represents the traditional relationship it figured in Act III, scene
ii. On its figural as well as literal progress, it accumulates other meanings and associations: cuckoldry and thus female unruliness, female
genitalia, woman's changeable nature and so-called animal temperament, her deceptiveness and potential subversion of the rules of possession and fidelity that ensure the male line.[12] By dressing up as a man
and arguing the law, by imaginatively expressing her own sexuality
with Balthasar – 'I had it of him. Pardon me, Bassanio,/For by this ring
the doctor lay with me' (V.i.258–9) – Portia refuses the role of subservient woman she played in Act III, scene ii. Now her speech is filled
with imperatives – 'Speak not so grossly ... Read it ... Unseal this
letter' (V.i.266, 267, 275). Having expressly given over her house to
Bassanio in Act III, scene ii, she says 'I have not yet/Entered my house'
(V.i.272–3). She emphasizes her power and secret knowledge by
giving Antonio the mysterious letter, but refusing to reveal how she
came by it: 'You shall not know by what strange accident /I chancèd
on this letter' (V.i.278–9).

It is often said that Act V of *The Merchant of Venice* is unusually
harmonious even for Shakespearian comedy; certainly the world of
usury, hatred, and aggression that characterizes Venice has receded
(Barber 1959: 187). But Act V is far from presenting the harmonious
view of love and marriage many have claimed, for even the idyllic
opening dialogue between Jessica and Lorenzo is troubled by allusions
to unhappy love and broken vows. Lorenzo mockingly calls Jessica a
shrew and the play ends on an obscene pun on 'ring' and a commonplace joke about female sexuality and cuckoldry, not on the

idealized pledges of true love that characterize III.ii.50–60. Portia's verbal skills, her quibbles and play with words, her duplicitous representation of herself as an unlessoned girl who vows 'to live in prayer and contemplation', even as she rules her household and prepares to argue the law, bring together contradictory attitudes and views towards women and their role and place both in drama and society. Bassanio accepts the oppositions that her play with language enacts: 'Sweet doctor, you shall be my bedfellow' (V.i.284), he says. But in an aside that scarcely requires a psychoanalytic gloss, Bassanio exclaims 'Why, I were best to cut my left hand off / And swear I lost the ring defending it' (V.i.177–8). Portia's unruliness of language and behaviour exposes the male homosocial bond the exchange of women ensures, but it also multiplies the terms of sexual trafficking so as to disrupt those structures of exchange that ensure hierarchical gender relations and the figural hegemony of the microcosm/macrocosm analogy in Elizabethan marriage. Instead of being 'directed, / As from her lord, her governor, her king' (III.ii.164–5), Portia resumes her role as lord of Belmont: 'Let us go in' (V.i.297), she commands. As Davis suggests, in the 'little world of the family, with its conspicuous tension between intimacy and power, the larger matters of political and social order could find ready symbolization' (Davis 1975: 150). The sexual symbolism of transvestism, the transgression of traditional gender roles and the figural transgression of heterosexual relations, the multivalence of linguistic meanings in women's and clowns' speech, all interrogate and reveal contradictions in the Elizabethan sex/gender system in which women were commodities whose exchange both produced and reproduced hierarchical gender relations.

Other *Merchant* Rings

However powerful a hermeneutic device for reading Shakespeare's play, 'the traffic in women' paradigm as it is currently used in feminist analysis is no longer tenable. Putting aside the very real risk of reinscribing a victim's discourse by repeatedly reading woman as the object of male exchange, reading women as objects exchanged by male desiring subjects, or even as I have done above, reading Portia as derailing that system by acting as a subject herself, partakes of a degraded positivism that relies on an outmoded, humanist view of identity characterized by a metaphysics of presence.[13] It assumes an unproblematic subjectivity for 'men' as desiring subjects and concomitantly assumes as directly accessible woman-as-object. It is as if there were two theoretical regimes uneasily conjoined in feminist analysis: one that recognizes and analyses the fragmentary, non-unitary subject in certain critical contexts; the other, governed by the exchange paradigm, that assumes untroubled, unified subjects exchanging women/objects. Contemporary theories of the subject and of the subject/object problem have rendered the 'traffic in women' paradigm as it is currently used untenable.

Revisiting *The Merchant of Venice* at the current critical moment compels analysis of Portia's disruption of the syntax of exchange not by pointing to her agency, her unruliness in playing the man's part, but by considering Portia's transvestism as a central aspect of the performative character of gender in the play. As Judith Butler (1989: 141) argues:

> That gender reality is created through sustained social performances means that the very notions of an essential sex and a true or abiding masculinity or femininity are also constituted as part of the strategy that conceals gender's performative character . . .

And not only gender, but also identity more generally as it is produced and traduced in the performance of class or status and degree, nationality, race and sexuality. The play can no longer be read by isolating the category of gender from those other categories of difference 'understood as historically contingent and relational rather than foundational concepts' (Ferguson 1991: 163). The exchange of women in *The Merchant of Venice*, after all, hinges upon the subjection of the body and property of the Jew, on the theft of Shylock's ring by Jessica and its circulation to one of Antonio's creditors in trade for a monkey. And Portia's part in the 'traffic in women', far from simply enabling or promoting homosocial relations, robs Antonio of his beloved, a theft poignantly rendered in the trial scene when he pleads, 'bid her be judge/Whether Bassanio had not once a love' (IV.i.273–4).[14] In the final scene, Antonio once again hazards his body on Bassanio's behalf:

> I once did lend my body for his wealth
> Which, but for him that had your husband's ring,
> Had quite miscarried. I dare be bound again,
> My soul upon the forfeit, that your lord
> Will never more break faith advisedly.

> (V.i.249–53)

Portia's response is 'Give him this/And bid him keep it better than the other' (V.i.254–5). Here Antonio, not Portia, is the conduit, the channel, the passage that secures their heterosexual union. Portia's ring is here again transmuted, but here it figures the anal ring Antonio must forgo.

SUPPLEMENT

NIGEL WOOD: As was the case with your earlier treatment of Portia's ring (Newman 1987), you seem here to show a great suspicion for studies of female exchange based on Stone's 'data', and you make the telling point that, while feminist analyses may decry the values that Stone espouses, many also seem not to be able to dispense with his anthropology. Can you explain this dichotomy? Can we or should we dispense with Stone's research?

KAREN NEWMAN: Stone is, of course, a social historian, not an anthropologist; he simply appropriates the rhetoric of anthropology in order to win support for his facile generalizations about the exchange of women in early modern England. I would also not want to seem to suggest that Stone 'espouses' the exchange of women; my sense is he believes he is 'telling it like it is', regardless of his personal views. Feminist critics first turned to Stone's work because he was one of the earliest of the social historians to study the family and marriage in the period, and because his book is so widely available. Nor would I discount the temptation offered by his copious detail and curious anecdotes. It's not that we should, or can afford to, dispense with Stone's research; we simply need to be aware of its limits as detailed by both Thompson and Wrightson, among others.

But your question raises a larger question about the uses of history by literary critics, particularly in the last decade and a half since the advent of 'cultural materialism' and 'new historicism', both critical approaches or methodologies concerned with history not simply as background or context, a set of facts that ground a literary text, but with *histories*, history as texts that are themselves interpretations, texts that must be read, and that are, as the saying goes, always already read. But the positivist pull of history continues strong, and for that generation of feminists concerned to make visible the past, the inequities between men and women, the ways in which the 'happily ever after' of marriage in Shakespeare's comedies seems to gloss over women's oppression, Stone's work seemed to provide proof of that oppression. My point is that we need to write different histories, literary and social, that reveal that exchange was never seamless, that there are other stories we can tell about the past.

NW: Portia may well 'derail' the cultural and patriarchal imperative that women become objects and men active subjects in public social ritual, but you could say that Shakespeare was simply availing himself of the comic form's holiday from high seriousness. Rosalind in *As You Like It* and Katherine from *The Taming of the Shrew*, for example, are *licensed* transgressors, and, especially in the latter case, notoriously conform. Does this point of view question a confidence in (to follow Judith Butler's coinage, quoted on p. 120) the performative freedoms of gender categories, in that comedies are not reliable indicators of seriously entertained propositions?

KN: As I've already said (pp. 115–16), I don't buy the claim that generic closure – shrew-taming, the convention of the boy page, fifth Act marriages and the like – simply contain 'transgression'. It is, of course, a theoretical commonplace to argue that transgression presupposes rules and norms and that ritual transgression of various kinds, and including Shakespeare's comedies, are 'safety valves' that secure order and stability. I agree with Jonathan Dollimore's important observation that such containing operations can never 'retrospectively guarantee ideological erasure' (Dollimore 1984: 61); there continue to be contestatory effects; change happens, after all.

NW: What do you think is gained in the portrayal of these forms of sexual politics by Shakespeare's Venetian setting?

KN: Of course it's always said that by locating his plays elsewhere – especially Italy, with all its reputation for vice, mercantilism, and so on – Shakespeare in some sense spares England and allowed his contemporary audience to stay at a comfortable distance from the conflicts he represents. Certainly such an explanation is plausible for *The Merchant of Venice*. Venice in particular represented commerce, exchange, usury, and also the 'other', the strange, the 'not me'. *Othello*, after all, is also set in Venice which, in the early modern period, was a crossroads, a city in which one might see people from Africa and the East, both near and far. And Venice was a city with a significant Jewish population. Clearly English anxieties around mercantilism and usury are projected on to Shylock and Italy.

NW: You do not, of course, have to be absolutely comprehensive in your account of the play's gender constructions, but, to my mind, there might be an opportunity to reflect on the intersection of class and race in the representation of femininity in a consideration of the roles played by Nerissa and (especially) Jessica. Is it now possible to portray their assimilation into married Belmont society as unproblematic?

KN: Certainly there are important ways in which what we now term 'class' and 'race' articulate with the category of gender in the play. Even before turning to Jessica and Nerissa, I would wish to think about how Portia and Shylock are related in important ways – through the motif of fathers and daughters, through the giving and loss of rings, through their celebrated riches, and so on. Nerissa is complicated since, as you know, companions of her sort were themselves often not of a lower social status or degree, but simply poorer than their masters or mistresses. In my view, the 'class' issues in the play are best discussed with relation to Launcelot and Gobbo. Jessica is another story, and would require perhaps another paper concerned with the way in which her plot is a kind of comic reversal of *Othello* in which the daughter is the 'Other', the Jew, who escapes her father's house, marries a Christian, and belies the cultural stereotype her father represents in conflating his daughter and his ducats by spending them wantonly. And one would want to consider as well the problem the daughter's loss – not, after all, uncommon in Shakespeare.

CHAPTER **4**

Heterology

SCOTT WILSON

[What *use* is further comment on Shakespeare? Or how valuable can it now be? One reassuring answer might be that the production of new readings of his work helps us rediscover their basic truths, sentiments that persist through time, even as they take on different temporal forms. Similarly, once Shakespeare is introduced as a historical (and verifiable) item in critical discourse, then that is eventually to disable the 'modern' view, and notions of our remoteness from the source of meaning in turn posit original meaning as our goal. On the other hand, if given this priority, such attempts to discover an original intention and yet also provide a unitary sense are bound to be simplifications, where 'Shakespeare' is eventually too protean a reference to merit a settled understanding. Here, in Scott Wilson's Bataillian terms, is a sun that can destroy as well as authorize or create, a light that is a merciless glare and a foundry of profligate production, expelling waste as it illuminates. 'Shakespeare' becomes the sheer weight of the accumulated cultural use of his undoubted aesthetic power. Even the decision to return to basics and produce an unvarnished text of his work is still undertaken in the midst of this always contemporary imperative: to recover a truth that might stand distinct from falsehood, the valuable from the gratuitous. As Steven Shaviro has recently understood it,

> truth in language is always a consequence of this violent making-absent, of domination enforced by the threat of murder. Such a relation of power, such violence, is present in any discourse of knowledge or of truth, as in any attempt to assign identities or names.
>
> (Shaviro 1990: 18)

The discovery of identity is also to realize what we expected to find embedded in the very terms of our enquiry, an eventual identity between question and answer.

For Georges Bataille, the truthful perspective should be one that entertains the prospect of intellectual *disorder* and of heterological disarray: 'it is the *foundation* of things that has fallen into a bottomless void . . . The human being arrives at the threshold: there he must throw himself headlong into that which has no foundation and no head' (Bataille 1985: 222). What is saved is the power of the *event*; history strives to enclose it in a series and in its periods, yet the *experience* of events traces no fault-line of causes or effects. Heterogeneity is qualitatively different from 'the abstract and neutral aspect' that homogeneity lends 'strictly defined and identified objects', in that it inevitably produces 'a force or shock. It presents itself as a charge, as a value, passing from one object to another in a more or less arbitrary fashion' (Bataille 1985: 143). When we link items of information we empower them to reassure us that reality is inherently meaningful; Bataille works against the identification of such trains of association as the discovery of the real or natural.

This has radical consequences for both criticism and scholarship, for if *we* are responsible for the consonance of reported events, the principles by which we construct coherence are in urgent need of investigation. Moreover, the consequences of not 'making sense' (refusing to decipher a pattern) produce a clearer realization that the practice of criticism can be an intervention in the traditional forms of textual commentary and thus a deliberate transgression. We should not be too surprised, therefore, if Bataille's writing appears unexpectedly imaginative and metaphorical. As founding editor of the journal *Critique* (1946–) and author of atypical 'philosophical' works, such as *L'Expérience intérieure* (1943; trans. 1988), *Le Coupable* (1944; trans. 1988) and *La Part Maudite* (1947; trans. 1988), his work is particularly hard to characterize, except by noting his great reliance on metaphor and connotation, which, quite calculatedly, stretches the resources of prosaic cognition. His erotic narratives, *Histoire de l'œil* (1928; trans. 1977) and *Madame Edwanda* (1941; trans. 1989), are as much concerned with demonstrating the arbitrariness of taboos as with depicting the enhanced delights that derive from their transgression (see the lucid accounts in Richman 1982: 100–11; and Pefanis 1991: 39–58).

As Richardson (1994: 23–39) has recently traced, Bataille's focus on the excess of meaning that all attempts at clarity produce is closely linked to his most seminal perception: that one's sense of identity (as any restricted economy) will be destabilized at some point by the unacknowleged excess (of the unintended, the apparently alien and the multivalency of expression) that proving such existence will inevitably entail. In his 1933 essay, 'The Notion of Expenditure' (Bataille 1985: 116–29), he is struck by how unmotivated and redundant most behaviour is. A minimal conservation of life (work to subsist, for example) hardly accounts for what we do at all. The inevitable superfluous expenditure of effort or loss of advantage/time/freedom actually involved in the activity decreed by this economy works against its defining logic. Such excess is radically irrational, and yet inevitable (see Richman 1982: 150–4; Botting and Wilson 1993: 196–8; and Denis Hollier, 'The Dualist Materialism of Georges Bataille', in Stoekl 1990: 124–39).

It has taken time for cultural studies to take stock of Bataille's contribution to more recent critical debate. Along with Maurice Blanchot, he was a major influence on post-structuralist assumptions about the necessity of the 'supplement' that language appends to any intended meaning. For Jacques Derrida, all attempts to instil language with inbuilt values or 'natural' tendencies merely draw out the self-projections of those who are using it; there is no 'presence' in linguistic traces, which Derrida terms 'logocentrism' or 'phonocentrism': the belief that the means of expression can ever be totally self-sufficient and transparent in its representation of 'the world' (see this volume pp. 4, 8–9.]

NIGEL WOOD

Heterology

The solar annulus *is the intact anus of her body at eighteen years to which nothing sufficiently blinding can be compared except the sun, even though the* anus *is the* night.

(Bataille 1985: 9)

Solar anus (heterology and Shakespeare)

As we know, in our solar system the sun is the origin, the cause and sustenance of all light and life. Even when this banal fact was not 'known' in the scientific sense familiar to the West, the sun's obvious and seemingly eternal ascendancy guaranteed that numerous societies, religions, philosophies and even individual monarchs would aim to legitimize and universalize their systems by associating themselves with the most valuable, mysterious, irreplaceable external referent. Georges Bataille, the French writer, sociologist, economist and philosopher was, in this respect, no different and the sun appears constantly in his work as one of his primary metaphors.

However, it is not as the origin of all production, all light and life, that the sun is granted prestige in Bataille's work; or rather, it is not *just* that. Associated, in Mithraic cult, in Aztec rituals, in Icarian myth, with slaughtered bulls, human sacrifice and fall, the sun, in its terrible noonday glare, is destructive as well as productive. For Bataille, it is *the* example of pure expenditure without profit or return. This wanton expenditure, which both exceeds and destructively negates its productive function, becomes the ambivalent principle upon which Bataille bases his social and political analyses. In a short article entitled 'Rotten Sun', Bataille (1985: 57) writes:

> If we describe the notion of the sun in the mind of the one whose weak eyes compel him to emasculate it, that sun must be said to have the poetic meaning of mathematical serenity and spiritual elevation. If on the other hand one obstinately focuses on it, a certain madness is implied, and the notion changes meaning because it is no longer production that appears in light, but refuse and combustion, adequately expressed by the horror emanating from a brilliant arc lamp.

If the sun illuminates, it also expends waste, 'refuse and combustion': it enlightens through the horrific force of an endless, violent excretion. The productive sun is connected to the contemplative eye, though the contemplative eye cannot look directly at it, but must ruminate in the shade. For to gaze directly at the sun invites dazzlement and madness. The rational work of cool reflection, on the other hand, requires averted eyes that symbolize, interiorize and 'emasculate' the sun's indifferent fury. Bataille, characteristically, genders ambivalently both the sun, as a castrating and castrated power, and the spectator, whose 'virility' (if such it is) seems to depend on a will to approach madness, horror and the impossible.

But what has any of this got to do with Shakespeare? Or with the study of Shakespeare? Well, Shakespeare is also a (phallic) sun, the most luminous star in the Anglo-American literary firmament. Shakespeare's genius and the magnitude of his work, it is conventionally claimed, enlighten the whole of the English language and illuminate every aspect of the human condition. As Ralph Waldo Emerson wrote in the mid-nineteenth century: 'Now, literature, philosophy, and thought are Shakespearized. His mind is the horizon beyond which at present we do not see ('Shakespeare or the Poet', in Emerson 1968, 4: 204). Yet, as this quotation indicates, if Shakespeare is a glorious sun illuminating the horizon of knowledge, his solar quality is also blinding: he demarcates a limit 'beyond which at present we do not see'. Shakespeare is, in a certain sense, just as ambivalent as Bataille's sun. Both productive and destructive, sacred and base, castrated and castrating, Shakespeare is impossible to look at directly, impossible to read out of the long shadows of commentary cast by the succeeding centuries. He is as temporally remote as the sun in space, empirically unknowable, as dead as it is possible for an author to be, yet all the more radiant for that. If we cannot have access to Shakespeare, cannot have access to his mind, his person, the world in which he lived, if we cannot have access to the pre-Shakespearized world in which his work first irrupted and almost completely disappeared, then we cannot properly know the meaning of Shakespeare or his work: Shakespeare himself, as a totality, as a work, is never properly present in discourse; there is certainly no access to the meaning of Shakespeare (Shakspere) or the work through the dead letters that signify them. Shakespeare, like the sun, is a metaphor; he always means something other than he is. Moreover, again like the sun, Shakespeare is a very special sort of metaphor. Jacques Derrida, a French philosopher who owes much to Bataille, has written on both the metaphoricity of the sun and the heliotropic nature of metaphor in his essay 'The White Mythology':

> Each time that there is a metaphor, there is doubtless a sun somewhere; but each time that there is a sun, metaphor has begun. If the sun is metaphorical always, already, it is no longer completely natural. It is always, already a lustre, a chandelier, one might say an *artificial* construction, if one could still give credence to this signification when nature has disappeared. For if the sun is no longer completely natural, what in nature does remain natural? What is most natural in nature bears within itself the means to emerge from itself; it accommodates itself to 'artificial' light, eclipses itself, ellipses itself, always has been other, itself: father, seed, fire, eye, egg, etc., that is, so many other things, providing moreover the measure of good and bad metaphors, clear and obscure metaphors; and then, at the limit, the measure of that which is worse and better than metaphor.
>
> (Derrida 1986: 251)

How much like the sun then is Shakespeare, whose endless proliferation as a metaphor in and of the English language also presently provides 'the measure of good and bad metaphors, clear and obscure metaphors'. Shakespeare provides the standard against which Anglo-American culture measures its cultural discourses in which Shakespeare is always already inscribed, empowering and negating the speaker.

In the quote above, Derrida makes a silent allusion to Bataille's *Story of the Eye*, an allusion that is picked up again at the end of the essay when the 'heliotrope' of Plato and Hegel is doubled and deferred by the 'heliotrope' of Nietzsche and Bataille, to illustrate that what is 'other' than the sun, what is dark, absent or unnatural, is seen to emerge from the sun itself, in its revealing and concealing movements, its metaphorical transformations and displacements. The sun exceeds and transforms itself 'as father, seed, fire, eye, egg, etc.', in a metaphorical chain driven by the force of erotic desire that charges each element with a surfeit of meanings that flow into one another, into other meanings, other objects. In the *Story of the Eye* (Bataille 1982) the sun becomes like a great eye that dispenses not light but tears of urine, and the eye loses its function of seeing to become, like an egg, rolled round the body of Simone as an erotic object of sexual play.

The metaphoricity of Shakespeare has expanded since his remains became the object of an institutionally channelled desire. Yet these institutionalized transformations have tended to move in one direction, they have homogenized Shakespeare's remains into a smooth cultural commodity and icon. Whatever there is in Shakespeare's remains that remains 'other' to Shakespeare, as he has come to be known and loved, is utterly heterogeneous to his homogenized cultural body.

This has, of course, been noted before. In his book discussing the 'Shakespearization' of America and the American institutionalization of Shakespeare, Michael D. Bristol examines the 'quasi-religious', 'erotic' investment in Shakespeare that turns his 'goodness' or greatness into a sort of tyranny. Bristol (1990: 17) argues that there

> is a normative distinction between loving Shakespeare and using him as a cultural commodity. Scholarship is committed to the intact body of the Shakespeare text, and to the absolute primacy of Shakespeare's cultural authority over that of his interpreters. The central imperative of humanism is not a search for determinate knowledge, but rather a submissive empathy with the transcendent source of aesthetic experience. That empathy, of love, must be kept chaste, and remain disinterested. In other words, there can be no intrusion of purely modern concerns or interests, no violation or degradation of the intact body of the text.

For Bristol American scholarship has developed a chaste, quasi-religious 'erotics of reading' that compels the critic or reader endlessly to affirm Shakespeare and the values he is supposed to embody, values inescapably associated with the past. Attending the intact body of

Shakespeare's text is an erotic, aesthetic yet blinding – or castrating – experience: scholars are impelled to accept 'the absolute primacy of Shakespeare's cultural authority' over them. It appears to be an anally erotic activity *par excellence*. Scholarly ordination and identity are established through close attendance to the anally intact body of the Shakespearian text. 'Nothing confirms a professional reputation', Bristol (1990: 91) notes, 'more securely than "doing an edition" '. The erotic, affirmative, male culture of Shakespeare scholarship attends, interprets and perfects the text; rather than using it, or – heaven forbid – violating it, humanist criticism and scholarship reduces the text to the general equivalent of literary and aesthetic exchange.

If, as Michael Bristol suggests, 'doing an edition' constitutes a sort of anally erotic or anally retentive activity, then Gary Taylor should know, since he has not merely done an edition of a particular play, but covered them all. Along with Stanley Wells, Taylor is the joint editor of the New Oxford edition of the *Complete Works*. In another of his books, *Re-inventing Shakespeare* (1990), Taylor reflects on the image he has of Shakespeare and also characterizes him as a sun, but a sun become so impossibly powerful that he has violently imploded into an astral singularity. Shakespeare, once the most vast, the most glorious sun in the galaxy, is now a collapsing star where matter is crushed by its own irresistible galaxy into literally zero volume. Shakespeare no longer emits light, but rather voraciously consumes it, sucking it in to a place where time has stopped:

> If Shakespeare has a singularity, it is because he has become a black hole. Light, insight, intelligence, matter – all pour cease-lessly into him, as critics are drawn into the densening vortex of his reputation; they add their own weight to his increasing mass . . . Shakespeare himself no longer transmits visible light; his stellar energies have been trapped within the gravity well of his own reputation. We find in Shakespeare only what we bring to him or what others have left behind; he gives us back our own values. And it is no use pretending that some uniquely clever, honest and disciplined critic can find a technique, an angle, that will enable us to lead a mass escape from this trap. If Shakespeare is a literary black hole, then nothing I, or anyone else, can say will make any difference. His accreting disk will go on spinning, sucking, growing.
>
> (Taylor 1990: 410–11).

This is a wonderful metaphor: Shakespeare is a dense, retentive abyss reflecting nothing but the horror, the impotent plight of the would-be uniquely clever, honest and above all disciplined Shakespeare scholar faced with over 4,000 items lodged by the World Shakespeare Bibliography every year and the certain knowledge that any and every interpretation evaporates the instant it is written, and that no edition can be definitive, not even one authorized by Oxford University. This ought to be encouraging: interpretation becomes self-defeating, an operation of loss rather than recuperation. Yet this loss, this self-sacrifice, remains a gift to the terrible god Shakespeare which does not diminish him. Instead, loss is recuperated in the expanding image and reputations and scholarly identities flicker in the dark iris of Shakespeare's blind yet endlessly illuminating eye: a black sun.

For Gary Taylor's novel image of Shakespeare is just as erotic, just as enabling/disabling as any other. After all, what beloved could be more remote yet so incessantly demanding? What lover could be as destined to be engulfed in the abyss of an impossible desire than the Shakespeare scholar faced with the blinding image of Shakespeare's intact yet devouring solar anus, the scholar's own narcissistic mirror-image? And all this, of course, in the name of science! The black hole is the mysterious figure of abstract astral physics. Taylor's intentionally iconoclastic image still exalts Shakespeare, even in the scientific image of an imploding sun, as a sacred, celestial icon, though he has now become neutrally profane, opaque and inscrutable. Notwithstanding astral physics, this image remains metaphysical: Shakespeare stands above and beyond the world turning ever inward towards the imploding ideality of his dissolving core.

Humanist criticism and scholarship are not the only activity that can be undertaken in relation to Shakespeare. Yet the question remains, though Taylor's image already answers it negatively: do any of the other more political, alternative or radical approaches to Shakespeare make any difference to his position of solar unassailability?

Mouth (Heterology and Marxism)

In Bataille's short articles on the 'Eye', the 'Big Toe' and the 'Mouth', he operates a symbolic transformation of a body image. The mouth, for example, becomes the pivot between two axes: a vertical and a horizontal or biological and ideological. The vertical axis, constituted by the polarity mouth/anus, marks the line of materially uttered rather than articulated sounds: bestial cries, laughter, vomit, spit, alongside ejaculation and excretion. The horizontal axis, in which the mouth is associated with the eyes, opens out on to the field of vision and rational discourse. Bataille's point, in the short article, is to attempt to force the horizontal axis back to the vertical in a spasm of pain or pleasure or in a burst of laughter, expression always having been linked to the vertical axis before its constant repression according to the functioning of discursive horizontality (Bataille 1985: 59–60; see also Hollier 1989: 80–1).

As an almighty mouth, a mouth all mighty, Shakespeare governs the horizontal axis of discursive eloquence. Terry Eagleton, in an 'Afterword' to *The Shakespeare Myth* (Holderness 1988), recalls how, at Cambridge in the early 1960s, he was baulked by the intimidating volume of Shakespeare's speech and that of the Bard's self-appointed heirs:

> in Cambridge the air was thick with convoluted syntax, elaborate expressiveness, lexical dexterity, rhetorical virtuosity ... Shakespeare's inability to shut up, his grating habit of rattling on through sub-clause after sub-clause with not an emotional nuance or conceptual aspect left unelaborated, struck me as peculiarly tactless and overblown, an excessive garrulousness for which the closest analogy seemed that endless middle-class gushing and twittering ... Shakespeare showed me two things: first, that language was power; secondly, that I had neither.
> (Holderness 1988: 203)

What is repressed by the academic establishment's celebration, co-option and servile imitation of Shakespeare's eloquence and the power it both legitimates and performs, is the vertical language of the body: the violent spits, the snarls, the vicious laughter and, as Eagleton himself argues, the 'erotic', 'perverse', 'libidinal excess which humanism recuperates, gullibly, as "human richness" or "sensuous concretion", blind to the mastery, violence and manipulation implicit in any such idiom' (Holderness 1988: 204).

Given humanism's virtually complete co-option of Shakespeare and his sacralization as humanism's guarantee, as its simple, paternal sign of universal homogeneity, it is difficult to see how any of the violent force of Shakespeare's initial irruption can be recuperated or traced. The lines are now so familiar, so deeply ingrained in the literary and polite discourse of every succeeding epoch. For if Shakespeare exerts mastery now (and he certainly does), it is largely because his mouth is shut. Shakespeare has 'the magisterial look of the face with a closed mouth, as beautiful as a safe' (Bataille 1985: 60). No longer belonging to an author, Shakespeare's safely dead, closed mouth locks the vault holding the accumulated dollars of a multinational industry. As such, Shakespeare's periodically reanimated, open and shut mouth becomes the image of late capitalist consumption: a mastication detached from any material, alimentary need, concerned only with the manipulation of status signs and the exchange of hollowed-out cultural values and meanings. For any of Shakespeare's 'perverse libidinal excess' to be experienced then surely that safe, closed mouth must somehow be torn open, must be made to choke, splutter, scream; it must be forced to make decidedly un-Shakespearian noises. But this certainly seems an unlikely prospect.

In his 'Afterword' to the *Shakespeare Myth*, Terry Eagleton declares that it is useless to go on criticizing Shakespeare. Eagleton, who has written two books of critical interpretations of Shakespeare, argues that interpretation has now reached its limit:

> How far can you go in critical interpretation given the political, cultural and ideological constraints and determinants signalled by the name 'Shakespeare'? To find a genuine new range of use-values for the text would involve, as a laborious preliminary operation, challenging and dismantling their present exchange-values.
>
> (Holderness 1988: 207–8)

If there is one Marxist imperative that has survived recent post-structuralist or cultural materialist revisions of Marxism, it is that all critical work should be useful, politically useful. On the face of it this statement appears to possess similar aims to those set out in Bataille's essay 'The Use Value of D.A.F. de Sade', namely: to expose the ideology of the author, to arrest the reduction of the texts to the categories of bourgeois literary and aesthetic exchange and to liberate their affective, revolutionary potential – or alternatively to demystify them as reactionary (Bataille 1985: 91–104). Yet Eagleton calls a halt to the productive academic energies of the Shakespeare industry – even its radical, alternative, historicizing wing – because he doubts that either Shakespeare or the products of interpretation can have any 'genuine' use-value. What does Eagleton mean by 'use-value'? And how does a 'genuine' or authentic use-value differ from a false or inauthentic one? Can something be useful, but not *really* useful?

At the beginning of *Capital*, Marx (1977: 421) argues that 'the utility of a thing makes it a use-value'. The use-value of historical artefacts, texts, play-scripts, documents, Grecian urns, suits of armour, privies resides in their initial material mode of existence, in the use for which they were designed, in their consumption and, indeed, destruction – for ultimately utility is a value things can only lose. Paradoxically, perhaps, genuine use-values only arise at the moment of destruction of the useful object. As Marx (1977: 421) writes, 'use-values become a reality only by use or consumption'. But if the object has been consumed in use, so has the moment when it was valuable: use-value, like the object with which it is realized, cannot be conserved or exchanged, it arises and disappears in a moment of expenditure.

As Terry Eagleton knows, for some time academic criticism has been anxious to account for the use-value of its textual objects, more or less at the expense of their aesthetic surplus value, as the condition of taking its own usefulness into account; for this form of criticism use-value is defined in terms of its usefulness to 'politics'. Criticism has become an academic struggle over the politics of (in this case) Shakespeare.

Yet 'given the political, cultural and ideological constraints and determinants' signalled by Shakespeare's name, Eagleton argues that there can be no access to a genuine Shakespeare, no reconstruction of the historical use-values of his texts upon which one might base a politics of change in the present. All scholarly talk of Shakespeare is useless. And one can certainly have no recourse to present uses of Shakespeare. Shakespeare can have no 'genuine' use for us in the present, we cannot experience, consume, or take any authentic pleasure from Shakespeare not because his plays have become commodified (they always were commodities), but because Shakespeare himself – that is, his name and the work authorized and circumscribed by his name – merely constitutes an empty signifier designating a value that is endlessly exchanged not for other things but for other equally empty or ideological values; Shakespeare is 'used' in a sense, but it is not really Shakespeare, it is a 'cultural token', a coin, a signifier that is used to purchase and guarantee ideological notions such as national identity, Western civilization, literary greatness, literature itself. We have no access to Shakespeare because Shakespeare must always mean, for us, something other than he apparently is, or rather was.

Yet there is hope. Perhaps, Eagleton offers, Shakespeare can be recovered, or reinvented so that he might be genuinely useful again. However, he warns, this is going to take a lot of work. Eagleton's statement, impeccably couched as it is in Marxist terminology, proposes (if not imposes) quite an intimidating regime in which the new use-values he promises do appear a trifle utopian. Is there not a danger that, like most moments of truth, they might prove to be infinitely deferred? This could mean that like so many Five Year Plans the 'laborious preliminary operation' will be interminable. Moreover, there is a further, methodological problem with Eagleton's proposed 'answer' which 'consists in replacing the study of Shakespeare with the (laborious) study of "Shakespeare" ' (Holderness 1988: 207). Eagleton's programme is, naturally, dialectical and therefore speculative. He speculates that a period of indefinite critical labour will sublate a negated and doubled, uncomma'd and inverted-comma'd, Shakespeare with a single useful one. This speculation aims for a return on the investment of our labour criticizing and negating 'Shakespeare'; our profit will be the return, one fine day, of the new/old(?) Shakespeare and/or his texts whom/which we will be able to use genuinely, take pleasure in once again, consume with good conscience and value accordingly. Until then, however, use, pleasure, consumption, value must all be deferred, delayed, invested, in fact, in the destruction of the cultural token, the ideological Bard we love to hate.

But can such genuine use-values be realized as the result of a dialectical speculation which must, of necessity, involve the texts in an economy genuine use-value can only deny? The expenditure which realizes use-value must not be conserved or invested otherwise it instantly becomes abstracted as exchange-value. Since dialectical negation conserves that which it negates, even as the error necessary to its truth, the exchangeable, ideological Shakespeare must remain necessary and internal to the material, useful one. Genuine use-values, located beyond the threshold of an economy based on the exchange of signs and cultural tokens, begin to look like an impossibility. As impossible, perhaps, as 'genuine' use-value itself which must disappear the moment it is realized. Use-values do not materially exist, they are absent until, in a moment of pure expenditure, they are realized in their destruction. If genuine use-values cannot be conserved or held in reserve (to be known), what use are they? Use-value, then, designates precisely the *impossible*, the very limit of (non-)legitimation against or in the name of which all forms of radical critical work are undertaken.

Eagleton's advocacy of new use-values for Shakespeare implies that we have a need for him. The satisfaction of needs has always been the fundamental political project of Marxism, and in this sense it can also be figured under the sign of the mouth – an open mouth signifying hunger and need, defined against the full mouth, the fat, gorged mouth of industrial capitalism. But what does it mean to suggest that we need Shakespeare? Is that not precisely what the Shakespeare industry depends upon, the universal acknowledgement of Shakespeare's necessity? If capitalism does not satisfy everyone's needs (and it certainly does not) it still requires the ideological positing of need – in every field – in order to keep the wheels of production rolling and the wine lakes, the mad cow mountains and the copies of Shakespeare's Complete Works piling up (Holderness 1988: 207).[1]

Bataille's notion of a self-destructive use-value in his essay on Sade is somewhat elusive; his equally problematic proposal was that the specific use-value of Sade he envisaged would precisely destroy the system of utility upon which both use- and exchange-value rest. Some of its suggestions may make it possible to pursue this question of use- and exchange-value in relation to heterology and so-called literary texts, or in this case dramatic works. The sacralization of Sade by his surrealist admirers, and their assimilation of his work into homogeneous orders of aesthetic value already prescribed for them, depend upon his simultaneous excretion as a sacred object, an excretion that renders him, like shit, completely useless. This is, *a fortiori*, true of Shakespeare. He is also a foreign body, remote, unapproachable, desirable, revolting, terrible, Other. Taking Shakespeare out of reserve as a paternal guarantee, as the Father of English Literature, and putting him back into the use circuit precisely requires putting him back *as* shit; and putting all of Shakespeare's shit, all that is remote, revolting, terrible, Other and so on, back into play.

In his essay on Sade, Bataille sets out the principles for a practical heterology or scatology, which includes this definition:

> Science of what is completely other. The term *agiology* would perhaps be more precise, but one would have to catch the double meaning of *agio* (analogous to the double meaning of *sacer*), *soiled* as well as *holy*. But it is above all the term *scatology* (the science of excrement) that retains in the present circumstances (the specialization of the sacred) an incontestable expressive value as the doublet of an abstract term such as *heterology*.
>
> (Bataille 1985: 102)

Heterology then, as a sort of scato-theology, puts the shit back into the sacred and the sacred back into use, thereby disrupting the sacred as general equivalent, the surplus which, held in reserve, guarantees universal homogeneity as the gold standard of exchange currency; heterology puts it back in use but only, it should be stressed, in order to destroy the rational system of utility upon which exchange-value is based. In so far as it is a 'science', heterology occupies the uncertain space within rationality where heterogeneity declares its necessity: 'the intellectual process automatically limits itself by producing of its own accord its own waste products, thus liberating in a disordered way the heterogeneous excremental element' (Bataille 1985: 97). That which criticism cannot or will not assimilate becomes the object of heterology's affirmative attention, whose approach, remaining below the threshold of assimilation, is inevitably affected by the virulent refusals of the heterological objects located.

In so far as it is possible, in relation to 'Shakespeare' as the locus of literary and aesthetic exchange-value, to approach 'his' texts below the threshold of the name, below the threshold of Shakespeare himself, heterology would attempt to examine the subterranean, heterogeneous effects of Elizabethan and Jacobean theatre at the moment of their initial irruption. When Bataille underscores the 'use-value' of texts and the affective work of language he is granting it its historical specificity. If use is to be made of Bataille in the analysis of texts, this is the first thing to stress in any approach. However, what 'history' might mean in any given context is another question fraught with problems of its own. For it is not a matter of lifting the veil of the edited text, prising 'Shakespeare' off the sixteenth and seventeenth centuries like a stone to see what crawls underneath. Shakespeare's texts are now inseparable from their accreted layers of representation, interpretation and adaption; he is nothing more than a massive, stratified nexus of writing, so mountainous and imposing that it exerts its own horrifying fascination. Too big to be taken in by any individual scholarly subject, Shakespeare is the critical/theatrical sublime, the pit and pinnacle of the writing subject. Consequently, Shakespeare must be regarded as one of the more implacable horizons of the Other to whom and from whom all writing proceeds.[2] And all writing, as Artaud famously asserted, is pigshit (Hirschman 1965: 38). Any question of historical specificity, then, has first to negotiate the heterogeneity of writing and representation.

All Writing is Pigshit (The Theatre and Evil)

Antonin Artaud's horror of writing and articulate speech derives from the despair that language is always already Other to the body of the writing or speaking subject. 'The whole literary scene is a pigpen,'

Artaud spat, 'especially this one' (Hirschman 1965: 38). Yet Artaud spent his whole tortured life trying to climb out of that pigpen through means designed precisely to keep him firmly in it: writing and acting. Writing, which is inevitably work, Artaud regarded as excrement expelled, or stolen, from his pure body; he wanted to free his body from the work of discursive terms and classifications, the work, essentially, of the Other which steals the body away from its owner at the moment of birth and renders it foreign in systems of representation. Writing can only express itself: as shit which is subject to the equally filthy scrutiny of 'bearded critics' (Hirschman 1965: 38). These critics stand in the place of the 'Other, the Thief, the great Furtive One' who has, of course, as Derrida (1981a: 180) notes, 'a proper name: God'. But God, in Artaud's scheme, as the Thief, as the shit collector extraordinary, is also the primary principle of evil, the dark monarch of representation.

Artaud's Theatre of Cruelty attempted to clear an anti-theological space for the pure bodily presence of life itself, free from the 'author-creator' (Derrida 1981a: 235). Following Artaud, then, a theatre that would make Shakespeare spit, snarl and scream would have to do without Shakespeare, would have to reside purely in the bodies of the (nevertheless) always already Shakespearized/Shakespearian actors. But perhaps it is more interesting to put Shakespeare's work to work not as the product of an 'author-creator', but as the Other, the source and destination of all our writerly excretions. If Shakespeare's plays, as a recent study has suggested, now signify nothing they consequently occupy the place of Macbeth himself, the problematic and negative place of evil. And this is where they began in the sixteenth century.

The Elizabethan theatre was a pigpen: an enclosure in which all the heterogeneous elements of society gathered together to laugh, spit and experience death's relentless work on the stage. A repository of plague, prostitution and rank aristocratic patronage, the theatre outraged the piety of the emerging forces of Puritan, bourgeois hegemony. Long before the notion of a dramatist as a godlike 'author-creator' was thinkable, the theatre itself appeared to clear a space for the Creator's Other: Elizabethan and Jacobean plays were, if anything, the product of evil. This, in any case, was the Puritan view and, when they had the power in 1642, they closed the theatres down. Shakespeare and his theatre were held partly to blame for the excesses of the Stuart monarchy. The Puritan John Cook, for example, claimed in 1649 that the execution of Charles would not have been necessary 'had [Charles] but studied Scripture half so much as *Ben: Johnson* or *Shakespear*' (Cook

1649: 13). The Elizabethan and Jacobean theatre was perceived as a wholly negative space in which negativity swelled in waves of evil, exciting the base and lascivious desires of the lower orders, flattering, corrupting and ultimately damning the aristocracy whose sovereign spirit atrophied to the point where, like Charles, it was condemned to death.

Evil, in the Christian universe, is deprivation, the negation of being, non-being itself, or rather, nothing. Thomas Aquinas sums up the conventional Christian conception of evil in the *Summa Theologica* like this: '*Malum est non ens*' ('Evil is not essence'). Evil can only come into being in the form of representation that actually represents nothing, manifesting itself as a 'shade of death' (Bataille 1973: 49). Popular forms of 'dramatic' representation, from which the Elizabethan theatre largely derives, owe their emergence to the place of evil allotted for them by the Church. Rather like the leering gargoyles that pock the façade of a great cathedral and function as (the comic) part of the sacred (in its repulsive aspect), so, on festival days, saints' days and holidays, profane representation took to the streets and performed the comic panoply of evil: as personifications of Sin, Vice, devils, fire-cracking demons.[3]

The great so-called 'characters' of English literature can be traced there. When Richard III snickers in solitude before the auditorium, he is not representing some real historical character, he is a Vice; when Macbeth frets and struts his hour on the stage, he signifies, as he says, precisely nothing: evil. These 'characters' are seductive masks veiling a void that leads straight down the mouth of hell, yet a mask so seductive and a void so powerful that it threatens to suck in enough desire and tumult to shatter the frail moral parameters of the play.

For Bataille, all 'literature' has this problem to a greater or lesser extent, the problem of the Sorcerer's Apprentice: in order to instruct for the good it must represent or perform evil – and evil can get out of hand. Milton, for example, was said by Blake in *The Marriage of Heaven and Hell*, to be of the devil's party without knowing it (Blake 1984: 150). For English Romantics like Blake, the 'use-value' of Milton's rebellious, revolutionary Satan superseded his author's 'exchange-value' as the devout father of parliamentarians.

Like Milton's Satan, there is an irreducible part of literature that will not serve:

> First of all, it is impossible to define just what propels the phenomenon of literature which cannot be made to serve a

master. NON SERVIAM is said to be the devil's motto. If this
is so, then literature is diabolical.

(Bataille, 'Letter to René Char on the Incompatibilities of the
Writer' in Stoekl 1990: 34)

For Bataille, literature will not serve the demands of the critic, will
not serve the demands of its author, will not serve the demands of
representing reality or mediating expression; instead it proliferates in
its own sovereign space, demonically betraying its function, becoming
its own likeness, devoid of origin and reference, a veil to nothingness,
a shade of death, exercising the work of death on authors and readers
alike, drawing subjects into the indeterminate realm of writing and
joyfully dispersing meaning and identity among a multiplicity of differences and significances.

Like Artaud, Bataille was interested in a form of 'communication'
which exceeded speech and the categories of rational discourse. But
unlike Artaud, he did not proceed by denouncing the shit that is
writing, but instead affirmed the heterogeneous force of the shit that
resides *in* writing: the excess that actuates laughter, anguish and loss
of self, not its pure, bodily recuperation. This, then, is the matter
under discussion in what follows in the reading of *The Merchant of
Venice*. However, alongside the analysis of the (formless) forms of
heterogeneity disclosed by the play, my reading will follow the
strategic movements of Shylock and Portia, who are read not as
'characters' but as textual points marking instances of objectification
through the social process of, respectively, exclusion and exchange.
Through the fatal seductions of love and hate, Shylock and Portia,
from their positions as objects of exclusion and exchange, attempt to
destroy the systems of value in which they are negated, drawing those
systems through their own momentum into the pair's heterogeneous
sphere of appearance, disappearance and death, a place, I will go on
to argue, possibly definable by Bassanio's phrase 'valour's excrement'
(III.ii.87). Naturally, this dual strategy requires that these two objects
be resolutely and irreconcilably opposed.

Laughter, Evil and Valour's Excrement: Forms of
Heterogeneity in *The Merchant of Venice*

*Unconstrained laughter leaves behind the areas that are accessible to
speech – and starting with its conditions, such laughter is an indefinable
leap. Laughter hangs suspended, it leaves you laughing in suspense.*

You can't keep up your laughter – keeping it up is ponderous. Laughter hangs suspended, it doesn't affirm anything, doesn't assuage anything.

(Bataille 1988a: 101)

It's not among those who laugh that the rupture takes place and otherness comes into the picture, but in the movement of the comic object.

(Bataille 1988a: 142)

The Merchant of Venice takes its place as a dynamic element in the general economy of Elizabethan society as a comedy, as a textual 'point' where diverse discursive elements clash in an explosion of laughter. What is the nature, or the function, of this laughter? Can its political effects be traced four centuries later, can its affective force even be appreciated when the play is now, for many reasons, no longer particularly funny? Responses based on personal experience will not take the investigation very far, neither will months sifting through the historical archives, though both might conceivably help. Laughter, paradoxically, for something that is so easily experienced and yet leaves speech behind, can perhaps only be approached theoretically; an approach that should no doubt result in a burst of laughter.

Laughter can be politically both a subversive and a reactionary thing, often simultaneously. For Georges Bataille, shared laughter extinguishes isolated existence; solitude emerges from itself, in a collective act of exclusion, to form a current of intense communication, a wave which flows and rebounds in an indefinable, precarious unity (Bataille 1988b: 95). This bonding effect can, of course, have the result of reinforcing or guaranteeing the constitution of society: laughter expels its comic objects to the periphery on the wave of its derision; yet, again like a wave, laughter also returns, necessarily, to the centre, in festivals, Saturnalias, satires and threatens to knock the centre off its perch. Laughter does not appear to be in any sense a positive thing, rather it swells in a perpetual and self-generating wave of negativity that produces nothing, that hangs in the air. It is not dialectical, though the production and containment of Saturnalias sometimes makes it seem so. Rather, 'laughter hangs suspended', neither affirming nor assuaging anything, marking and patrolling the limit with the beyond.

Shared laughter appears to assume the absence of anguish, light-heartedness, but Bataille (1988b: 96) argues it has no other source than anguish. At the heart of this anguish is, of course, the fear of death, the fear of that loss of selfhood, that laughter seems to dispel in precisely the performance of that loss. Like an orgasm, a burst of laughter is also a little death, a momentary loss of (self-)consciousness. And again, like the amorous relationship, this ecstasy, this ecstatic expression of fear, involves a confrontation with otherness.

The objects of comedy are perhaps more interesting than the audience or spectators, the subjects who laugh. Formed to excite laughter, comic objects achieve, in the act of laughter, a state of formlessness, becoming heterogeneous vehicles of pure affect. In this they mirror the precarious unity of the subjects that have dissolved in laughter. Through exciting and suspending laughter in turn, the comic object, in the otherness of its movements, lures the audience along a fatal trajectory of helplessness and loss.

The Merchant of Venice, in so far as it is a comedy, establishes bonds between and within its audience. It also stages the formation and deformation of bonds and attachments, as it also stages the production of value, its exchange and its sudden reversals. The argument that follows, then, is predicated on the assumption that the play enacts something like the experience of laughter, in the form of the ambivalent bonds that it both establishes and breaks, and that through its comic objects the play unleashes the effects of otherness on to the audience, thus compelling it to confront and experience the force of its political, racial and sexual anxieties.

Various bonds are established in *The Merchant of Venice*: legal bonds, bonds of love and friendship, bonds of hate and revenge, marital bonds, financial bonds and bonds between evil and laughter that operate in the general economy established in the play. 'General economy' signifies not just the flow of goods and money, not just the production of wealth, but also the exchange of values and affections: the economy of love and hate, of inclusion and exclusion; and how the body, as always with Shakespeare, exists, along with money, as the medium for these exchanges.

'I am a Jew.' says Shylock.

> Hath not a Jew eyes? Hath not a Jew hands, organs, dimensions, senses, affections, passions ...? If you prick us, do we not bleed?
>
> (III.i.55–7, 60–1)

Guffaws from the crowd. Shylock tickles the audience and makes them laugh, disavowing his evident and alarming alterity, suggesting that he is just like them, suggesting that he has, in common with both the audience and the Christians in the play, a sentient body. Oh yes?

So what! If this spirit of revenge in the form of a Jew is suggesting a parity with Christians on the basis of the parts and functions of his body his argument is absurd. Everyone knows that in a universe regulated by ideological notions of good and evil the materiality of the body does not count. Indeed, the body is itself merely the veil or the representation of the soul – or of the lack of a soul. Shylock, from the beginning, is characterized by the Christians as evil and inhuman, body or no body. To Launcelot 'the Jew is the very devil incarnation' (II.ii.25); to Solanio he is 'the dog Jew' (II.viii.14) and 'the devil ... in the likeness of a Jew' (III.i.19–20). Evil, incarnate in the form, the 'likeness', of a criminal Jewish body is merely the veil to a lack that must be filled by Christian goodness and mercy.

Nevertheless, the often shocking corporality of Shylock's comic arguments frequently has considerable force, and they establish a bond with the audience not because he and they have life in common, but because they have death, couched in the intimate relation established by revenge. This stage Jew with his sentient yet soulless body, who is merely the simulacrum of a man, has a devastating proximity to death; he is 'fatal' in every sense. By Act IV, the drama having unfolded in its inexorable way, Shylock brings to court his sentient but simulating body, a harbinger of death wrapped in black Jewish gaberdine, along with his knife and prepares to exercise its keen threat right into the heart of Venetian society and to reveal death, in all its objectivity, as Christian flesh.

If Shylock has a devastating and fatal relation to death, then so does Portia, as Shylock discovers to his cost. Since Freud's famous essay on 'The Theme of the Three Caskets' (1913), psychoanalysis, at least, has acknowledged that Portia is also a veil to death. According to Freud, desire, by means of a double reversal, elaborates a fiction in the form of a choice between three women in which the choice of the most beautiful, or best woman, masks the necessity of death:

> Choice stands in the place of necessity, of destiny. In this way man overcomes death, which he has recognized intellectually. No greater triumph of wish-fulfilment is conceivable. A choice is made where in reality there is obedience to a compulsion; and what is chosen is not a figure of terror, but the fairest and most desirable of women.
>
> (Freud 1953–74, 12: 299)

Thus Freud discovers the latent meaning in the manifest text in a manner, Sarah Kofman has ironically noted ('Conversions: *The*

Merchant of Venice under the Sign of Saturn' in Collier and Geyer-Ryan 1990: 142–66), not dissimilar to Bassanio who precisely rejects the surface glitter of gold and silver in favour of the more pale and deathly lead. Kofman argues that what Freud, following the imperative of the text, perceives to be latent is actually quite manifest and evident in the text. She argues that *The Merchant of Venice* does not re-enact unconscious process (and she contends that Freud actually abandons this model a little way into his essay), but rather arranges itself according to the ancient and even structural principle of the ambivalence of love and death in which love is identical to death. Freud acknowledges that the goddess of love had once been the goddess of death, before Aphrodite 'surrendered her chthonic role to other divine figures, to Persephone, or . . . Artemis-Hecate' (Freud 1953–74, 12: 299). Moreover, the great mother goddesses of the oriental peoples all seem to have been both creators and destroyers, goddesses of life, fertility *and* death.

In order for this point to be made, it is not, I think, really necessary to go back into ancient history and assert some universal structuring principle originating with the figure of woman. Yet the construction of woman as an ambivalent figure, both sacred and base, creative and destructive, castrated and castrating, does appear to be a recurrent theme of various patriarchal cultures in different epochs. Portia is no different. Kofman notes that access to Portia demands that her suitors risk their lives, or at least their love-lives, as a precondition of their entry into the game. Moreover, when Bassanio finally opens the leaden casket he compares her image to that of a fatal spider's web:

> Here, in her hairs
> The painter plays the spider and hath woven
> A golden mesh t'entrap the hearts of men
> Faster than gnats in cobwebs.
>
> (III.ii.120–3)

Sarah Kofman argues that a theory of 'general ambivalence' orders the play, yet the logic of this order is also, presumably, quite undecidable since it is not one in which harmony is restored through ambiguity or compromise, but rather one in which order hangs suspended in paradox:

> While ambiguity, in an equivocal fashion, may equally well signal one meaning *or* another, ambivalence *simultaneously* asserts two opposed meanings, sense and non-sense; not love *or* death but love *and* death. The structure of ambivalence is the uncom-

promising structure of a two-faced Janus, precisely that, according to Freud, of the joke.

(Collier and Geyer-Ryan 1990: 146)

Certainly both Portia and Shylock assert their ambivalence and their
seductive charm through jokes, enlisting not only their fellows but
also the audience into the dangerous logic of their fatal strategies.

Portia, as a woman, as a very beautiful, very rich, very powerful,
very clever and (for these very reasons) castrating woman, is still
merely an object and not primarily a subject. She is an object of
exchange. The whole plot of *The Merchant of Venice* is based upon the
central exchange of Portia to Bassanio via the caskets, an exchange over
which she ostensibly has no control. Yet Portia achieves power over
Antonio, Bassanio and even the whole of Venice through subverting
the patriarchal system of exchange and her place in it as a woman,
precisely as an object of exchange. She achieves this initially by seizing
control of her father's wealth at the very moment of giving it away,
and maintains hold of her wealth by 'killing' or castrating the male
members of the cast through her cunning, particularly by means of
exploiting the signifying potential of a bawdy joke in which woman,
or a woman's body, is the degraded comic and fatal object.

This reading of Portia relies on two recent interpretations by Karen
Newman and Coppélia Kahn. Newman (1987) reads the economy of
the play as primarily articulated by gift exchange, an economic principle first discussed at length by the French anthropologist Marcel Mauss
(1954). Mauss argues that social exchange in archaic societies is
dominated by, indeed structured around, the practice of giving,
receiving and reciprocating gifts. Lévi-Strauss (1969) adopted the idea
and argued that marriage is the most fundamental form of gift
exchange, and women the most basic of gifts. The bonds and relations
of power-organizing society are exercised by and forged between men
by means of the exchange of wealth and women through marriage,
in which women figure only as objects in these exchanges, never as
partners. The central exchange of Portia to Bassanio via the caskets
requires Antonio to give Bassanio the money he has secured from
Shylock so that Bassanio can, in turn, arrive at Belmont laden with
enough gifts to appear an impressive suitor. These gifts hope for a rich
return, of course. Portia is the object of Bassanio's desire not least
because she is, as he says, 'richly left' (I.i.161). Marriage with Portia
would enable Bassanio to reciprocate the many gifts lavished on him
previously by Antonio. Portia seems to be merely the means, the

bounty, by which the two men can continue and maintain their affectionate relationship. However, in the absence of a living father who would be present to exchange her as a gift, Portia intervenes into this patriarchal system of exchange by herself giving her father's wealth and even more importantly by giving herself, her body, in the symbolic form of a ring:

> I give them with this ring,
> Which when you part from, lose, or give away,
> Let it presage the ruin of your love
> And be my vantage to exclaim on you.
>
> (III.ii.171–4)

Portia gives the gift of herself and her wealth in an act, Newman suggests, reminiscent of *potlach*: the non-reciprocal gift that empowers the giver. Portia gives more to Bassanio than he can ever return. The act initiates a series of gifts that ultimately gains her power over Venice when she rescues Antonio and the integrity of Venetian law. 'In giving more than can be reciprocated', Newman (1987: 26) argues, 'Portia short-circuits the system of exchange and the male bond it creates, winning her husband away from the arms of Antonio'.

Bassanio, on receipt of the ring, naturally vows that he would die rather than give it up:

> when this ring
> Parts from this finger, then parts life from hence.
> O, then be bold to say Bassanio's dead.
>
> (III.ii.183–5)

The ring seals the bond between Portia and Bassanio and subsequently, through her own manipulations, becomes the means by which Portia guarantees her hold over Bassanio and remains her own lord and master of Belmont.

This is so because Bassanio does, indeed, give the ring away; and his gift to Balthasar does bring vantage, that is advantage, to Portia. She wins power over his life. Moreover, the nature of the bond symbolized by the ring has now changed, as has the significance of the ring. Coppélia Kahn argues in her essay 'The Cuckoo's Note: Male Friendship and Cuckoldry in *The Merchant of Venice*' (in Erickson and Kahn 1985: 104–12) that the ring always had a double significance. On the one hand, the ring represents the marriage bond as it does in the wedding ceremony, but on the other, it has a specifically sexual meaning. As Kahn notes, rings, circles and Os are frequently, in

Shakespeare's works and elsewhere, metaphors for female sexual parts (Erickson and Kahn 1985: 109–10). In the last scene, speaking to Bassanio, Portia refers to the ring as 'your wife's first gift' (V.i.167), that is, her virginity. In fact the whole ring plot plays upon the sort of bawdy story you would find in a Tudor jokebook, the point being that the only way a husband can be sure of not being cuckolded is to keep his finger in his wife's 'ring'. And since Bassanio does not, the ring, according to Karen Newman, goes on a promiscuous journey, accruing, in its comic movements, associations of disturbing otherness: 'cuckoldry and thus female unruliness, female genitalia, woman's changeable nature and so-called animal temperament, her deceptiveness and potential subversion of the rules of possession and fidelity that insure the male line' (Newman 1987: 31). Portia takes this bawdy commonplace which denigrates women and turns it to her own advantage, and returns to Belmont, Newman suggests, as the unruly woman who now rules both the roost and the rooster. Kahn argues that the resonances of this comic reversal reverberate right to the final lines of the play:

> Well, while I live I'll fear no other thing
> So sore as keeping safe Nerissa's ring
>
> (V.i.306–7)

These lines, spoken by Graziano, far from expressing harmony, suspend the play on the crest of a wave of male desire, fear and anxiety, the stuff of all good jokes, at least according to Freud.

Neither Karen Newman nor Coppélia Kahn has much to say about Shylock. Indeed, Newman excludes him from her gift economy presumably because he does not appear to give anything away; on the contrary, his daughter is 'stolen' from him along with the ring that Leah, his wife, gave him, and which is consequently sold for a monkey in Genoa. Interestingly, Walter Cohen, in his essay 'The Merchant of Venice and the Possibilities for Historical Criticism' (Cohen 1982), a Marxist reading which concentrates on the bourgeois economics of the play, also excludes Shylock from the dominant mode of production and exchange in Venice as a historical anachronism. Within the economy of the play it is not even usury, as such, Cohen suggests, that marks Shylock out as something different, but rather his peculiar refusal of it: 'the penalty for default on the bond is closer to folklore than to capitalism: stipulation for a pound of flesh, after all, is hardly what one would expect from *homo economicus*' (Cohen 1982: 769). For Cohen, Shylock's insistence on his bond takes him out of the 'bounds of rationality' and into the mists of medieval folklore, a place more remote even than Jewish quasi-feudal fiscalism.

So can no tolerable sense be made of Shylock's bond with Antonio? Does this bond, which refuses interest, refuses the production of a surplus, exist outside both the capitalist mode of production and the aristocratic economy of the gift? The bond is certainly extraordinary, it turns medieval folklore at a stroke into something devastatingly and menacingly contemporary. Shylock's bond literalizes an old commonplace, gives it flesh and blood, and thus comically transforms it. Just like Portia. By literalizing the old and traditional conceit that the Jewish moneylender always gets his pound of flesh, Shylock threatens to short-circuit the conventional modes of representation in which he is inscribed as a Jew, and by making the phrase flesh, by turning the sign into the thing, he sets himself up as the destiny of the racist Antonio. It is the fatal strategy of the object, here of exclusion, an object that seduces the subject to experience its own death. Shylock challenges Antonio: what I am you must be. Your body may also be rendered 'foreign' and exterior to you, and we will be bound together in death, in the ultimate demonstration of human reciprocity.

Far from existing outside the economy of the gift, Shylock's bond seems to me to be an example of a social principle called symbolic exchange that Jean Baudrillard claims was lost, or rather massively repressed by successive rationalist, pragmatist and functionalist systems, yet which has remained to haunt them ('Symbolic Exchange and Death' and 'Fatal Strategies' in Baudrillard 1988).[4] This principle engages the elements which remain unassimilable to the systems of equivalence that govern a rational or market economy. It is a principle of loss, frequently involving transgression, sacrifice and death. In an economy based on the gift, symbolic exchange takes the form of a 'counter-gift' which enacts a dangerously ambivalent challenge, a counter-movement which becomes privileged above all other moments and modes of exchange, since it actuates a sudden reversal and destruction of value. The counter-gift is the gift returned as excess, poison and defiance, the response which 'raises the stakes', and by this ensures communication and a profound human reciprocity beyond the hierarchical systems of value and status that regulate society.

Shylock's bond performs many of these functions, establishing a deeply ambivalent exchange of reciprocities. For the first time and just like the Christian Antonio, Shylock agrees to lend money gratis, free: there is to be no profit, no return ... except, as a 'merry sport' (I.iii.142); should the money not be returned, there will be a token

charge, which, in the context of the business exchange, is completely
valueless. As Shylock himself points out: 'If he should break his
day, what should I gain/By the exaction of the forfeiture?'
(I.iii.160–1). What can you do with a useless lump of flesh? What
can you buy with a mutilated corpse? The bond is a gift, given,
Shylock says, in 'friendship' and 'love'. Does Shylock mean it? Is
Antonio taken in? The bond *is* a gift, but a defiant and poisonous gift
whose excess raises the stakes between Shylock and Antonio, and cunn-
ingly places all that defines them as different and opposed under
erasure:

ANTONIO:　　　　Hie thee, gentle Jew.
　　The Hebrew will turn Christian: he grows kind.
BASSSANIO: I like not fair terms and a villain's mind.

(I.iii.174–6)

If the bond began as a joke, a 'merry sport' with little thought of
the possibility of a default, if it was conceived merely as a challenge,
a barbed comedy that simultaneously inscribed a vicious threat into
an act of generosity, by the time the news of Antonio's ships has
arrived, it has taken on a deeper significance. Shylock has also lost
heavily. The metaphor Shylock merrily made between money, produc-
tivity and life in Act I (money breeds like sheep) has fast become concrete by the end of Act II: money is no longer money but his own
flesh and blood – his daughter, his ducats, his manhood (the two bags
of gold signifying his testicles, of course) have all been seized from
him by the Christians. He has been castrated, placed beyond the world
of value, use and usury. The price of Venice itself now is meaningless,
since Shylock, in his sacred rage, has become utterly heterogeneous
to the state, and all he has left is his bond with Antonio. So he under-
takes to make use of his heterogeneity, of his uselessness, with the
effect of bringing down the whole economic system of use- and
exchange-value. Shylock's relentless pursuit of his forfeiture threatens
symbolically to destroy the hierarchy of value that holds them apart.
Money is now meaningless, it becomes a non-equivalent. All the
money in Venice cannot buy Antonio's life and a pound of flesh is
worth nothing – a waste of 3,000 ducats. The dramatic fulfilment of
the bond would destroy the system of value regulated by economic
exchange, and would consequently negate the hierarchical social code
that separates merchant and usurer, Christian and Jew, and subor-
dinates the latter to the former.

　What is at stake, then, is more than just a legal bond, though for strategic reasons Shylock stresses its legality, pushing the law to the limit with his threatening challenge: 'If you deny me, fie upon your law!/There is no force in the decrees of Venice' (IV.i.100–1). Yet its legality is perhaps not strictly necessary, and ultimately of course undoes it. More than just a legal contract, Shylock's bond addresses the principle of human bonding itself ambivalently expressed in the form of symbolic exchange.

Antonio, alone of the Venetians, understands the bond. It is significant that he not only accepts the bond readily, but even perceives 'kindness' in it in the alternative sense, played on previously in the scene, of 'kinship'. Furthermore, Antonio may hope to gain some 'vantage' through the bond himself. Antonio loves Bassanio, loves him, at the very least, with an ardent and chivalrous passion, and he has demonstrated and sustained his love through the aristocratic means of gift-giving. Since their different classes make the relationship unequal, Antonio has constantly to increase the debt he is owed to maintain the balance, in order to maintain the bond of gratitude and obligation that Bassanio owes him. On the verge of losing Bassanio and the means of maintaining this bond, Antonio makes a last gesture in which that bond is pushed to the ultimate limit; for if Antonio seriously accepts the risk implied in Shylock's contract then he does so purely for the sake of his emotional bond with Bassanio. It is a form of communication which places being itself at the limit of death, a form of communication that can at last leave speech behind and the limits and obstacles speech always creates for communication.

Antonio is seduced into the bond; he does not, presumably, have to take it. Bassanio objects: 'You shall not seal to such a bond for me./I'll rather dwell in my necessity' (I.iii.151–2). But Antonio insists: his ships will come in – and Bassanio's gratitude will be deeper for the risk of his life. By accepting the terms of the bond as a practical means of expressing his love, Antonio seals his own fate. Moreover, when the time comes to pay up, he seems to accept his fate and acknowledge his own heterogeneity in relation to homogeneous society: 'I am a tainted wether of the flock,/Meetest for death' (IV.i.113–14). In fact, his primary concern appears to be only that Bassanio be present to see the ultimate demonstration of his love: 'Pray God Bassanio come/To see me pay his debt, and then I care not!' (III.iii.35–6). If Antonio's life is saved he knows he must lose his love, but in death his own love's debt is eternal. Bassanio could never repay him so their bond would be sealed for ever.

The single act of destruction, sealing the bonds of love and hate, in which a merchant and a usurer symbolically shatter the economic system they inhabit, does not take place. The bond is brought to court and the law takes over. Portia's ruling, by destroying the spirit and indeed the legality of the bond (which both Shylock and Antonio accept), destroys the bond itself. So Shylock decides to cut his losses. But the state, in an excessive act of revenge, strips him of everything, even his own life. Then, crucially, the Christians are merciful. Mercy, the gift of God, the non-reciprocal gift that empowers the Christian God and all those who derive their legitimacy from Him, gives Shylock back his life along with half his wealth on the condition that he gives it in turn to Lorenzo and Jessica, and on the fundamental condition that he converts to Christianity. This non-returnable 'gift' of Shylock's own life guarantees his humiliation and submission.

Portia's ruling, from a non-Christian position, takes *The Merchant of Venice* beyond a joke. This sudden reversal that appears to mark the end of the Saturnalias and the reassertion of mastery, forcing Shylock to espouse a despised faith, many modern viewers find 'unbearable' (Kofman, in Collier and Geyer-Ryan 1990: 161). For us, Portia's dialectical reversal raises not the spirit, but the gorge. Whether this would be the case with a contemporary audience is hard to say, though it is unlikely. No doubt a large proportion would, like Graziano, be cheering: 'O learnèd judge! Mark, Jew – a learnèd judge!' (IV.i.314). Yet, if the Bassanios and the Grazianos in the audience have their peckers up at this point, Portia very quickly deflates them with another turn of the wheel, another reversal.

Portia cuts the men to the very quick of their being in the court scene, 'emasculating' them even as she saves Antonio's skin. Balthasar's ruling, which breaks the Shylock–Antonio–Bassanio bonds, is more than comic. Beyond a joke, it is decisively anti-tragic. It firmly arrests the tragic principle of loss and the *risk* that throughout the play has been the virile imperative of aristocratic male sovereignty: the willingness to risk death, which distinguishes the master from the slave, has been placed in reserve in a servile act of recuperation, in the name of the bourgeois law and state. Yet Balthasar is not quite the state and not quite the law: he is a woman. As Balthasar, Portia assimilates everyone in the name of the law, she severs the Christian men from the heterogeneity/sovereignty they had established in relation to Shylock, with the result that the bourgeois state reasserts its mastery. But then, for her own purposes as a woman, Portia–Balthasar seduces the heroes into risking everything once more, luring them into her field of deception so that in the next Act she can excrete them once again as heterogeneous base matter and sovereignly put them to use.

At Bassanio's moment of truth in Act III, the moment where he has to risk everything and finally choose a casket, he anxiously reflects on the show and substance of valour:

> How many cowards, whose hearts are all as false
> As stairs of sand, wear yet upon their chins
> The beards of Hercules and frowning Mars,
> Who inward searched have livers white as milk?
> And these assume but valour's excrement
> To render them redoubted.
>
> (III.ii.83–8)

'Excrement' does not, of course, mean shit here. It means hair, in particular, facial hair or beard,[5] the conventional signifier of male virility. The word certainly *could*, in the sixteenth century, signify a whole manner of waste products: phlegm, choler, urine, sweat, snivel, spit, milk and so on, as well as ordure, since all these things were seen as the dregs or excrements of digestion. Here, the term signifies beard, but in a pejorative sense, I would suggest, with strong resonances of the base material the word could also signify. As an outgrowth of valour, this 'excrement' is merely a misleading signifier, not the thing itself, just like the gold casket. Bassanio doubles the riddle of the caskets with the image and substance of valour and thus wins Portia through imaginary identification. He affirms and performs the valour that lies imaginarily at the deathly hollow of his being and wins Portia and the gold, which ironically is, naturally, the outgrowth, the rotten, shimmering 'excrement' of pale and deathly lead.[6]

Subsequently possessed, in the play, with, or rather *by* the gold, valour lies like lead in the limbs of Bassanio. Time and again he (and Graziano) bravely boast they will sacrifice their lives, wives and wealth for Antonio, and at any time they can do this simply by killing the Jew, but they do not. In Act V, in an aside to the audience, Bassanio confides: 'Why, I were best to cut my left hand off/And swear I lost the ring defending it' but of course he does not because he did not (V.i.177–8). Instead he whinges interminably.

A woman has tricked and confounded him, he has betrayed his vow and become, effectively, lead in the water. Valour – the imperative mode of male sovereign existence – is expelled by Portia's cunning gifts, her ruling at court and her rule in Belmont. Valour is now reducible to the golden shimmer of Belmont's glittering aristocratic surface, or rather, having grown beyond or out of itself, to its own 'excrement'.

After the recuperation of Shylock's threat in the court scene, the subsequent scene playfully mocks the tragic bonds of love. A succession of great tragic heroes are paraded before us, mythological figures who risked everything for love: Troilus and Cressida, Pyramis and Thisbe, Dido, Medea, ... and Jessica and Lorenzo.

The musical harmony of the spheres is invoked, but they cannot be heard:

> Such harmony is in immortal souls,
> But whilst this muddy vesture of decay
> Doth grossly close it in, we cannot hear it.
>
> (V.i.63–65)

Then we hear it. Or do we? Is the introduction of a few earthly trumpets soothing here or just plain funny? In any case, no one is pacified. Instead a lovers' quarrel ensues in which the women shimmer and the men feel like shit. The (woman's) body, that 'muddy vesture of decay', returns as the final focus and limit of the play, suspending the action in a bawdy pun and the deferred prospect of carnal pleasure, in which the audience could have no doubt who would be on top.

Evil laughter from the women.

Conclusion: *Trompe le Monde*

> *Here is my table, my chair, my bed. They are here as a result of labor ... As a matter of fact I myself had to work to pay for them, that is, in theory, I had to compensate for the labor of the workers who made them, with a piece of labor just as useful as theirs ...*
>
> *Now I place a large glass of alcohol on my table.*
>
> *I have been useful. I have bought a table, a glass, etc.*
>
> *But this table is not a means of labor: it helps me to drink alcohol.*
>
> *In setting my drinking glass on the table, to that extent I have destroyed the table, or at least I have destroyed the labor that was needed to make it ...*
>
> *In this world there is no immense undertaking that has any other end than a definite loss in the futile moment.*
>
> *(Bataille 1989: 101–2)*

I don't wear pyjamas in bed, I am naked.

Then I read, generally – about four lines. I'll read a page occasionally and realise I haven't taken any of it in. So I go back to the start of the page again. I've been reading the same page for about 15 years now.

(*Reeves 1991*)

This essay, indeed this book, is designed for students to use. Readers will have noticed that I have largely neglected the pedagogical implications for literature students of this theory-as-practice which I have called, after Georges Bataille, 'heterology'. I have neglected to talk much about it partly because I am myself very unsure of its practicality. The primary aim of the book is to help students apply theory to literary texts, in this case *The Merchant of Venice*, yet heterology is not a literary theory. Bataille's interest in heterogeneity took him into the fields of sociology, economics and anthropology rather than literary theory. To locate the historical effects of an Elizabethan play properly, as a form of heterological practice, with its own dynamic force in the general economy of its society, would require an interdisciplinary study that crossed many related fields in which specifically 'literary' problems would be likely to dissolve.

Bataille's views on the importance of art and literature have little to do with their formal, aesthetic qualities so much as their material social effects on the one hand and their affects on an individual subject on the other, neither of which are reducible to so-called expressed meaning or the formal properties in which that meaning is produced. Hence, in his own fiction, Bataille takes literature into the field of eroticism not in order for eroticism to become the subject of literature, but for literature itself to become transformed into an erotic, untransposable practice (of reading/writing) that would transgress the polite, individual limits enclosing those beings it brings into play. To form or extrapolate a literary theory purely on the untransposable effects of literature at any point in time or on any particular subject, collective or otherwise, is, then, neither possible nor desirable. It would only set about to re-enclose, in a structure or syntax, the beings brought into play as subjects of discourse. Moreover, if literature is the same as eroticism, then I do not want to do it in the classroom.

The project in the 'theoretical' section of this essay (as opposed to its application as 'practice' in the reading that followed) was to provoke, through its intentionally irreverent and gratuitously scatological approach, a desire to read Shakespeare differently from a position sovereign, in its foul-mouthed irreverence, to the mastery of the Bard: to treat him lightly while granting him his full cultural and institutional weight. One of the reasons why I did this was to foreground the limits placed on reading in the context of academic seriousness and pedagogy. The way any text is approached and read is over-determined to a significant degree by the conditions in which that reading takes place and what sort of, for example, pedagogical demands are placed on that reading to begin with. At college one always reads with a set of institutional demands and expectations already in place. All these things direct reading towards the elucidation of some sort of institutionalized truth about literature, one way or another. One must read closely, think rigorously (of course), but to what end: to understand more fully and appreciate the outpourings of genius or to unearth another set of contradictions? Or, more ambitiously, to locate the struggle for and over meaning inherent in texts and society at large, to trace the relations of force that construct configurations of meaning into discrete knowledges that include and exclude, empower and disempower the subjects and objects of such knowledges. Certainly. Yet we are here close to pedagogical practice itself.

Power, as Portia demonstrated, addresses itself rigorously to details, to the very letter of the text, in order to exert its force in the name of the truth of that text. Yet, as every student knows, a text is certainly not something to which one can remain true in any ultimate sense. Each reading, each use of a text is always to some extent a betrayal of it, a resistance to the set of determinations, the relations of power, that inform and authorize that reading and that text; it involves a drifting off, a loss of interest, where other texts, other associations and resonances interrupt . . . in a voice squealing like a pig being roasted on a spit:

> I had me a vision
> there wasn't any television
> from looking into the sun
> looking into the sun
> we got to think quick
> says blind st. nick hey!
> from looking into the sun
> looking into the sun
> we got to get some beer
> we got no atmosphere
> from looking into the sun

looking into the sun
I had me a vision
there wasn't any television
from looking into the sun.

(The Pixies 1991)

You have to hear it, but this is, I think, the position I would suggest readers take in relation to Shakespeare: outface the sun with music blaring; think quick according to the blind and ambivalent principle of good/evil (adopt simultaneously productive and destructive strategies); get drunk (on alcohol and/or the text). But now I have just done what I said I would not do and laid down some theoretical rules. In fact, the mild 'shock' I experienced was not necessarily one of delight at this sudden coincidence of theme between some of the matters I raised earlier in the essay and this song by the Pixies which happened to be playing as I wrote. On the contrary, the particular texts, books, songs, poems (popular or canonical) that give me the most pleasure are more 'useful' to me if I do not attempt to use them for some other end, if I do not attempt to interpret precisely why they give me so much pleasure. So I am uneasy about reframing the Pixies' song as an 'approach to Shakespeare' even humorously in an academic exercise. The music I play, for example, is not supposed to complement or confirm my reading, it is meant to distract me. I began reading English literature at the age of 15 for O level: Jane Austen. For many reasons, I found it helped if I listened to the Sex Pistols at the same time. Fifteen years later, the idea that these two disparate but simultaneous pleasures have decisively converged is, for me, a bad sign. It signals that everything is becoming grist to the interpretative mill.

I always attempt when writing about literature within the academic institution of English, to make some productive use of it. I modestly endeavour to produce something in the tradition that unworks the Great Tradition, something alternative, political or radical. But this project is necessarily, and *at the same time*, undertaken ambivalently, with an accompanying sense not of futility, but of joyful indifference: listening to some obnoxiously loud pop music I don't give a shit about the institution of English, I don't give a shit about literature, history or traditions great, alternative or otherwise. I don't give a shit about my career. Strangely enough it is, for me, the best way to get ideas, such as they are. The struggle to think productively and differently can often best be achieved through reverie and loss. Thought must be methodical and concentrated, of course, but it is also always the product of absent-mindedness, distraction, indifference, loss: precisely and paradoxically the product of non-productive expenditure. One must be infused with pressures, forces and pleasures outside the institution to do any productive work within it. Every student knows that.

Incidentally, the phrase 'I don't give a shit' implies that to give one is an act of engagement, rather like the punk practice of gobbing spit at one's favoured performers. Giving a shit is, of course, the Freudian act of infantile love: a gift to the Other, a demand for the desire and approval of the Other. Since we all want to be loved we all give our shit, but perhaps it must be precisely shit that we give, or a gob of spit. For the receivers, such a gift is ambivalent: parents no doubt greet the child's rituals of potty prestation with a mixture of delight and revulsion; punk performers, leaning into wave after wave of flying phlegm, found the approval gratifying but the experience tiresome. Yet they had to put up with it because it was part of a symbolic exchange.

One of the most important of the many gifts the generous Antonio gives in *The Merchant of Venice* is his spit. For Shylock, these gifts of spit 'upon my Jewish gaberdine', and 'rheum upon my beard' demand a return (I.iii.109, 114). So Shylock sets up his seductively generous and poisonous bond. Elsewhere in the play (IV.i.279-84) Bassanio hollowly threatens to sacrifice Portia to Shylock to save the life of her rival. When Portia gives Antonio back to Bassanio she realizes his empty threat. She makes Bassanio give her away, but back to herself, thus giving himself, his own life, away. As objects of exclusion and exchange, Shylock and Portia exploit their positions of alterity in relation to the homogeneous order of the state and turn the laughter of the audience back on itself, at least for a time in Shylock's case. Their strategies all involve gifts, deception and ambivalence. They play the game of the Other, enlisting its power, as that which both exceeds us, excludes us and determines our movements, to turn its law back on itself.

If I were to extract a use-value on the basis of these internal strategies, or at least an uplifting conclusion, it would be that our gifts to the Other (in the shape of the institution that defines us) are also conceived in the spirit of a challenge or a deception, a challenge to the system in which the Other uses us. *Trompe le monde*!

SUPPLEMENT

NIGEL WOOD: You seem to stress the need for a resistant ('heterological') reading of the play by pointing out the heterodox nature of many of the narrative topoi, for example how Shylock's 'gift' of his bond unsettles the Christian moral economy. How would you regard the closing promise of celestial, or at least Belmont, music in Act V, scene i, that would underpin the escape of the iniquities of Venice? As Portia puts it, 'the greater glory' can 'dim the less' (V.i.93) when placed in a true comparison. Surely there is evidence here of an attempt to transcend and harmonize?

SCOTT WILSON: I've always been a bit perplexed by the apparent complacency with which the so-called harmony of Belmont has been accepted. The lovers spend most of their time quarrelling, after all, no doubt in order to generate the 'heat' necessary for a successful consummation of their marriages.

But if we accept that there is an attempt to 'transcend and harmonize', how does it occur, and what is the relation between 'the greater glory' and 'the less'? I argued that through her ruling at the court in Venice Portia in effect produced a 'new' Belmont, a new heterogeneous space over which she is sovereign. This space is produced as an effect of her legal work which homogenizes everyone as lawful, Christian subjects. Everyone, that is, except Portia who was not there. If we acknowledge that she was indeed there, in disguise, then her ruling can only be illegal since she has no authority to judge. Shylock has been the victim of a confidence trick, a fraudulent deception. Illegality, fakery, lies at the heart of Portia's successful ruling yet goes unperceived and renders everyone subject to the law. Now there is nothing particularly attractive to the aristocrats about this 'subjection' to a law which renders everyone servile and bourgeois. Portia herself 'transcends' the law because she is double, she is not a 'subject', she is both the mistress of Belmont and Doctor Balthasar: the fake instigator of the law, the law's beautiful, and beautifully deceptive, double.

This is precisely Belmont's 'transcendent' and 'harmonious' relation to Venice. Act V opens with the comic affirmation of law-breaking. Comparing themselves to legendary tragic lovers of the past, Jessica and Lorenzo congratulate themselves on how transgressive, extravagant and insincere they have been:

> LORENZO: In such a night
>   Did Jessica steal from the wealthy Jew
>   And with an unthrift love did run from Venice
>   As far as Belmont.
> JESSICA: In such a night
>   Did young Lorenzo swear he loved her well,

Stealing her soul with many vows of faith
And ne'er a true one.

(V.i.14–20)

If Shylock's unfortunate bond were rendered illegal by Portia, his heirs would celebrate their own good fortune by glorying in their illegality. This is how the 'greater glory [doth] dim the less'. Portia's two examples further illustrate how glory achieves its greatness through doublings and deceptively stealing from, the less. Moreover, Portia's analogies curiously grant precedence to the artificial over the natural, bringing the naturalness of the natural into question: the moon exceeds the candle by doubling its brightness to the extent that the candle is deceptively eclipsed; the king derives his brightness from his substitute (the king is the double of his double) by draining his state 'as doth an inland brook/Into the main of waters' (V.i.93–7).

These are images of a transcendence that 'harmoniously' repeats what it surpasses in a dubious economy in which interest is gained, and credit doubled, through deception. Portia describes how this sort of 'credit' accumulates most succinctly during the ensuing lovers' quarrel. Bassanio is attempting to swear by Portia's eyes never to break another oath. Portia interrupts him delightfully:

Mark you but that!
In both my eyes he doubly sees himself,
In each eye one. Swear by your double self,
And there's an oath of credit.

(V.i.243–6)

Bassanio's oath accumulates credit through deceit. Rendered two-fold by Portia's two eyes, the oath doubles, yet since the reflected 'I(s)' that made it are also doubled, the oath is two-faced and insincere. And these doublings can be multiplied even further when we remember, as Bassanio will soon remark, that Portia is Doctor Balthasar as well as his wife. The oaths double and redouble through a reflected, amorous gaze that divides and displaces any stable or singular relation between a subject who could swear and an object whose eyes could be sworn on. Portia is beyond the law, she can no longer be bound.

So if there is a certain 'harmony' to these repetitions and doublings which echo, repeat and displace each other within a Belmont that is itself an echo of its former self (where Portia was first bound to the will of a dead father and then, through marriage, to Bassanio), it is a harmony that reverberates with an eternally false ring.

NW: Let's tackle the rest of my questions together. First, you conclude with a determination to 'challenge . . . the system in which the Other uses us'. Are you claiming that the only possible resistance is a discursive (rhetorical) one? And could you give examples of the Other in operation within the academy, that is, how it may be said to affect you on a daily basis?

Second, most accounts of the play are particularly reticent about the Gobbos. They seem unlikely material for what we might now call 'comic relief'. Do you regard them as part of the central issue? I'm not asking you to incorporate reference to them if you feel they do not rate an honourable mention, but, if that is the case, can a reading of a text be fully persuasive if it's not comprehensive, i.e. assigning a role for every textual item?

Third, you doubt that 'heterology' is 'practical' in interpretative work. Is it worth it, then, for most of the purposes of tertiary study of literature?

SW: I will answer your first and third questions with reference to your second and *The Merchant of Venice*, Act II, scene ii.

Yes, I certainly should have done something with the Gobbos. How can one not, with a name like that, grant them an honourable mention in an essay so alert to the importance of spitting in the play? While the term 'gob' did not become a verb until the nineteenth century, as a noun, in the sixteenth century, the word signified a lump or clot of slimy substance, usually phlegm or blood. For the Irish the term could also signify 'mouth'. Indeed, in the late seventeenth century the charming phrase 'the gift of the gob' appears, according to the *Oxford English Dictionary*. John Russell Brown, the editor of the Arden edition of *The Merchant of Venice*, suggests that Gobbo is a version of *Iobbe*, the Italianized form of Job. The range of possible significations, then – base matter, language, mouths, the gift of speech, suffering and servile work – establishes an irresistable heterogeneous assemblage that it would be shameful not to note.

Nevertheless, in general, I don't think a reading of a text need assign a role to every textual item, I don't think a reading need be 'comprehensive' in that way in order to be persuasive. This is surely a leftover from new criticism: the text must ultimately be harmonious in spite of local ambiguities and contradictions. In contrast, some of the best work of the latest critical fashion, new historicism, makes a virtue out of reading apparently minor elements of a range of disparate texts and connecting them in a surprising and illuminating way.

Having said that, I really do not think I should have omitted the Gobbos. However, I think I know why I did. I could not write about the Gobbos because, I have realized, the Gobbos occupy the place from which I imagined I wrote. I'll explain that and in the process try to answer all the other questions concerning the Other and the academy with close reference to Act II, scene ii of *The Merchant of Venice*, the scene in which both Gobbos appear.

In this scene the young Launcelot Gobbo, like most servants or 'slaves' in a Hegelian sense, is in a position where the 'other' is his master. His master, Shylock, is 'other' also in respect of his Judaism. In the Lacanian system, specific 'others' stand in the place of the Other which constitutes the locus of the signifier along which, in this scene, Launcelot's 'fiendish' desire must travel. In the scene Launcelot is trying to make up his mind whether or not to leave the service of his master, Shylock. He admits that his 'conscience' can only counsel what the 'fiend' (the desire of the Other?) would have him do anyway; whether he leaves the Jew or remains, he will still be serving evil: 'to run away from the Jew, I should be ruled by the fiend who, saving your reverence, is the devil himself' (II.ii.22–4).

Launcelot is interrupted by his father who arrives to give Shylock a present, and there are some comic confusions as they re-establish their kinship. Then they come across Bassanio, another master, to whom Launcelot decides he would like to belong, but it is not up to him to make the proposal: 'I serve the Jew, and have a desire, as my father shall specify' he says hopefully (II.ii.122–3). So old Gobbo's gift of the dish of doves goes not to Shylock but to the fortunate Bassanio who repays him by giving his son Launcelot a new livery and possibly the promotion to 'fool' in his retinue.

I am going to draw an analogy. I function in an academic institution in which a fairly recent, 'radical' body of critical writing has emerged in opposition to more 'conservative' or 'traditional' approaches. As this volume, series and others like it demonstrate, the former is now fairly well established. Indeed, at both undergraduate and postgraduate levels I was taught by radical Shakespearians who reached a certain prominence in the 1980s and who continue to publish groundbreaking new work. In this work the theoretical notion of the Other is broadly used to designate that which is excluded or repressed by a subject, collective or otherwise, as it attempts to homogenize itself and establish its individual or communal ('national', say) identity. The Other in this case constitutes all the heterogeneous elements that are thus expelled, ignored or demonized: the unconscious, base matter, waste, non-productive elements, so-called undesirables, people of different races, sexualities, classes or 'underclasses' and so on. As defining 'others' these elements are crucial to the subject and necessarily render the apparently seamless nature of its identity radically unstable.

Alternative, radical and political approaches to Shakespeare do not, in a simple sense, 'serve' these 'others', as Launcelot serves Shylock his master, they do not write *for* or *on behalf* of heterogeneity, but such approaches do involve examining and contesting the ways in which institutions homogenize themselves through their various processes of exclusion, denial and rejection. They also attempt to offer, through the (largely textual) means at their disposal, ways of resisting such repression. In this sense, then, such writing is a 'gift' – perhaps not exactly a dish of doves – but a collection of analyses, alternative histories and different reading strategies that may be put to use by those who would learn and

accept them. For better or worse, such writing also sires and nurtures subjects like me.

But on the way to Shylock the gift gets deflected. And I have a desire
that my 'father' shall specify.

From the radical position, the homogeneous, conservative academy is
'other'. Both the radical and conservative positions, however, are functions of the Other in the shape of the institution in which all academics
work. In this sense then, the Other *is* my 'daily basis', is *me* on a daily
basis as, among other things, a signifying function of the academy. The
Other is the Master that distinguishes one master from another, Shylock
from Bassanio, radical from conservative, and puts all the academic
Gobbos into service – indeed, which seigneurally *allows* them to work
(readers are no doubt very well aware how difficult it frequently is to per-
suade the Master to come up with some gainful employment). The Other,
in the shape of the institution, is the object of professional desire and
demand for approval (or disapproval), promotion, money and so on: the
institution is the Master who makes us work slavishly for a living. In so
doing, the institution ceaselessly (and 'fiendishly' perhaps) homogenizes
itself through the very mechanisms of power and governmentality that
make it 'work'; it redefines itself once again against the useless, the unac-
ceptable, the heterogeneous. In its 'radical' form the institution puts the
heterogeneous *to use* in an academico-political project, puts it to work
in its (written) work and then offers that work to the heterogeneous as
a *gift*, thereby maintaining its institutional power and prestige.

It is not easy (or even possible?) to escape this given the role of servile
master that state or 'service' institutions such as universities have in
society. To be neither a master nor a slave one has, according to Bataille,
to be sovereign, that is not 'be' at all in the terms that define us as
academics or students. Because we are not just academics or students,
we are all 'other' to the institution, just as we are all 'other' to ourselves,
in a multiplicity of different ways. One of the most effective ways in which
this alterity or heterogeneity is disclosed in academic discourse is through
the effects of ambivalence and deception: that was the point of my
conclusion.

When I expressed reservations about the practicality of heterology as
a mode of interpretation or literary theory it was this problem that I had
in mind. One cannot write 'on' the heterogeneous or the untransposable
effects of literature without homogenizing them as objects of institutional
knowledge, without carving up 'heterogeneity' into various disciplines.
Nevertheless, given that one writes from a particular academic position,
within a certain discourse, it should be possible to trace or account for
the historical, social, political and 'literary' effects of heterogeneity, and
literature's emergence as a heterological practice. Perhaps 'heterology' is
not, after all, quite the correct term, implying as it does (with its 'ology')

a complete or completable project for knowledge. An alternative term, suggested to me by Fred Botting, might be 'heterography' since that would signal that such a practice was always working within and along the threshold of writing in the expanded Derridean sense.

It is in this expanded sense, which would far exceed the limits of academic discourse, that I would argue that resistance is indeed primarily 'rhetorical' given that one of the main weapons in this rhetorical armoury is reason. Yet even in a narrow sense, if we accept that in the West the most visible terrain of the political and the most effective means of political intervention is apparently 'the media' and media representations, then naturally the most important thing for any oppressed group is to gain access to it and use it. Of course one cannot use or manipulate the media in any simple way; the best one might hope for is to develop the ability to use it even as it uses you. This is not to say that there is not what used to be called 'direct action', but it seems to me that even this can be understood as rhetorical, in an expanded sense. There is also silence, blunt recalcitrance, mute rage, passivity, apathy, indifference: resistances that are, for one reason or another, 'unspeakable'. Yet frequently the 'unspeakable' merely designates that which cannot be amplified, heard, understood or granted status, seriousness, legitimacy or utility. Discourse functions in a restricted economy that 'works' or circulates primarily for those who work. For a relatively small cost – the price of a newspaper – anyone can listen in. But the large cost of this economy is paid for by those rendered useless, superfluous, unemployed and unemployable, those 'under' or outside (or to one side of) the class system whose silence or inaudibility is its very foundation. I would argue that it is precisely the degree to which the 'democratic' or 'market' economies of discourse produce and maintain these silences as their basis, as their very condition, that defines the intolerable.

Endpiece

NIGEL WOOD

In Umberto Eco's *The Name of the Rose* (first published in 1980), the climax of the narrative surrounds the discovery of an Aristotelian treatise on comedy. That the form might have some serious philosophical purpose akin to tragedy, and that its democratic impulse to unveil mysteries and parody authority should have such powerful sanction is dangerous enough to inspire its destruction. A licensed feast of fools would be something for the Church even to promote: the grotesquerie of carnival, a day's holiday from the social order where fools change places with kings – this inverts, but does not ultimately question, hierarchies and the present distribution of power. For Jorge, the monk who fully understands the threat posed by the book and who is its 'defender', comedy need not simply invert; on the contrary, laughter possesses the potential to strike at the root, to challenge authority's weapons of fear and ideologies of natural subservience and inherent orders of humanity:

> Laughter, for a few moments, distracts the villein from fear. But law is imposed by fear, whose true name is fear of God. This book could strike the Luciferine spark that would set a new fire to the whole world, and laughter would be defined as the new art, unknown even to Prometheus, for canceling fear.
>
> (Eco 1983: 474–5)

All the more reason to rid the world of this threat, if you conclude that *all* order would be cancelled. Where and when should the laughter stop? Cicero advised the best orators to practise restraint in 'jesting', lest they lost the esteem of their audience by attacking objects of either general approbation or deep misery. 'Ugliness' and 'physical blemishes' are comic material, yet one must not at the same time cross the line to 'bad taste', where one's comic talents become merely 'buffoonery' or 'mimicking' (*De Oratore*, in Cicero 1942, 2: 375). Where Aristotle does touch on the 'Ludicrous' in his *Poetics* he concludes that comedy is an imitation of 'characters of a lower type' and that it had an ingredient of ugliness: 'the comic mask is ugly and distorted, but does not cause pain' (Aristotle 1895: 19). Jorge's definition of Aristotelian comedy is a more basic critique. There have been classicists ready to hazard guesses as to just what rules such comedy might obey (see Cooper 1922), but the threat posed in Eco's terms runs against all rules – favouring perhaps ultimate goals rather than standards or laws. There is almost something fitting for any comic formulae to be lost: what is mysterious cannot ever be completely neutered or appropriated by masterful interpretation.

Cleopatra is so perturbed at a guying of herself by 'quick comedians' (*Antony and Cleopatra*, V.ii.216) at Rome that she eventually finds it a 'liberty' to determine her own fate by suicide: 'I am marble constant' (V.ii.237, 240). The serendipity of *commedia* artists is not divorced from the stage practices of a Robert Armin or Richard Tarlton on the Elizabethan stage. Folio or quarto texts are snapshots of performance, not exhaustive or definitive versions. For Cleopatra, the audience for her prospective burlesquing is distinctly unruly:

> Mechanic slaves
> With greasy aprons, rules, and hammers shall
> Uplift us to the view. In their thick breaths,
> Rank of gross diet, shall we be enclouded,
> And forced to drink their vapour.
>
> (V.ii.209–13)

There is certainly a fear here that part of this mistreatment by proxy will be at the hands not only of those who are of inferior class but also of those whose unruly antagonism will infect her person and force 'her' to 'drink their vapour'. Mimicry is a form of appropriation; like any theatrical image, it will pose as content but never shake off the status of being form. Cleopatra aspires to self-identity yet cannot prevent her valency in unthought-of contexts.

If we identify comedy merely by a fortuitous conclusion, where, against all the (constructed) odds, poetic justice is seen to be done, then this closing romantic consonance and melody hardly helps define the more visceral and disturbing force feared by Cicero. Quite accurately, Moisan (1991) has recently identified indices of class as well as race in the play (see also Ferber 1990), and this is a consideration taken further by both John Drakakis and Graham Holderness in this volume. For Drakakis, there is ever the temptation to join the drift towards mythography where basic economic and lived relations within a given society *at a particular historical juncture* get explained away as a perennial syndrome, an unchanging pattern unalterable because true of a transhistorical tendency lodged within humanity. At the same time criticism (if it is to retain the name) needs to avoid 'complicity' with the texts it regards in order to evade its prejudices (pp. 52–3). For Holderness, the route back to this raw comedy and its effect on present as well as past audiences is not to 'don intellectual doublet and hose' (pp. 65–7), but to strive to be conscious of historical difference, not to efface it but exploit it. History for both Drakakis and Holderness is not a one-way street.

The same could be said of both Karen Newman and Scott Wilson, but that would be less than helpful and visit a conformity on their essays that eventually would be uncritical. Newman is conscious of the hyperbolic role afforded most sociological enquiry into gender difference, Lawrence Stone's work in particular. Newman reads the role of Portia and her significant cross-dressing in Act IV, scene i, as exceptions that question the 'rules' of female exchange. Empirical investigation can suffice for only the most basic of leads into the comprehension of fictive documents; their 'factual' strategies are still open to ideological colouring and our critical faculties must be turned on the background 'tie-breaking' sources as much as the fictive texts they are deployed to help elucidate. Scott Wilson aims to withstand another potent authority, 'Shakespeare', in reading the play. This is so as to bypass a consideration of the accepted estimates of the 'formal, aesthetic qualities' of his work in order to assess 'its material social effects' and specifically its work upon an 'individual [human] subject' (p. 154). We should not, therefore, rush to predict a response from a typical audience, because that general description already predicts an answer that might leave out of account the non-erotic and engaged in favour of the banal and abstract.

If theory in these instances has appeared to be too curious and ingenious for such a 'low' form as comedy, then that is an image that the form could be said to entertain for its own ends. On the other hand, the sudden laugh can be a complex act, both as regards its causes and its eventual effects, either in political or apparently 'personal' terms. Its comparative accessibility is no more a route to an understanding of its social and historical location than the plot synopsis of a narrative is of the artistry that renders it emotive material. This might leave us with a reading of Shakespearian comedy that is attuned to its 'cover story' – one part disarming good humour, one part disruptive festivity. Structure is set against effect. As Lisa Jardine has made clear, the movement of the play towards closure (neatness, coherence) is no direct guide to the drama and dialectic that has *actually* been the sum of any audience's experience in the theatre. Thus, Graziano's last lines may underscore husbandly ownership and control, yet telling is not showing; the husbands have not been cuckolded, that much is clear in Act V, yet at the same time as there is a slackening of tension on that score there is their unanswered and so unresolved reinscription 'in a position of servitude to the wives who are revealed to have rescued them from dishonor' (Jardine 1987: 17). Bassanio may end up as lord of Belmont, and that could well have been an answer perfectly satisfactory to that monolithic polite fiction, the Elizabethan audience, yet it is also the case that he is so according to the wishes of his independent and learned wife. In Carol Leventen's reading of the play's forces of 'Patrimony and Patriarchy' the portrayal of femininity is split between Portia (the dutiful daughter) and Jessica (the runaway). Both could serve patriarchal agendas: Portia as the obedient daughter, who uses her new-found independence only to offer it up immediately to a husband; Jessica as the unfilial traitress, who while excusable on one level (she leaves the Jew) is also profligate with his wealth given the chance and so is the ambiguously independent female, a convert but yet not ever the 'natural' Christian ('Patrimony and Patriarchy in *The Merchant of Venice*', in Wayne 1991: 55–79). Both are taken care of by the plot, they are both there in Belmont and married, yet the tacit suggestion that transgression might yield reward (true also of Bassanio) cannot be wished away.

If this is a manufactured 'contemporary' reaction, then so be it, yet it is all the same derived from not only the figural power of the text but also its continued existence through time. Yet Norman Rabkin's objections to the theme-hunters, explored in the opening chapter of his *Shakespeare and the Problem of Meaning* (1981), that they reduce all to rationality and away from direct experience of the aesthetic artefact, can eerily be like a Derridean sensing the undertow of the 'supplement'. Authorial meaning, for Rabkin, is also a cause we ascribe to incompatible effects and inexhaustibility: 'The essence of our experience is our haunting sense of what doesn't fit our thesis we are tempted at every moment to derive' (Rabkin 1981: 23). Thereafter, Rabkin may consider meaning as dynamic and poetic, yet he may be disappointed to discover that he is in an uncanny agreement with many theorists on that score with this important reservation: he may cease questioning much sooner than they, because he believes himself clearer about limiting factors such as authors and humanity.

A little earlier in the same year as Rabkin wrote his timely admonition against critical reason, Arnold Wesker wrote a review article for *The Guardian* (29 August) about John Barton's RSC production of the play which had then reached London. Wesker's own riposte to Shakespeare, *The Merchant*, had opened in Stockholm in 1976, with its English premiere in New York a year later (later revised as *Shylock* (1989)). For Wesker, Shakespeare had supplied a coarse stage Jew, a gesture which could not be rescued by protestations that it was actually liberal for its time and could be part of a wider debate about usury or legal interpretation. The path back to an Elizabethan *Merchant* was barred: 'perhaps it is impossible to think straight about *The Merchant of Venice*. The Holocaust could be viewed as the ball and chain to all attempts at reason. There are only a few positions to take and each of them is bound to be unnatural' (Wesker 1990: 179; see also Wesker's debate with David Thacker in *The Guardian*, 13 April 1994). A 'doublet and hose' *Merchant of Venice*, if at all possible, would surely be both unnatural and intolerable.

Notes

Introduction

1 It is revealing to note that, despite the widespread critical observation that Portia utters New Testament sentiments (see, for example, Coghill 1950), the most direct model is Seneca's *De Clementia*, I.xix:

> Eo scilicet formosius id esse magnificentiusque fatebimur, quo in maiore praestabitur potestate, quam non oportet noxiam esse, si ad naturae legem componitur. Natura enim comment est regem, quod et aliis animalibus licet cognosecere et ex apibus . . .

> (This quality is the more beautiful and wonderful, the greater the power under which it is displayed; and this power need not be harmful if it is adjusted to Nature's law. For Nature herself conceived the idea of king, as we may recognize from the case of bees and other creatures.)
> (Seneca 1928, 1: 408–11; see also 1: 414–17)

2 See also Oliver's comment in *As You Like It*, IV.iii.129–30 ('kindness, nobler ever than revenge,/And nature, stronger than his just occasion') and the injunction from Ariel to Prospero to consult 'human' affections: Prospero concludes that he ought to 'take part' with his 'nobler reason 'gainst [his] fury', because the 'rarer action is/In virtue than in vengeance' (*The Tempest*, V.i.26–8).

3 This gap in the play between apparent intention and rhetoric has been explored in predominantly non-Derridean terms by Jonathan Goldberg, in his 'Shakespearean Inscriptions: The Voicing of Power', in Parker and

Hartman 1985, esp. pp. 120–5. If language is composed of relational traces (i.e. of other texts, there being no original urtext), then difference can be as easily a result of those who wield power as of some 'nature' of language itself (see Culler 1983: 89–110 on this).

4 A similarly significant pun occurs in Portia's comment to Bassanio (V.i.199) that if he 'had known the virtue of the ring', he would never have parted with it. 'Virtue' here is a conflation of potency or simply power with moral quality. The reiteration of anaphora and epistrophes (beginning and ending clauses with repeated phrases – V.i.193–7, 199–202) obeys the law of diminishing returns. The ring ceases to be the object in question.

5 The mix of danger with deliverance that is introduced in Lorenzo's duet with Jessica is analysed by Catherine Belsey (1991: 43) (see also Jardine 1987; Newman 1987; and Dunlop 1989):

> Love in *The Merchant of Venice* means marriage, concord, consent, and partnership. It means mutual compatibility and sympathy and support. But the older understanding of love leaves traces in the text, with the effect that desire is only imperfectly domesticated, and in consequence the extent to which Venice is superimposed on Belmont becomes visible to the audience.

6 For Paul de Man (1979: 10), this confusion between the figural and the literal meaning is not open to resolution, as it 'radically suspends logic and opens up vertiginous possibilities of referential aberration'. This blindspot of referentiality is frequently described using the Aristotelian term of *aporia*.

7 The alternation between those speeches assigned to Shylock and those to the 'Iew' in both the first and second quarto and Folio editions show a similar duality. The use of 'Iew' in the first quarto follows (loosely) those instances when Shylock is most tribal in his allegiances, for example, I.iii.28ff., II.v.1, III.iii.i and throughout most of the trial scene (this latter item also true of the Folio).

8 That this could have been the case in the immediate acting context has been valuably advanced by Hotine (1991), who points out that no Jews practised usury in Elizabethan London, and that anti-Semitism was far more likely to emanate from stage traditions than observable cultural conditions.

9 That Shylock may embody 'mercantile logic' is one of the arguments of Leonard Tennenhouse's chapter on 'Staging Carnival' in his *Power on Display* (Tennenhouse 1986: 56). See also Holmer (1995: 29–39). Thomas Wilson's objections against usury might be set against Francis Bacon's recognition that it was inevitable in his essay 'Of Usury' (see Bacon 1625: 242–6).

10 The most thorough account is provided in McPherson (1990: 36–8, 56–61).

11 Not a material, but rather a loose garment, which stressed general Eastern origins. Caliban wears a gaberdine when we first meet him (*The Tempest*, II.ii.37).

12 The hidden agenda explored in the play between gentility and the gentiles (referred to by Graham Holderness, this volume, pp. 90) is surely part of the byplay in Act I, scene iii, where 'kind' is repeated with interest (I.iii.138–40, 150, 174–5). Well may the Duke 'expect a gentle answer' from Shylock at the trial (IV.i.33).

13 The fixing of these gender stereotypes may be questionable, though, especially as Portia clearly converts 'her' Belmont holdings to Bassanio (III.ii.163–71).

14 This sense is clearest in *Venus and Adonis*, 11.375–6: 'O give it me, lest thy hard heart do steel it,/And being steeled, soft sighs can never grave it' (*The Poems*, p. 99). See also *Richard II*, I.iii.74 and V.ii.34.

15 The determination to provide Jessica with a knowledge of Boethius was started first by Danson (1978: 187–8). Does she feel what Lorenzo immediately explains, that her 'spirits are [merely] attentive' (V.i.70) to human music? There is no gesture of assent.

16 The clearest description, and exploration of its consequences for the task of criticism, is provided by Norris (1983: 25–30).

17 The temporizing of both the Friars Jacomo and Bernardine is an obvious example, yet there are other areas of Christian venality in the play; see Act II, scene ii and Ferneze's behaviour to the Turks and the parody of Christian sanctimony at IV.i.174–204. The oft-quoted controversy excited by the trial for treason of the Portuguese Jewish convert, Roderigo Lopez (the Queen's physician), in 1594 has been amply recorded in Sinsheimer (1964, 62–8). It is not as often remarked that for a Marrano Jew to achieve such high office is no mark of deep-seated national prejudice. See Hotine (1991) and Popkin (1989) for more on the surrounding events.

18 One voice that showed early commiseration for Shylock at this time was that of Richard Hole in his 'Apology for the Character and Conduct of Shylock' from his *Essays by A Society of Gentlemen at Exeter* (1796). He even imagines a sequel, written by Shylock, that would explore his viewpoint, and visit remorse on his vilifiers.

19 It is at about this time that certain significant excisions begin to alter the balance of the Shakespearian text. First to go are usually Shylock's 'If I can catch him once upon the hip,/I will feed fat the ancient grudge I bear him' (I.iii.43–4), his dream of 'money-bags' (II.v.18), and Jessica's testimony that her father had rather have 'Antonio's flesh' than twenty times the sum owed him (III.ii.282–8).

1 Historical Difference and Venetian Patriarchy

1 See also Adorno (1982: 34): 'To write poetry after Auschwitz is barbaric'. But see also Bond (1976: vi): 'What Adorno and Auden said about poetry and Auschwitz misses the point. They would have hit it only if Auschwitz had been the summing up of history – and of course it wasn't.'

2 Cf. Brown (1962: 74), where some residual guilt remains on the part of the critic that the aesthetic judgement he has himself made, savours of less than charity:

Shakespeare does not enforce a moral in this play – his judgement is implicit only – but as the action ends in laughter and affection at Belmont we know that each couple, in their own way have found love's wealth. We know too that their happiness is not all that we would wish; as they make free with Shylock's commercial wealth, we remember that they lacked the full measure of charity towards one who, through his hatred and possessiveness, had got his choice of that which he deserved.

3 But see also Shapiro (1992: 3), who argues that there were Jews in England, though

Virtually all those Jews practised their faith in secret – since most were of Spanish or Portuguese descent, *marranos*, they surely had had enough experience with disguising their beliefs because of their experience of the Inquisition, far harsher than any repression they might face in England.

4 It is also worth remembering that at a purely phenomenological level this battle was constantly fought out in the institution of the Elizabethan theatre itself in connection with the reduction of the 'play' to the status of a printed text, with *The Merchant of Venice* not being printed until 1600, some three or four years after its first performances.

5 *The Oxford English Dictionary* lists as one meaning of 'purse', 'The scrotum'. This raises the prospect of 'legitimate' as opposed to 'illegitimate' insemination; in mercantilist practice there is a legitimate way of making money 'breed', that of Antonio, which is closely aligned with friendship, contrasted with Shylock's illicit practice, articulated as a form of sexual licence.

6 Cf. Sonnet 6, where the distinction is made between 'usury' and progeny:

Make sweet some vial; treasure thou some place
With beauty's treasure ere it be self-killed.
That use is not forbidden usury
Which happies those that pay the willing loan –
That's for thyself to breed another thee,
Or ten times happier be it ten for one.

(II.3–8)

7 Cf. the role of the Duke in *Romeo and Juliet*, or, more problematically, the Duke in *Measure for Measure*.

2 Shakespeare on Marx

1 'Marlowe, Marx and Anti-Semitism', in Greenblatt (1990: 40–58 (particularly 40–2)).
2 The term, New Historicism, was coined by Stephen Greenblatt (1988), where the method is best exemplified.
3 Stephen Greenblatt's essay 'Marlowe, Marx and Anti-Semitism', in Greenblatt, (1990), adopts this position. Greenblatt (1990: 40–2) finds both Marlowe and Marx contaminated by racism. Racism presupposes at least a preference for one race over another. Since 'On the Jewish Question' is more scathing towards Christian culture than towards Judaism, and clearly envisages a necessary emancipation of humanity from both religions, Greenblatt's is an extraordinary misreading.
4 Marx comments on this passage in 'Excerpts from James Mill's *Elements of Political Economy*' in Marx (1977: 114–23).
5 Venetian merchants established a credit system known as the Monte de Caritia specifically to subvert by the provision of interest-free loans the business of Jewish usurers; see Pullan, (1971).
6 See Marx (1977: 51): 'If you Jews wish to achieve political emancipation without achieving human emancipation, then the incompleteness and contradiction does not only lie in you, it lies in the nature and category of political emancipation'.

3 Reprise: Gender, Sexuality and Theories of Exchange

1 This essay is based in part on two previously published articles (Newman 1987; 1990).
2 There are numerous exceptions to the claim that 'feminists ... have reproduced the paradigm of exchange', but I am describing a dominant approach employed particularly within white Anglo-American feminist critical practice, based in anthropology and history, and which often recuperates radical appropriations of Lévi-Strauss's paradigm to its own empiricist ethos.
3 See the work of the Cambridge demographers on age at marriage in the early modern period, especially Laslett (1984: 81–90).
4 Appropriately unmarked since in Tudor and Jacobean England, marriages were arranged for men as well as women, and they were arranged by both male and female 'more prudent and mature heads', not just by fathers as Stone implies (see Wrightson 1982: 71–9; see also Byrne 1981: 198–9).
5 See among others work by Dash (1981), Erickson (1985), Kahn (1981), Neely (1988), Novy (1984) and Williamson (1986).

6 On the seeming centrality of the woman as desired object, see Kristeva (1970: 60, 160).

7 See E.T., *The Lawes Resolution of Womens Rights* (1632), also known as *The Woman's Lawyer*, which gathers together in one volume contemporary laws about women, property and marriage. In Bk. II, xxxii, there is an extended discussion of the gifts given at marriage.

8 Kenneth Burke (1962: 508) calls this figure the

> 'noblest synecdoche,' the perfect paradigm or prototype for all lesser usages, [which] is found in metaphysical doctrines proclaiming the identity of 'microcosm' and 'macrocosm.' In such doctrines, where the individual is treated as a replica of the universe and vice versa, we have the ideal synecdoche . . .

9 For a contemporary discussion of the giving of rings, see Swinburne (1686); see also Parten (1976).

10 Virgil knew the simile from the end of Hesiod's prologue to the *Theogony*, but Shakespeare would only have known it, of course, through Virgil.

11 Quoted in Jordan (1983: 192). On the position of the learned lady in the Renaissance, see Jardine (1985).

12 Holland (1966: 238–331) reviews the psychoanalytic accounts of the link between rings and female sexuality; for folk-tale sources, see, for example, the Tudor jestbook *Tales and Quick Answers* (1530) cited in Parten (1976: 27).

13 See in particular Engle (1986: 37) who argues for Portia's 'absolute mastery' in Act V, and Horwich (1988: 199) who claims that the ring trick is 'a device by which she may exercise her free will'.

14 Commentators have often remarked on Shakespeare's introduction of the theme of friendship in the relation between Antonio and Bassanio, a shift from the paternal/filial relationship of *Il Pecorone* usually recognized as *The Merchant of Venice's* primary source. Recent critics who explain Antonio's melancholy as a loss of friendship and/or who argue that their relationship is homo-erotic include Midgley (1960); Auden (1963); Hyman (1970); Tennenhouse ('The Counterfeit Order of *The Merchant of Venice*' in Schwartz and Kahn 1980: 57–66); Geary (1984); and MacCary (1985).

4 Heterology

1 For Baudrillard (1975, 1981), use-value is the 'real' value promised but deferred by exchange-value; it is the fantasy that capitalism itself constructs as the impossible object of desire for its never satisfied consumers. And Marx and Marxism fall for it along with everyone else.

2 Jacques Lacan's conception of 'the Other' is another ambivalently gendered figure, which is to say it has both genders and neither. The Other is 'the locus of the signifier' whose Law is appropriated by the Father who 'assumes its authority', yet it is the Mother 'who is actually led to occupy

the place of the Other' (Lacan 1989: 310–11). From the position of the critical or pedagogical subject, Shakespeare as one threshold of the Other becomes both the Law, the measure of Anglo-American cultural discourse, and the object of scholarly desire and institutional demand. For Lacan on *Hamlet* see 'Desire and the Interpretation of Desire in *Hamlet*', in Felman (1982: 50).

3 For the importance of these popular forms of medieval 'street theatre' for Shakespeare see Spivack (1978).

4 A recent example of the power of the symbolic act or utterance – not here in the form of a gift – can be seen, according to Baudrillard, in the effects the Ayatollah Khomeini's *fatwa* on Salman Rushdie has had on the West:

> Quite apart from performing a *tour de force* whereby the West has been obliged to hold this particular hostage itself, whereby Rushdie has in a way been obliged to hold himself entirely hostage, the Ayatollah has offered spectacular proof of how possible it is to overturn all existing power relations through the symbolic force of an utterance.
>
> Confronting the entire world, his tally utterly negative in the distribution of political, military and economic forces, the Ayatollah had but one weapon at his disposal . . .: the principle of Evil. The negation of all Western values – of progress, rationality, political ethics, democracy and so on. By rejecting the universal consensus on all these Good Things, Khomeini became the recipient of the energy of Evil, the Satanic energy of the rejected, the glamour of the accursed share . . . Of course we still have the power to destroy him, but on the symbolic level he is the victor, and symbolic power is always superior to the power of arms and money.
>
> (Baudrillard 1993: 81–3)

Could it be argued that Shylock, in a certain sense, takes Antonio 'hostage' through his insistence on his bond?

5 The term crops up five times in Shakespeare's work, mostly signifying hair. Interestingly, the line which editors usually use to illustrate this meaning (which includes the *Oxford English Dictionary* itself) is one from *Love's Labour's Lost*: 'It will please his grace . . . to . . . dally with my excrement' (V.i.91, 93). Scholarship, here, seems to abandon disinterested historical elucidation and reverses itself in laughter. We are compelled by laughter to think, in its baser sense, a line that seems more appropriate to *One Hundred and Twenty Days of Sodom*, except that 'my excrement' means 'my mustachio'. In the play, hair does have its own heterogeneous force. Portia's hair constitutes the deadly spider's web, and Shylock's beard is one of the objects of loathing that Antonio spits on.

6 Sarah Kofman brings out the ambivalence of gold in her essay.

> Despite appearances, *gold* . . . is not the opposite of pale and base lead. Its perfection is the result of a slow gestation, a transformation of low

> metals. It is ... this base origin of gold that explains its symbolic equivalence with the basest thing of all, excrement.
>
> (Collier and Geyer-Ryan 1990: 151)

It is possible to make this symbolic equivalence tighter by changing the metaphor from 'gestation' to 'digestion'. Lead turns to gold through the work of digestion in the bowels of the earth. Gold, like shit, is essentially waste matter, it is not *usable* in any productive sense, it is generally held in reserve while silver, that 'pale and common drudge/'Tween man and man' (III.ii.103–4), does the work of exchange.

References

Unless otherwise indicated, place of publication is London.

Adorno, Theodor (1982) *Prisms*, trans. Samuel and Shierry Weber. Cambridge, MA.

Althusser, Louis (1977) *Lenin and Philosophy and Other Essays*, trans. Ben Brewster.

Aristotle (1895) *The Poetics of Aristotle*, trans. S.H. Butcher.

Auden, W.H. (1963) *The Dyer's Hand, and Other Essays*.

Bacon, Francis (1625) *The Essays or Counsels, Civill and Morall*.

Barber, C.L. (1959) *Shakespeare's Festive Comedy*. New York.

Barnes, Julian (1984) *Flaubert's Parrot*.

Barthes, Roland (1973) *Mythologies*, trans. Annette Lavers.

Bataille, Georges (1973) *Literature and Evil*, trans. Alexander Hamilton.

Bataille, Georges (1982) *Story of the Eye*, trans. Joachim Neugroschal (with essays by Roland Barthes and Susan Sontag). Harmondsworth.

Bataille, Georges (1985) *Visions of Excess: Selected Writings 1927–39*, trans. Allan Stoekl. Manchester.

Bataille, Georges (1988a) *Guilty*, trans. Bruce Boone. San Francisco.

Bataille, Georges (1988b) *Inner Experience*, trans. Leslie Anne Boldt. New York.

Bataille, Georges (1989) *Theory of Religion*. New York.

Bate, Jonathan (1989) *Shakespearean Constitutions: Politics, Theatre, Criticism, 1730–1830*. Oxford.

Bate, Jonathan (ed.) (1992) *The Romantics on Shakespeare*. Harmondsworth.

Baudrillard, Jean (1975) *The Mirror of Production*, trans. Mark Poster. St. Louis. MO.

Baudrillard, Jean (1981) *Critique of the Political Economy of the Sign*, trans. Charles Levin. St Louis, MO.

Baudrillard, Jean (1988) *Selected Writings*, ed. Mark Poster. Cambridge.

Baudrillard, Jean (1993) *The Transparency of Evil*, trans. James Benedict.

Bauer, Bruno (1843) *The Jewish Question*.

Belsey, Catherine (1991) 'Love in Venice', *Shakespeare Survey*, 44: 41–53.

Berry, Philippa (1989) *Of Chastity and Power: Elizabethan Literature and the Unmarried Queen*.

Bindoff, S.T., Hurstfield, J. and Williams, C.H. (eds) (1961) *Elizabethan Government and Society*.

Blake, William (1984) *The Complete Works*, ed. Geoffrey Keynes. Oxford.

Bloom, Harold (1973) *The Anxiety of Influence: A Theory of Poetry*. New York.

Bond, Edward (1976) *The Fool and We Come to the River*.

Book of Homilies, The (1594).

Botting, Fred and Wilson Scott, (1993) 'Literature as Heterological Practice: Georges Bataille, Writing and Inner Experience', *Textual Practice*, 7: 195–207.

Bourdieu, Pierre (1977), *Outline of a Theory of Practice*, trans. Richard Nice (*Studies in Social Anthropology* 16). Cambridge.

Braudel, Fernand (1982) *Civilization and Capitalism: 15th–18th Centuries*, trans. Sian Reynolds, 3 vols.

Brecht, Bertolt (1977) *Brecht on Theatre*, trans. John Willett.

Bristol, Michael (1990) *Shakespeare's America, America's Shakespeare*.

Brown, John Russell (1961) 'The Realization of Shylock', in *Early Shakespeare* (Stratford-upon-Avon Studies, no. 3), pp. 187–209.

Brown, John Russell (1962) *Shakespeare and his Comedies*.

Brown, John Russell (1964), 'Introduction', in *The Merchant of Venice* (ed. Brown). Harmondsworth.

Brown, John Russell (1966) *Shakespeare's Plays in Performance*.

Bulman, James C. (1991) *Shakespeare in Performance: The Merchant of Venice*. Manchester.

Burke, Kenneth (1962) *A Grammar of Motives and A Rhetoric of Motives*. Cleveland, OH.

Butler, Judith (1989) *Gender Trouble*. New York.

Byrne, Muriel St Clare (ed.) (1981) *The Lisle Letters, an Abridgement*, Chicago.

Caesar, M. Phillippus (1578) *A General Discourse Against the Damnable Sect of Usurie*.

Callaghan, Dympna, Helms, Lorraine and Singh, Jyotsna (1994) *The Weyward Sisters: Shakespeare and Feminist Politics*. Oxford.

Carlyle, Thomas (1829) 'Signs of the times', *Edinburgh Review*, 49: 439–59.

Chambers, David and Pullan, Brian, with Jennifer Fletcher (eds) (1992) *Venice: A Documentary History, 1450–1630*. Oxford.

Chambers, E.K. (1923) *The Elizabethan Stage*, 4 vols.

Cicero (1942) *De Oratore*, trans. E.W. Sutton and H. Rackham.

Coghill, Nevill (1950) 'The Basis of Shakespearean Comedy: A Study in Medieval Affinities', *Essays and Studies*, n.s., 3: 1–28.

Cohen, Walter (1982) '*The Merchant of Venice* and the Possibilities of Historical Criticism', *Journal of English Literary History*, 49: 765–89.

Cohen, Walter (1985) *Drama of a Nation: Public Theater in Renaissance England and Spain*. Ithaca, NY.

Collier, Peter and Geyer-Ryan, Helga, (eds) (1990) *Literary Theory Today*. Cambridge.

Cook, John (1649) *King Charls his Case: or, an Appeal to all Rational Men, Concerning His Tryal*.

Cooper, Lane (1922) *An Aristotelian Theory of Comedy*. New York.

Culler, Jonathan (1983) *On Deconstruction: Theory and Criticism after Structuralism*.

Danson, Lawrence (1978) *The Harmonies of 'The Merchant of Venice'*. New Haven, CT.

Dash, Irene (1981) *Wooing, Wedding, and Power: Women in Shakespeare's Plays*. New York.

Davis, Natalie Zemon (1975) *Society and Culture in Early Modern France*. Stanford, CA. First published 1965.

de Beauvoir, Simone (1988) *The Second Sex*, trans. H.M. Parshley. Harmondsworth. (1st edn 1949).

de Man, Paul (1979) *Allegories of Reading: Figural Language in Rousseau, Nietzsche, Rilke and Proust*. New Haven, CT.

Demetz, Peter (1967) *Marx, Engels and the Poets: Origins of Marxist Literary Criticism*, trans. Jeffrey L. Sammons. Chicago.

Derrida, Jacques (1976) *Of Grammatology*, trans. Gayatri Chakravorty Spivak. Baltimore.

Derrida, Jacques (1977a) 'Signature Event Context', *Glyph*, 1: 172–97.

Derrida, Jacques (1977b) 'Limited Inc', *Glyph*, 2: 162–254.

Derrida, Jacques (1981a), *Writing and Difference*, trans Alan Bass.

Derrida, Jacques (1981b) *Positions*, trans. Alan Bass. Chicago.

Derrida, Jacques (1986) *Margins of Philosophy*, trans. Alan Bass. Brighton.

Dobson, Michael (1992) *The Making of the National Poet: Shakespeare, Adaptation, and Authorship, 1660–1769*. Oxford.

Dollimore, Jonathan (1984) *Radical Tragedy*, Chicago.

Dollimore, Jonathan (1986) 'Subjectivity, Sexuality and Transgression: The Jacobean Connection', *Renaissance Drama*, n.s., 17: 53–82.

Dunlop, William (1989) 'The Virtue of the Ring', *Modern Language Quarterly*, 50: 3–22.

E.T. (1632) *The Lawes Resolution of Womens Rights*.

Eagleton, Terry (1986) *William Shakespeare*. Oxford.

Eagleton, Terry (1991) *Ideology: An Introduction*.

Eco, Umberto (1983) *The Name of the Rose*, trans. William Weaver.

Emerson, Ralph Waldo (1968) *Collected Works of Ralph Waldo Emerson: Centenary Edition*, ed., A.R. Ferguson, 12 vols. New York.

Engle, Lars (1986) ' "Thrift is Blessing": Exchange and Explanation in *The Merchant of Venice*', *Shakespeare Quarterly*, 37: 20–37.

Erickson, Peter (1985) *Patriarchal Structures in Shakespeare's Drama*. Berkeley, CA.

Erickson, Peter (1991) *Rewriting Shakespeare, Rewriting Ourselves*. Berkeley, CA.

Erickson, Peter and Kahn, Coppélia (eds) (1985) *Shakespeare's Rough Magic: Renaissance Essays in Honor of C.L. Barber*. Newark, DE.

Felman, Shoshana (ed.) (1982) *Literature and Psychoanalysis*. Baltimore, MD.

Ferber, Michael (1990) 'The Ideology of *The Merchant of Venice*', *English Literary Renaissance*, 20: 431–64.

Ferguson, Margaret (1991) 'Juggling the Categories of Race, Class and Gender: Aphra Behn's *Oroonoko*', *Women's Studies*, 19: 159–81.

Fiedler, Leslie A. (1973) *The Stranger in Shakespeare*.

Foucault, Michel (1977) *Language, Counter-Memory, Practice*, trans. Donald F. Bouchard and Sherry Simon. Oxford.

French, Marilyn (1982) *Shakespeare's Division of Experience*.

Freud, Sigmund (1953–74) *The Standard Edition of the Complete Psychological Works*, ed. J. Strachey, 24 vols.

Geary, Kenneth (1984) 'The Nature of Portia's Victory: Turning to Men in *The Merchant of Venice*', *Shakespeare Survey*, 37: 55–68.

Granville-Barker, Harley (1930) *Prefaces to Shakespeare*, Vol. 1.

Greenblatt, Stephen (1988) *Shakespearean Negotiations*. Oxford.

Greenblatt, Stephen (1990) *Learning to Curse: Essays in Early Modern Culture*. New York.

Gross, John (1992) *Shylock: Four Hundred Years in the Life of a Legend*.

Halio, Jay L. (1994) 'Introduction', In *The Merchant of Venice*, ed. Halio. Oxford.

Hardison, O.B., Jr (ed.) (1967) *English Literary Criticism: The Renaissance*.

Hawkes, Terence (1992) *Meaning by Shakespeare*.

Hazlitt, William (1930–4), *Complete Works*, ed. P.P. Howe, 21 vols.

Hill, Christopher (1982), *The Century of Revolution: 1603–1714*. New York.

Hirschman, Jack (ed.) (1965) *Artaud Anthology*. San Francisco.

Holderness, Graham (ed.) (1988) *The Shakespeare Myth*. Manchester.

Holderness, Graham, Potter, Nick and Turner, John (1987) *Shakespeare: the Play of History*.

Holland, Norman (1966) *Psychoanalysis and Shakespeare*. New York.

Hollier, Denis (1989) *Against Architecture: The Writings of Georges Bataille*, trans. Betsy Wing. Boston.

Holmer, Joan Ozark (1995) *The Merchant of Venice: Choice, Hazard and Consequence*.

Horwich, Richard (1988) *Shakespeare's Dilemmas*. New York.

Hotine, Margaret (1991) 'The Politics of Anti-Semitism: *The Jew Of Malta* and *The Merchant of Venice*', *Notes and Queries*, 38(1): 35–8.

Hyman, Lawrence W. (1970) 'The Rival Lovers in *The Merchant of Venice*', *Shakespeare Quarterly*, 21: 109–16.

Irigaray, Luce (1985) *This Sex Which Is Not One*, trans. Catherine Porter with Carolyn Burke. Ithaca, NY.

Jameson, Fredric (1981) *The Political Unconscious: Narrative as a Socially Symbolic Act.*

Jardine, Lisa (1983) *Still Harping on Daughters: Women and Drama in the Age of Shakespeare*. Brighton.

Jardine, Lisa (1985) ' "O decus Italiae virgo", or the Myth of the Learned Lady in the Renaissance', *Historical Journal*, 28: 799–819.

Jardine, Lisa (1987) 'Cultural Confusion and Shakespeare's Learned Heroines: "These be old paradoxes" ', *Shakespeare Quarterly*, 38: 1–18.

Johnson, Samuel (1986) *Selections from Johnson on Shakespeare*, ed. Bertrand H. Bronson with Jean O'Meara. New Haven, CT.

Jordan, Constance (1983) 'Feminism and the Humanists: The Case of Sir Thomas Elyot's *Defence of Good Women*', *Renaissance Quarterly*, 36: 181–201.

Kahn, Coppélia (1981) *Man's Estate: Masculine Identity in Shakespeare*. Berkeley, CA.

Knox, John (1558). *The First Blast of the Trumpet Against the Monstrous Regiment of Women*. Geneva.

Kristeva, Julia (1970) *Texte du roman*. The Hague.

Kristeva, Julia (1991) *Strangers to Ourselves*, trans. Leon Roudiez. New York.

Kuhn, Annette and AnnMarie Wolpe (eds) (1978) *Feminism and Materialism*.

Lacan, Jacques (1989) *Ecrits*, trans. Alan Sheridan.

Laslett, Peter (1984) *The World We Have Lost*. New York.

Leggatt, Alexander (1974) *Shakespeare's Comedy of Love.*

Lelyveld, Toby (1960) *Shylock on the Stage*. Cleveland, OH.

Lévi-Strauss, Claude (1969) *The Elementary Structures of Kinship*, trans. James Harlie Bell and John Richard von Stermer. Boston.

Luther, Martin (1962) *Works: The Christian in Society*, 6 vols. Philadelphia.

Lyotard, Jean-François (1990), *Heidegger and 'the Jews'*, trans. Andreas Michael and Mark S. Roberts. Minneapolis, MN.

MacCary, W. Thomas (1985) *Friends and Lovers: The Phenomenology of Desire in Shakespearean Comedy*. New York.

Macherey, Pierre (1978) *A Theory of Literary Production*, trans. Geoffrey Wall.

Machiavelli, Niccolò (1970) *The Discourses*, trans. Bernard Crick. Harmondsworth.

McPherson, David C. (1990) *Shakespeare, Jonson, and the Myth of Venice*. Newark, NJ.

Marx, Karl (1963) *Early Writings*, ed. Tom Bottomore.

Marx, Karl (1977) *Selected Writings*, ed. David McLellan. Oxford.

Marx, Karl (1981) *Capital, Volume III*, trans. David Fernbach, Harmondsworth.

Mauss, Marcel (1954) *The Gift: Forms and Functions of Exchange in Archaic Societies*, trans. Ian Cunnison.

Merchant, Moelwyn (1967) 'Introduction', in *The Merchant of Venice* ed. Merchant. Harmondsworth.

Midgley, Graham (1960) '*The Merchant of Venice*: A Reconsideration', *Essays in Criticism*, 10: 119–33.

Moisan, Thomas (1991) ' "Knock Me Here Soundly": Comic Misprison and Class Consciousness', *Shakespeare Quarterly*, 42: 276–90.

Montrose, Louis Adrian (1980) 'Gifts and Reasons: The Contexts of Peele's *Araygnment of Paris*', *Journal of English Literary History*, 47: 433–61.

Moulton, Richard G. (1906) *Shakespeare as a Dramatic Artist*. Oxford.

Neely, Carol Thomas (1988) 'Constructing the Subject: Feminist Practice and the New Renaissance Discourses', *English Literary Renaissance*, 18: 5–18.

Newman, Karen (1987) 'Portia's Ring: Unruly Women and Structures of Exchange in *The Merchant of Venice*', *Shakespeare Quarterly*, 38: 19–33.

Newman, Karen (1990) 'Directing Traffic: Subjects, Objects, and the Politics of Exchange in *The Merchant of Venice*', *differences*, 2: 41–54.

Norris, Christopher (1983) *The Deconstructive Turn: Essays in the Rhetoric of Philosophy*.

Norris, Christopher (1987) *Derrida*.

Novy, Marianne (1984) *Love's Argument: Gender Relations in Shakespeare*. Chapel Hill, NC.

Nuttall, A.D. (1983) *A New Mimesis: Shakespeare and the Representation of Reality*.

Parker, Patricia and Hartman, Geoffrey (eds) (1985) *Shakespeare and the Question of Theory*. New York.

Parten, Anne (1976) 'Re-establishing Sexual Order: The Ring Episode in *The Merchant of Venice*', *Selected Papers of the West Virginia Shakespeare and Renaissance Association*, 6: 27–34.

Pêcheux, Michel (1983) *Language, Semantics, Ideology*.

Pefanis, Julian (1991) *Heterology and the Postmodern: Bataille, Baudrillard, Lyotard*. Durham, NC.

Pixies, The (1991) 'Distance Equals Rate Times Time', *Trompe le Monde*. Rice and Beans Music.

Popkin, Richard (1989) 'A Jewish Merchant of Venice', *Shakespeare Quarterly*, 40: 329–31.

Pullan, Brian (1971) *Rich and Poor in Renaissance Venice: The Social Institutions of a Catholic State*. Oxford.

Rabkin, Norman (1981) *Shakespeare and the Problem of Meaning*. Chicago.

Reeves, Vic (1991) 'A Day in the Life of Jim Moir', *Sunday Times Magazine*, 10 November.

Reiter, Rayna (ed.) (1975) *Towards an Anthropology of Women*. New York.

Richardson, Michael (1994) *Georges Bataille*.

Richman, Michele (1982) *Beyond the Gift: Reading Georges Bataille*. Baltimore, MD.

Schneider, Ben Ross, Jr (1993) 'Granville's *Jew of Venice* (1701): A Close Reading of Shakespeare's *Merchant*', *Restoration*, 17: 111–34.

Schwartz, Murray M. and Kahn, Coppélia (eds) (1980) *Representing Shakespeare: New Psychoanalytic Essays*. Baltimore, MD.

Sedgwick, Eve Kosovsky (1984) 'Sexualism and the Citizen of the World: Wycherley, Sterne and Male Homosocial Desire', *Critical Inquiry*, 11: 226–45.

Seneca (1928) *Moral Essays*, trans. John W. Basore, 3 vols.

Shapiro, James (1992) *Shakespeare and the Jews* (The Parkes Lecture). Southampton.

Shaviro, Steven (1990) *Passion and Excess: Blanchot, Bataille, and Literary Theory*. Tallahassee, FL.

Sher, Anthony (1987) 'Shaping up to Shakespeare: Anthony Sher in Interview with Mark Lawson', *Drama*, 4: 27–30.

Sinsheimer, Hermann (1964) *Shylock: The History of a Character*. New York. (Orig. edn pub. 1947).

Spencer, Christopher (ed.) (1965) *Five Restoration Adaptations of Shakespeare*. Urbana, IL.

Spivack, Charlotte (1978) *The Comedy of Evil on Shakespeare's Stage*.

Stoekl, Allan (ed.) (1990) *On Bataille* (*Yale French Studies*, no. 78). New Haven, CT.

Stoll, E.E. (1960) *Shakespeare Studies: Historical and Comparative in Method*. New York (2nd edn; orig. edn pub. 1927).

Stone, Lawrence (1965) *The Crisis of the Aristocracy, 1558–1641*. Oxford.

Stone, Lawrence (1977) *The Family, Sex and Marriage in England, 1500–1800*. New York.

Swinburne, Henry (1686) *Treatise of Spousals or Matrimonial Contracts*.

Tawney, R.H. (1947) *Religion and the Rise of Capitalism*. New York.

Taylor, Gary (1990) *Re-inventing Shakespeare*.

Taylor, Ronald (ed.) (1980) *Aesthetics and Politics*.

Tennenhouse, Leonard (1986) *Power on Display: The Politics of Shakespeare's Genres*.

Thompson, E.P. (1977) 'Happy Families', *New Society*, 8 September, 499–501.

Tillyard, E.M.W. (1950) *Shakespeare's Problem Plays*.

Tuvill, Daniel (1635) *St. Pauls Threefold Cord*.

Vaughn, William (1600) *The Golden Grove*.

Vickers, Brian (1974–81) *Shakespeare: The Critical Heritage 1623–1801*, 6 vols.

Virgil (1971) *The Aeneid*, trans. Allen Mandelbaum Berkeley, CA.

Wayne, Valerie (ed.) (1991) *The Matter of Difference: Materialist Feminist Criticism of Shakespeare*. Ithaca, NY.

Weimann, Robert (ed.) (1978) *Shakespeare and the Popular Tradition in the Theater*. Baltimore, MD.

Wesker, Arnold (1990) *Shylock and other Plays*.

Wilders, John (ed.) (1969) *The Merchant of Venice* (Macmillan Casebook).

Williams, Raymond (1980) *Problems in Materialism and Culture: Selected Essays*.

Williamson, Marilyn (1986) *The Patriarchy of Shakespeare's Comedies*. Detroit.

Wilson, John Harold (1934), 'Granville's "Stock-Jobbing Jew" ', *Philological Quarterly*, 13: 1–15.

Wilson, Sir Thomas (1572) *A Discourse Upon Usurye*.

Wing, John (1620) *The Crowne Coniugall, or The Spouse Royall*.

Wrightson, Keith (1982) *English Society, 1580–1680*. New Brunswick, NJ.

Young, Robert (ed.) (1981) *Untying the Text: A Post-Structuralist Reader*.

Further Reading

1 Historical Difference and Venetian Patriarchy

C.L. Barber, *Shakespeare's Festive Comedy* (New York, 1959).
An influential treatment (before the advent of Mikhail Bakhtin's analysis of the carnivalesque) of Shakespeare's comedies, including a chapter on *The Merchant of Venice*, where Barber adopts a dual perspective on Shylock, part scapegoat, part ironic doubling of gentile behaviour in Venice.

Roland Barthes, *Mythologies*, trans. Annette Lavers (London, 1973).
A very astute account of how societies create 'myths', and of how 'myths' stand in for, and seek to mediate, histories.

Walter Cohen, *Drama of a Nation: Public Theater in Renaissance England and Spain* (Ithaca, NY, 1985).
A very wide-ranging treatment of Renaissance theatre, which includes an acute Marxist reading of the play.

Jonathan Israel, *European Jewry in the Age of Mercantilism: 1550–1750* (Oxford, 1985).
A clear historical account of the Jews in a European context. To be augmented by John Edwards's *The Jews in Christian Europe, 1400–1700* (London, 1988).

Julia Kristeva, *Strangers to Ourselves*. trans. Leon Roudiez (New York, 1991).
An account of 'foreignness' informed by psychoanalytic theory.

Pierre Macherey and Etienne Balibar, 'On Literature as an Ideological

Form', in Robert Young (ed.), *Untying the Text* (London, 1981), pp. 79–99.

A supplement to Macherey's earlier *A Theory of Literary Production* (first published in 1966; London, 1978), where there is renewed stress on how Marxists are to develop a theory of how literature 'reflects' reality, and what ideological colouring lingers in the concept of 'literature', especially in education.

James Shapiro, 'Shakespeare and the Jews', The Parkes Lecture (Southampton, 1992).

A short, detailed treatment of the history of the Jews in Renaissance England, and a particularly perceptive reading of Shylock's bond and its significance in (and outside) the play.

2 Shakespeare on Marx

Terry Eagleton, *William Shakespeare* (Oxford, 1986).

A series of short and provocative pieces which does not take on trust the common understanding of Shakespeare that he upholds stability and order. Particularly good on law in the late comedies (pp. 35–63).

Jean E. Howard, *The Stage and Social Struggle in Early Modern England* (New York, 1994).

Some original research into antitheatrical prejudices in the early modern age and the coded way that drama provided a response. The fifth chapter, 'Power and Ethos: Crossdressing in Dramatic Representation and Theatrical Practice' (pp. 93–128), is nearest the concerns of this volume.

Christopher J. McCullough, 'The Cambridge Connection: Towards a Materialist Theatre Practice', in Graham Holderness (ed.), *The Shakespeare Myth* (Manchester, 1988), pp. 112–21.

A preliminary outline of how a materialist critique might proceed as regards the current British theatrical establishment.

Steven Mullaney, *The Place of the Stage: License, Play. and Power in Renaissance England* (Chicago, 1988).

A committed set of new historicist readings that open up several Shakespeare plays to their riddles and possible transgressions of theatrical 'good form'.

Edward Pechter, 'Against "Ideology"', in Ivo Kamps (ed.), *Shakespeare Left and Right* (New York, 1991), pp. 79–97.

A contentious collection of essays. Pechter's analysis of American academic politics should have resonances for others, too. It regards the woolly definitions that the term 'ideology' provides and shows how they actually foster inexact readings of Marx.

Frank Whigham, 'Ideology and Class Conduct in *The Merchant of Venice*', *Renaissance Drama*, 10 (1979), 93–115.

Excellent in isolating the factors involved in the 'ideology of harmony' visited on the play. Whigham traces a contrary current of demystification – especially of gentile manners.

3 Reprise: Gender, Sexuality and Theories of Exchange

Douglas Bruster, *Drama and the Market in the Age of Shakespeare* (Cambridge, 1992).

An important study of economies of market exchange in Elizabethan and Jacobean England.

Jonathan Goldberg, *Queering the Renaissance* (Durham, NC, 1993).

A collection of essays on the history of sexuality in the early modern period.

Goldberg, *Sodometries* (Stanford, CA, 1992).

A groundbreaking study of gender and sexuality in Shakespeare, Spenser and colonial American texts.

Ania Loomba, *Gender, Race, Renaissance Drama* (Manchester, 1989).

As its title suggests, a consideration of gender and race, primarily in Shakespeare.

Valerie Traub, *Desire and Anxiety: Circulations of Sexuality in Shakespearian Drama* (London, 1992).

Considers both the intersections and contradictions between sexuality and gender in the early modern period.

4 Heterology

Jean Baudrillard, *Critique of the Political Economy of the Sign*, trans. Charles Levin (St Louis, MO, 1981); and Baudrillard's, *The Mirror of Production*, trans. Mark Poster (St Louis, MO, 1975).

Baudrillard's two books on political economy rework Bataille's model of an expanded economy – which includes non-productive expenditure, non-utility, excess and the 'symbolic' destruction of all value – into a critique of Marxism.

Fred Botting, *Making Monstrous* (Manchester, 1991).

Botting's book looks at the social, literary and critical production of heterogeneity from the Romantic period, using Shelley's *Frankenstein* as a paradigm.

Jacques Derrida, 'From Restricted to General Economy. A Hegelianism

Without Reserve', in *Writing and Difference*, trans. Alan Bass (London, 1981), pp. 251–300.

Derrida's celebrated article on Bataille reads his texts within Hegel's system, pushing that system to its limit by reworking key Hegelian concepts in regard to that which is expelled by his system. Both here and elsewhere, Derrida uses Bataille's work to theorize the economic workings, unworkings and detours of *différance*. Most recently, Derrida has sought to deconstruct the notion of the 'general economy' itself through readings of Marcel Mauss (on the gift), Lévi-Strauss and Baudelaire's prose-poem *Counterfeit Money* (in *Given Time: 1. Counterfeit Money*, trans. Peggy Kamuf (Chicago, 1992)).

Michel Foucault, 'A Preface to Transgression', in *Language, Counter-Memory, Practice*, ed. Donald F. Bouchard, and trans. Bouchard and Sherry Simon (Ithaca, NY, 1977), pp. 29–52.

Foucault's essay on Bataille is significant not only because of its prophetic ability to predict Bataille's re-emergence in a culture for which 'the experience of transgression' replaces (dialectical) contradiction as its major theme, but also for the key place it marks in Foucault's own work on sexuality.

Denis Hollier, *Against Architecture: The Writings of Georges Bataille* (Boston, 1989).

The major work on Bataille by Hollier, the editor of his *Œuvres Complets*.

Steven Shaviro, *Passion and Excess: Blanchot, Bataille and Literary Theory* (Tallahassee, FL, 1990).

Situates Bataille alongside his one-time friend and fellow novelist Maurice Blanchot, and skilfully educes the debt owed by post-structuralism to both.

Index

Figures in parentheses after note entries indicate the relevant chapter number.

(3)

THE TEMPEST

Nigel Wood (ed.)

The Tempest is a powerful yet complex network of myth, symbol, romance
and broad comedy. For generations, its gallery of characters has suggested
a series of contrasts between Nature and Art, Community and Absolute
Power and, most recently, between the fear of alien savagery and the necessity
of colonial guilt. For Caliban, Prospero's Island is both enchanted and a
prison; for Ariel and Miranda, it is merely a place from which to escape; and,
for Prospero, it is a landscape both alien and spiritual. This volume of specially
commissioned essays contains examples of how the newest critical positions
may be brought to bear in practice on *The Tempest*. Sections in each essay
locate a context for the theories adopted and explain any unfamiliar terms.
There then follows an interpretation of the work guided by these theoretical
concepts. An introduction by the volume editor supplies an account of the
critical history of the play, an overview of its most recent criticism, and an
indication of how these have affected practical approaches to *The Tempest*.

Contents

Contributors

Howard Felperin, Charles H. Frey, John Turner, Richard P. Wheeler.

c.208pp   0 335 15688 6 (paperback)

HENRY IV PARTS ONE AND TWO

Nigel Wood (ed.)

In Falstaff, Shakespeare provided a potent and popular symbol of carnival and misrule. Largely Shakespeare's creation, he is a guiding spirit in a comprehensive staging of the dissolution of the feudal world and the birth of early modern perspectives on honour and kingship. Does he invalidate or strengthen Tudor myths? How can Hal, as Henry V, legitimate his rule? These questions are posed, and set in different lights, by these specially commissioned essays, which contain examples of how the newest critical positions may be brought to bear in practice on *Henry IV*. Sections in each essay locate a context for the theories adopted and explain any unfamiliar terms. There then follows an interpretation of the work guided by these theoretical concepts. An introduction from the volume editor supplies an account of the critical history of the play, an overview of its recent criticism and some indication of how these have affected practical approaches to the work.

Contents

Editors' preface – Preface – How to use this book – A note on the texts used – Introduction – Hal's desire, Shakespeare's Idaho – Uses of diversity: Bakhtin's theory of utterance and Shakespeare's second tetralogy – The future of history in Henry IV – Henry IV and epic theatre – Endpiece – Notes – References – Further reading – Index.

Contributors

Jonathan Goldberg, Ronald R. Macdonald, Kiernan Ryan, Peter Womack.

208pp   0 335 15690 8 (paperback)